NO SAFE PLACE

PLACE

Murdered by
our father

NO SAFE PLACE
Murdered by our father

Bekhal Mahmod

with

Dr Hannana Siddiqui

AD LIB

First published in 2022 by Ad Lib Publishers Ltd
15 Church Road
London, SW13 9HE
www.adlibpublishers.com

Text © 2022 Bekhal Mahmod and Hannana Siddiqui

Paperback ISBN 9781913543051
eBook ISBN 9781802470772

A CIP catalogue record for this book is
available from the British Library.

Every reasonable effort has been made to trace copyright-holders
of material reproduced in this book, but if any have been
inadvertently overlooked the publishers would be
glad to hear from them.

Printed in the UK
10 9 8 7 6 5 4 3 2 1

This is a true story. Some names, sequences and details have been changed for security and dramatic purposes.

This book is dedicated to the memory of Banaz Mahmod and Rahmat Suleimani – may they be together, free and at peace.

No Safe Place is also dedicated to all other victims of so-called 'honour killings' and their bereaved family and friends.

Foreword

by Dr Hannana Siddiqui

Background

Bekhal Mahmod is the sister of Banaz Mahmod, who was brutally raped and murdered aged twenty in 2006 in a so called 'honour' killing. Her Iraqi Kurdish family and community, based in South London, felt she had dishonoured them after leaving her allegedly abusive husband, to whom she was married as a seventeen-year-old child. They also did not want her to re-marry her 'prince', Rahmat Suleimani, whom her family said was 'unsuitable' as he was from a different tribe from Iran, and not a strict Muslim.

Seven male relatives were convicted of Banaz's murder or related crimes. In 2007, her father and uncle, a powerful community leader who instigated the crime, were unanimously convicted of her murder at the Old Bailey. They were sentenced to life imprisonment with a minimum term of twenty and twenty-three years respectively. One cousin pleaded guilty to murder at this trial and another was convicted of conspiracy to pervert the course of justice. Three other men, all cousins, were also convicted of murder, or other crimes, in two further trials in 2010 and 2013. In a first of its kind, two of the killers were extradited from Iraq, where they had fled after the murder.

According to the investigating officer, DCI Caroline Goode, there were up to fifty men from the community involved in the murder, or its cover up, in a 'web of lies'. Although Goode and her team were committed to achieving justice for Banaz, this high-profile case was a landmark for showing the failure of the police to protect Banaz before her death. She had reported multiple rapes, violence, attempted murder and threats to her life five times. In 2008, misconduct allegations against six officers were found to be substantiated. Despite this, two officers with the 'worst' failures only received 'words of advice' in disciplinary action.

The case led to a national outcry and measures to improve the policing of honour violence.

At great risk to themselves, two witnesses bravely gave prosecution evidence which led to the convictions. Bekhal gave crucial evidence against her father and uncle. She was the first daughter in this country to do so in an honour killing against her own family. Bekhal is now in hiding on a witness protection scheme with a new unknown identity. Rahmat also gave vital evidence and was in witness protection until his tragic suicide in 2016. He was heartbroken about the loss of Banaz and once said there was 'no life' left for him.

This book is about Bekhal's remarkable life story as she fled from home as a teenager after years of violence and a threatened forced marriage. There had been attempts by her family to kill her too for having shamed them. Bekhal has featured in numerous media interviews, including the Emmy Award-winning documentary Banaz: A Love Story, *and depicted by Rhianna Barrato in the popular ITV drama* Honour *in 2020. The drama also starred Keely Hawes and attracted nearly seven million viewers. Bekhal is now campaigning to introduce a 'Banaz's Law' with Hannana Siddiqui, a leading expert and activist, who works at the renowned group, Southall Black Sisters. Hannana supported her through the criminal trial and beyond, and recently formulated Banaz's Law, aimed at preventing the use of misogynous cultural defences to mitigate male violence against women and girls. The new law will regard such defences as an aggravating factor, attracting longer sentences, and re-frame violence in the name of 'honour' as a crime of 'dishonour'.*

Foreword

The first time I met Bekhal Mahmod, we just clicked. It was June 2006, and the body of her sister, Banaz, had only recently been found. Bekhal was pregnant and looked vulnerable, but also was open and easy to talk to. I sensed she instinctively trusted me. Her life was in danger because she was helping the police to investigate Banaz's death and she had herself fled from home some time ago after suffering years of abuse. My main concern was about Bekhal's safety and support. I would also normally advocate – meaning that I would advise and represent the client to outside agencies. But I could see that while I wanted to ensure that the police were doing all they could to protect Bekhal, and to bring those who killed Banaz to justice, that my intervention was not as much in need as it had been in other cases. The Metropolitan police appeared to be doing well on both counts. Indeed the lead officer, DCI Caroline Goode, had agreed to bring me in to support Bekhal on the recommendation of the honour-based abuse specialists at New Scotland Yard: Yvonne Rhoden and Yasmin Rehman. They knew of my expertise gathered from over many years of working at Southall Black Sisters. I think they also wanted someone from outside the close-knit Iraqi Kurdish community to support Bekhal. Confidentiality and the safety of all involved was paramount. So, while I kept a watching brief on the investigation, it was the support I gave together with Sarah Raymond, the kind and loving Police Family Liaison Officer, which proved vital to Bekhal. It pulled her through the harrowing experience of Banaz's death and giving evidence as a lead prosecution witness against her own father and uncle, which ultimately led to achieving justice for her beloved sister.

Based in Southall in West London, which has a large South Asian population, I have, in the main, been working with women in these communities, who have much in common with those from Middle Eastern backgrounds as they share similar cultural and religious values and practices. Although Bekhal's life was confined by conservative interpretations of women's role in Islam, codes of honour cut across different religious groups and can extend to other ethnic minorities. My work included handling extreme cases of serious violence, including rape, forced marriage, domestic homicide, suicide and honour killings. I had supported women or their bereaved family and friends through the criminal, inquest and civil justice system. Before Banaz's death, I had advised the police on the honour killings of Heshu Yonis, Surjit Kaur Athwal and Samaira Nazir, which helped to bring their killers to justice.

So-called 'honour killings' are used to preserve or restore the collective honour of the family and community. Honour rests on the behaviour of women, especially their sexual conduct.

Women are expected to conform to traditional gender roles as obedient and dutiful wives, mothers, sisters, daughters and daughters-in-law. Unmarried women are expected to be virgins and married women must be faithful at all costs. Divorce or separation is a stigma and women are blamed even if they leave an abusive relationship, which they are expected to endure in silence. Women are accused of bringing shame and dishonour, even if the allegations are merely suspected or untrue. They are 'punished' through being treated as social outcasts, harassed, assaulted, raped, murdered or driven to suicide. These conservative interpretations of honour are imposed by the male community and religious leaders or elders; and although women can also be perpetrators or collude in honour violence, this is within a patriarchal system where men have all the power to use honour to control women's autonomy and sexuality.

Bekhal was labelled as a 'troublemaker' from a young age, and repeatedly told that she would 'not enter heaven'. Her family feared losing control over her and so attempted to assert their power by striking fear of God into her heart. As a rebel, Bekhal posed a threat to male power. Southall Black Sisters also represent black feminist women's struggles of resistance and for women's empowerment. They have sought to subvert notions of honour by questioning who is being honourable or who dishonorable. Progressive women's groups and activists are the liberal sections of communities which believe in women's human rights – that it is not women as survivors of abuse or victims of honour killings who bring dishonour, but the perpetrators. It is not the abusers who should be celebrated as being heroes, but the abused who are the real heroes for refusing to be silenced and oppressed because they are our inspiration and symbols of 'true honour'.

What I admired about Bekhal was her defiance in the face of danger. Her courage was remarkable, and her anger at her family for killing Banaz was deep but restrained. When I met Bekhal, she would cry at times, and was afraid of exposing herself and her unborn child to danger by giving evidence for the prosecution. But she could not forget or forgive, even her own father, who she had loved in childhood. She longed for loving parents, and grandparents for her child, but knew that would never be a possibility given the abuse she had suffered from them in her own childhood and teenage years. I was shocked to find out later about the severe violence Bekhal had suffered at home and that there had been several attempts on her life. She was the original target for an honour killing but escaped this fate as her defiance and beatings had also taught her that in order to survive, she had to leave the very people she loved.

Given her history, it is therefore no surprise that Bekhal constantly worries for her safety, but she also wants change. Sometimes this creates contradictions. I have been campaigning against religious fundamentalism for many years, and so imagine my horror when Bekhal came up with the idea that she will wear the full burqa covering her from head to toe in order to give evidence in court and for media interviews. To me, 'the veil', as it is commonly known, was a historical symbol of women's oppression, so why would I support this? Bekhal insisted that although she too did not believe in women being forced to wear the veil, she felt safer doing so as it concealed her face and body. This meant that she could not be identified in public. 'Surely,' I asked, 'there are other ways of covering yourself?' But no, according to Bekhal, there were not, and while I supported her decision, as it made her feel safer and comfortable, it was nevertheless ironic, and comic too.

At court, however, the comedy ended when I experienced some of the aggression from Bekhal's family and community firsthand. At the sentencing hearing, while sitting in the public gallery, I, along with Diana Nammi from the Iranian and Kurdish Women's Rights Organisation (who led the Justice for Banaz Mahmod Campaign), were targeted by them with verbal abuse and threatening behaviour. We were escorted out through the back door by staff at the Old Bailey. But it was Bekhal's personal impact statement which really affected me at this hearing. In this statement, Bekhal laments that Banaz had not come into her dreams. After all these years, I still ask if Banaz has come into her dreams and the answers is invariably a tearful 'no'. In this context, until writing this book with her, I did not tell Bekhal about the medium who once told me that there was: 'A young woman with me and, although she was unhappy about how she died, she is alright.' I could not be sure if this was Banaz or even a real person – so I did not tell Bekhal about it so as to avoid giving her more pain. When I did tell her, I saw the hurt in Bekhal's eyes. I know that Bekhal once heard Banaz's voice at a moment when she was very frightened and anxious. Maybe the healing will only start when Banaz visits her – in dream or spirit form. But we both like to think that after Rahmat's tragic suicide ten years after their separation, the couple may well be together now. Bekhal told me about a dream she had at the time of Rahmat's suicide which was of two hummingbirds – one pink, one blue – flying out of the window after the pink bird came into the room to fetch the blue one where it was hovering. In Bekhal's culture, hummingbirds symbolise love. At the same time, whilst dozing, I also heard two small voices saying 'goodbye' to me. I know this sounds like seeing things through rose-tinted glasses, but even if these dreams just help us to come to terms with their sad and infuriating deaths, perhaps they are a sign of them both at last being free and at peace.

The police had failed to inform Bekhal about Rahmat's death. I told her about this after the *BBC London News* suddenly called me for an interview. They asked for my reaction, but I also had not until then heard about it. We were both shocked and devastated and questioned whether Rahmat had been provided with enough support in witness protection. He was heartbroken about losing Banaz and was known to be suicidal. Bekhal too complains about living without family and old friends. She also lives in constant fear of her life. Even recently Bekhal wore the burqa when appearing on *BBC News* with Victoria Derbyshire in 2020 after the airing of the ITV drama, *Honour,* based on Banaz's case.

Whilst welcomed, the shortfall of the drama was that it failed to tell Bekhal's story, although she was, according to *The Guardian* newspaper review, the real hero. Bekhal contacted me at this time so that she could use the opportunity to campaign for women's rights. We also revived the idea of writing a book – long mooted, but not then achieved due to other pressures. Bekhal's memory is incredible, as she remembers so much detail from her past and wants to recount it. This is amazing considering the beatings she received.

Sometimes memory of abuse is blocked out or knocked out, but at other times it can be vivid with frightening flashbacks where the victim relives the abuse. In childhood, Bekhal seems to have bounced back like a ragdoll, the damage being invisible, but started to show more of her injuries later on, when she was a teenager. She now has long-term trauma and physical ill-health. I therefore hope writing this book will be a cathartic experience for her. Moreover, it is good to know that, despite bouts of depression, Bekhal receives regular counselling and is sustained by her daughter and her passion for wanting change. It has been an emotional journey for both of us, and we have grown in love and respect for each other; we've formed an alternative family – I am a 'sister' in name or an 'aunty' in age. Bekhal continues to inspire and confound me with her views on life and deeds in action, which contain amazing wisdom, compassion, generosity, love and a strong sense of justice. For instance, I cannot help smiling at the way she does not ask for fees for interviews and, whenever possible, insists that journalists make a donation to Southall Black Sisters. She has achieved justice for Banaz and is now taking forward a legacy in her name by calling for a 'Banaz's Law' to protect other women and girls, and to bring justice for all.

Dr Hannana Siddiqui
14 July 2021

As I write these book sections, I notice, although it is entirely coincidental, today is the birthday of Shafilea Ahmed, who was killed by her parents when she was aged only seventeen. In 2015, this date was chosen to mark the National Day of Memory for Victims of Honour Based Abuse.

Prologue

NAZCA

South London, May 2005

'Bekhal, Miss, Madam, you fucking whore-child, you *bitch*. Come home now or you're dead. I have people on you. I have paid for them. They will bring you to me, alive or in a body bag!'

His threat echoed in my head as I got off the bus in Lewisham. '*Gahba* [bitch]. *Qehpik* [whore]… they will bring you to me. Even if it's only your head.'

That voice, loud and terrifying, tortured me through childhood, puberty, adolescence and beyond. A voice I could still smell and feel. Breath like stale lamb stew mixed with fag ash. Phlegm, crackling in his throat before he spat in my face. Evil, disgusting. The voice belonged to my father, Mahmod Babakir Mahmod.

Almost five years had passed since Dad left that message on my phone, but still his lethal words turned my blood and bones to ice. That had been one of several death threats I received after I first ran away from home as a teenager. And trust me, they were not empty threats; the thirteen stitches in my scalp served as a brutal reminder of my brother Bahman's attempt to kill me at Dad's behest.

I powered along Lewisham High Street with my head bent, hoodie pulled down to my eyebrows, even though it was boiling outside – well into the seventies. How I longed to be in a little summer dress, feeling the kiss of balmy air on my bare legs, hearing the lazy, carefree nip of my flip-flops. Imagine? I'd be wearing that dress for my death if a man in my family spotted me. You see, I'm from Iraqi Kurdistan, born to strict Sunni Muslim parents who advocate forced marriages, child marriages and female genital mutilation. Plucking my eyebrows or painting my nails would earn me several smacks around the head in our family home. I'm not kidding.

When I was fifteen, my parents tried to send me back to Iraq to marry my first cousin, Akam, a big, balding man almost double my age. No way did I want to marry Akam, and I told my parents as much. 'No, definitely *no*,' I said. 'If I do ever get married, I want it to be to somebody that I love – not my *blood* relative.' I endured subsequent beatings and threats from Dad before I finally fled home, having 'dishonoured' and 'shamed' our family. A crime worthy of an 'honour killing' in our misogynistic, hypocritical, and totally fucked-up culture.

Today, I was visiting one of my younger sisters, Banaz, whom I hadn't seen in over four years. Admittedly, my going to her flat was a move you might describe as dicing with death. I would routinely be followed by Kurdish men, often my uncles and cousins, who would report back to my dad with tales of my alleged despicable deeds that would, heaven forbid, ruin his 'reputation'. Should the Kurdish community find out that I'd as much as spoken with Banaz, a price would probably be put on both of our heads.

Seriously, Bekhal, are you mental or what? Yeah, I know you're thinking this too. But here's the thing: I never chose to be estranged from my siblings. I missed Banaz so much, just as I missed my two other younger sisters, Payzee and Ashti. So, when Amber, a family friend of mine and Banaz, had called a few days ago with shocking information about her and Payzee, I was there like a shot. Death threats or not.

Amber said Banaz and Payzee had been forced into arranged marriages at seventeen and sixteen respectively. Bile hit my throat when I heard this. Banaz, a couple of years or so younger than me, would be twenty in December. Payzee had just turned eighteen. 'They're both married to much older men and the four of them live together,' said Amber. 'Banaz's husband, Binar, is the worst... oh God...' I came off the phone thinking, *This is all my fault. I must help my sisters.*

When I reached the address – a soulless building resembling an eighties office block – I texted Amber. As planned, she had popped in to see Banaz, and would rush me into the flat as she left. Payzee and the two husbands would not be at home, she'd explained, and Banaz was unaware I was coming. The door buzzed. In I went.

'She's in there,' whispered Amber, tilting her cloaked head in the direction of a door, slightly ajar at the end of the skinny hallway. I waited for Amber to leave, then took a deep breath. Mm, dolma. *Smells just like Mum's cooking*, I thought, as I made my way towards the vertical strip of light and watery noises: *plunge, drip, plunge, drip*. Gently, I pushed the door and there she was: my darling Banaz, kneeling over a sickly green bathtub filled with clothes and soapy water, her arms like knitting needles, plunging in and out of the suds. Her hair was scraped into a messy knot at the back of her head, with wavy tendrils falling around her petal ears. Wet shirts hung slimily from a makeshift washing line above the bath. Tears blurred my eyes. 'Nazca,' I said, using Banaz's nickname, which means beautiful and delicate in Kurdish.

Banaz gasped and turned. 'Bakha [my childhood nickname], oh my God, is that really you?' she said.

I spread my arms wide, nodding, tears and snot streaming down my face. 'Banaz, my love,' I said, and we came together in the tightest hug you could ever imagine. I kissed her wet face all over, sobbing. I kissed her neck and inhaled her flowery scent: Kenzo, her favourite. She used to have to hide the bottle at home. Banaz kissed me too, both of us saying, 'My darling, my love, my beautiful sister,' over and over through tears.

'Where's Amber?' said Banaz when we finally let go of one another. But my sister's words flew past me as I got a proper look at her face. Banaz's stunning features were ever present – the high, contoured cheekbones and full, curvy lips; her perfectly shaped eyebrows, that cute little dimple in her chin – but she looked different. Worn out, ill even. She had a few marks on her face, small grazes and scratches. Black trousers clung for dear life to her hips. Her hazel eyes looked dark and sunken. When she attempted a smile, I noticed a few of her teeth were chipped. I touched her arm and we sat on the lip of the bath.

'Amber's gone,' I said, 'but she told me about you and Payzee, about Dad forcing you into marriages, and I had to see you. I'm so, so sorry. I'm so sorry, Nazca.' Again, my eyes spilled. I looked up, sniffing, and that's when I noticed a washing machine in the far corner of the bathroom. I wiped my face on my sleeve and asked Banaz, 'Why are you bending over backwards to wash your husband's clothes when you can just chuck them in the washing machine?'

I felt Banaz's thighs tighten and shake. Her shoulders trembled too. 'He doesn't... you know... he doesn't like me to use the washing machine or anything like that,' she said into her lap. She was picking at the thin white scar on her right index finger – an injury from accidentally slamming her hand in a fire door in Iran years ago. 'He likes me to wash his clothes by hand. He... he says, "you're not going to sit around and do nothing... or meet up with friends." I have to do all his cooking and cleaning and lay with him, like, have sex, whenever he wants. It's like I'm his glove or his shoe... that he can wear whenever he chooses. And, if I don't do what he wants, he beats me up and stuff.'

I took Banaz's scarred hand and held it in my lap. 'Fucking animal,' I said, 'I swear, if I see him, I'll kill him.' I sprung from the bath, pulling Banaz with me. 'C'mon,' I said, 'we're going for a walk.'

'But I have to finish the—'

'We're going,' I said firmly, 'just to the shop at the end of the road.' Granted, I knew we might not be entirely safe outside, but me being inside that flat with Banaz, I suddenly realised, was more dangerous. It would be hard to escape if people came to kill us.

'OK,' said Banaz, 'I can get chewing gum.'

The shop was less than a two-minute walk from the flat, but we were barely out of the communal door before Banaz's mobile started ringing. I remember the ringtone – one of a baby crying. Of course, it was Binar calling her. 'I'm just walking to the shop to get a drink,' Banaz told him. It was like he had eyes on her, literally. She hung up and we hurried into the shop with our heads down. 'Binar's on his way back,' said Banaz, her voice loaded with panic. 'I have to get home before him.' Banaz bought her chewing gum, bless her, and we headed out of the shop, into the blazing afternoon. And all I could think was, *I can't let Banaz go back to that heinous pig of a husband.* About halfway between the shop and her flat, we stopped behind a bus shelter to say goodbye. I grasped her shoulders and pleaded and pleaded with her. I said, 'I can't believe you're still here, living this life. Living with a brute who's beating and raping you. Please, come with me now. Get away. Please, I want to get you out of this before it's too late.'

Banaz looked first at the pavement, then at me, her eyes watering. 'Bakha, you're so brave for walking away, but I couldn't do that.'

I folded her hands in mine and tried once more: 'Please, Nazca, please come with me. I can help you. There are refuges for women in your situation. Please, Nazca, I promise I'll look after you.'

'I'm sorry,' she said then, brushing away her tears, and whispered, 'Can I see you again, Bakha?'

I threw my arms around her. 'I hope so,' I choked, 'let's try.'

Then I felt Banaz's lips on my face, and her voice, cracking like fine bone china in my ear. 'I love you, Bakha. Goodbye, my love.'

'I love you too, Nazca,' I said, and I stood there, behind the shelter, crying into my hoodie as I watched my Banaz running away from me. And, to my dying day, I shall always regret not forcing Banaz on to a bus with me that afternoon.

For that was the last time I saw my beautiful Nazca alive.

Chapter One

MASHALLAH?

Bump, bump, jiggle, I'm going, the world swaying above me in crisp blue and white. I'm wearing baggy trousers and a flowery top and I'm giggling away. Everything is perfect.

My carriage is a plastic basket, also blue with circular holes. I poke my dimply fingers through these gaps and try to lift myself. More, I want to see more.

Blue turns to green as I land with a soft thud in my basket. I'm giggling again and wriggling my legs as a gentle breeze tickles my bare feet. Next, a familiar face appears over my head, and frizzy black hair froths into the basket. My dayik [mum]. She picks me up, smiling and cooing, then plonks me on the grass. Baba [Dad] is there too. He cuddles Mum and they become one big, fuzzy shape in the bright sun. More figures appear, tall with high-pitched, sing-song voices. They're saying things like, 'Isn't she cute,' and, 'she's so pretty,' and they give me Arabic sweets. Soon, my face and hands are all gooey. Mum and Dad laugh, and I hear them chant my nickname, 'Bakha, Bakha, hello little one.'

The other figures clap and cry, 'Mashalla, mashalla [this is what God has willed].'

Everything is perfect.

I swear to God, the scene I describe above is my earliest memory. About six years later, I relived this moment to my mum, Behya, who laughed so hard her mountain-clay eyeliner ran down her cheeks. Though, to be fair, Mum often has bouts of uncontrollable laughter for no reason whatsoever. 'Really, Bakha,' she said, 'on Allah's name that can't be so?' Then she gave me a look that read, *you're a strange child* and, wiping her eyes, muttered between tuts, 'No Allah, how on earth do you remember all that, Bakha? You were no older than one and a bit.' She laughed again, then straightened her face and confirmed every detail of my memory as true.

The basket I mention was one of those eighties jelly bags: baby blue, with round holes in its sides. Mum still had it in the house somewhere, she said, along with the trousers and top that once belonged to my older sister, Kejal. On that day, Mum had bundled me into the bag and taken me to visit Dad at the college where he taught maths at that time. 'Your dad was on his lunch break, so we joined him for a picnic,' said Mum. 'The women who gave you sweets were students. They thought you were adorable. We let them pick you up and cuddle you, too.'

I never found out which college Dad taught at, but that day remains vivid as ever in my mind. A memory drenched in love and kindness. It's a place I can revisit time after time in my head and still, I hear, 'Mashallah, mashallah.' Oh, what I wouldn't give to go back to that day. If only life had stayed that way.

A few family photographs capture my happy era. In the pictures, taken in Iraq, Mum's wearing her headscarf tied back, so the fabric covers only the crown of her head, and her black hair whirls about her face and shoulders. A bit risqué, but after being photographed, she would have covered her hair again. Another picture shows Kejal, swathed in a white gown and perched on Mum's left knee, while my brother Bahman, as a toddler, grins into the distance as he clings to Mum's right arm and Dad, wearing traditional Kurdish clothes and a slight smile beneath his treacly moustache, cuddles Mum and Kejal. There's a similar snap featuring me as a baby on Mum's lap, with Kejal and Bahman either side of Mum, pulling funny faces. That picture makes me want to laugh and cry at once. In those photos we look like a regular happy family. It's deceiving until you learn the truth.

Mum and Dad got hitched in the mid-seventies. It was an arranged marriage, meaning they had been picked for each other by their families. At one of their several ceremonies, Mum sat while dozens of guests festooned her with gold – bangles, rings, and coins, and also pinned paper money to her wedding dress. She might even have been gifted a sheep or two (although, please don't quote me on that). In Sunni Islam, arranged marriages are often keeping-it-in-the-family affairs, too, and my parents' nuptials were no exception.

Behya and Mahmod are first cousins. Mum's mum, Hadlah, and Dad's dad, Babakir Mahmod, were sister and brother. So, Mum's uncle became her father-in-law and Dad's Aunty Hadlah morphed into the role of mother-in-law. When we kids came along, those two grandparents were also our great aunt and great uncle. Which means our parents are also our second cousins. It's confusing, I know, not to mention fucked-up. I've heard countless stories where kids from cousin marriages were born with twelve toes or with one leg longer than the other, on top of myriad other health issues. In the Arab-Muslim world, cousin marriages are generally considered ideal, pure, and honourable. Cousin marriages cement family ties and keep wealth within the family, they say. In other cultures, the act of getting it on with your cousin is often called incest. Honestly, do not get me started.

Bizarrely, Mum and Dad made their marriage work. Not that Mum would have had a say in the matter. Her job was to cook and clean, obey my father, and look after us children how he saw fit. I remember Dad once told me that he and Mum were not in love on their wedding day but 'grew to love each other over time'. I couldn't get my head around that idea. I still can't and never will. But, looking at early photographs of them together, Mum and Dad look so loved-up. They went on to have six children, and, as far as I know, they're still 'happily' married today.

Unbelievable.

I'm the third child of Behya and Mahmod. My brother Bahman is the eldest, and Kejal came along about a year before me. My parents named me Bekhal after the beauty spot in the mountains of northern Kurdistan where they honeymooned. I've never been to the Bekhal Summer Resort, but a Google search reveals stunning photos of a dramatic natural waterfall (Bekhal Waterfall) tumbling down the centre of a mountain. Unlike most Kurdish names, I can find no specific meaning for Bekhal – other than 'waterfall'.

When I was old enough to understand, Mum told me I had a twin sister. Her name was Berry, and she was born with only one kidney. At nine-pounds-something, I was a heavy baby, but poor Berry was severely underweight and, tragically, her one kidney failed, and she died at forty days old, bless her. I often think about little Berry and wonder how our relationship would have been had she survived. Apparently, Mum also suffered several miscarriages over the years.

Mum and Dad are both from big families from the Mirawaldy tribe. It's mental how huge Mum's side is. She's one of at least fifteen kids – some of whom are her stepbrothers and stepsisters because, just to complicate matters further, Mum's father Ahmed was simultaneously married to three women. Ahmed died around the time I was born, but Hadlah, Mum's late biological mother, was a lovely grandmother – unlike the evil witch who gave birth to my father and his five younger siblings.

It sounds harsh, I know, but, as you will learn, my reasons for hating Grandma Zareen are justified. In Kurdish, Zareen means 'golden child', but I can't think of a more inappropriate name for my grandmother. Zareen had four boys and two daughters and consequently resented Mum for having so many girls and only one boy. My grandmother was vocal about this, too; when my twin sister Berry died, Zareen told Mum: 'Good, I'm glad she's dead. That's one less pussy in this house.' Zareen died a few years ago. I can't believe that horrible woman lived to be 103.

As is traditional in our culture, Mum moved in with Dad's parents once she was married. They lived in a house built by Dad and his brothers in Qalat Dizah, an Iraqi Kurdistan town engulfed by mountains north of Sulaymaniyah, and close to the Iranian border. This would be my home for the first six-and-a-half years of my life.

The house was basically a wooden frame with mud walls and, like all buildings in Iraq, had a flat roof. Inside, the clay floors were covered with Persian rugs that you had to beat clean over the wall outside. Electricity came in the form of a noisy generator connected to our tiny black-and-white television or the ceiling fan in the men's lounge – via a long cable that stretched across the dusty road. Those were our only two electrical appliances; we had no overhead lights inside, so we made do with oil lanterns. There was no running water in the house either, so our supply was the Little Zab River, which tumbles into Kurdistan from Iran. We would trek across barren countryside to the river, where we'd wash our clothes, and collect water in buckets. We'd then carry those heavy pails home and heat the water in a metal tank over the outdoor picnic gas.

I clearly recall the layout of our home. It was on one level, and the front door gave way to the communal lounge, which had a Kurdish flag pinned to the back wall. Behind the lounge was the kitchen, where Mum would cook – and cook and cook and cook. My God, the aromas that used to fill that house. You know when you're on holiday somewhere hot – Turkey, for example – and you get hit by all the amazing smells from the restaurants at night? It smelled like that in our house twenty-four-seven. The dining room was through the lounge on the left. Mum would lay dishes on a big plastic tablecloth on the floor, and we'd all sit around the edges and tuck in – eating with our hands, always. A door linked the dining room to a separate men-only lounge at the back of the house, where there were also four bedrooms. I shared a bedroom with my siblings, and we slept on the floor on mattresses made from duvets stitched together in layers.

Our toilet – a hole in the ground that fed into a concrete sewer pipe – was in a wicker-style shack outside, nestled among the chicken coop, cowsheds, and donkey and horse stables. Actually, 'hole in the ground' is the polite term for what we called the 'shithole' – because that's what it was. You had to squat over the hole to relieve yourself, then tip a bucket of water down the hole to flush your excrement away, while centipedes and earwigs scuttled over your feet and bluebottles span around your head. And those weren't the only unwelcome visitors we encountered; we'd often see rats, mice, scorpions, snakes, and cockroaches. They'd come indoors too. Once, we found a baby rattlesnake in the larder and Mum screamed the house down. But what scared me most – more than those disgusting cockroaches who'd swarm over my mattress at night – was the monster called Reş who allegedly haunted the sewer pipe beneath the shithole. Reş, which means black or blackness in Kurdish, was a hairy beast with jagged nails. The story went that Reş's big hairy arm would shoot up the hole and pull you into the sewer. Some children never returned from the shithole after falling prey to him. I was so petrified of Reş that I used to make my older sister or cousin wait outside whenever I needed the loo.

Grandpa Babakir Mahmod Aghr (Aghr is an honorary term in Kurdish) was head of the household. He owned lots of gold and was highly regarded within the Kurdish community. I never had any problems with Bapîr (Grandpa) Babakir – he loved me. Oh my God, he was so tall, like six-foot-six or so. He had kind, sleepy eyes and deep, symmetrical creases that ran from his outer nostrils to either side of his jaw. I remember running up to him, then going on my tiptoes to reach for his hands, my head level with his knees. Grandpa would chuckle and stoop and say, 'Hello, Bakha.' I'd grab his fingertips and look up, and his face would crease further as he smiled. It was like looking up at a wise, old tree. Grandpa Babakir was definitely my favourite grandparent.

Dad's youngest brother, my uncle Zoran, also lived with us. I think this was because he hadn't found a wife yet. Other relatives

– too many to mention at once – were based in and around Sulaymaniyah, while my uncle Afran, another of Dad's brothers, lived just 600 yards away from us with his wife, Alal, and their four kids – two girls, Miriam and Shanar, and sons Daryan and Eylo. Miriam was of similar age to me – and we would become a mischievous pair.

Life in Qalat Dizah was primitive, but I knew no different at the time. And whenever I look back on my first five years in Iraqi Kurdistan, my heart glows and a massive smile fills my face. Perhaps that's why my early memories are so sharp – because I associate them with those happy, innocent days.

Back then, I was a proper Daddy's girl; he would bounce me on his knee and let me play with his moustache and sideburns. His facial hair fascinated me, especially his immaculate moustache, which felt so silky. My favourite game, however, was when Dad threw me up into the air and caught me. I loved that so much – the weightless sensation as I took flight, followed by my tummy flipping before I free-fell into Dad's arms. 'Bakha is flying, Bakha is flying,' he'd shout, and I'd giggle so much and beg him to toss me into the air again and again and again.

Another of my earliest memories is sitting on Mum's lap and pushing my hands and head into her huge, springy belly, which grew as the days went by. And while I don't remember her exact words, I do recall Mum telling me, as I prodded her tummy, 'Careful, there's a baby in there, Bakha.' I didn't understand what Mum was saying because I was only two-and-a-half, but, soon after, she disappeared for a day or so and returned home with what looked like a bundle of washing in her arms. She lay the bundle on the floor in the lounge, where the family was gathered. The sight shocked me. There on the floor, wrapped in cloth like a mummy, was a tiny person. It had tufts of black hair and rosy lips and, despite being so little, it screamed a lot. I remember pointing at the bundle on the floor and asking, 'What's that?' and everybody laughed at me. 'Bakha, my darling, my love,' Mum said, smiling first at me and then the miniature person. 'This is your little sister, Banaz.'

Yeah, it took me a while to comprehend how a little sister had come from my mum's stomach, and I admit I was jealous of Banaz at first. Mum was always cooking and cleaning, and suddenly my little sister had taken my position on Dad's knee. Then, less than two years later, Mum pulled the same stunt again: her belly grew and along came another sister, Payzee. By now my envy had passed, and I was chuffed to have two little sisters. In fact, I loved being part of a big family. I enjoyed the company – even though we siblings would fight at times, especially Kejal and me.

At that age, about four, I was a happy, bubbly kid. I had two toys – a wooden rocking horse and one of those battery-operated yapping dogs. Both were hand-me-downs from my brother via Kejal. The horse was scuffed and chipped, the dog's brown fleecy fur all matted, and I think I only witnessed it yap and jump once or twice as batteries were not staples in our mud house, but I adored those toys with all my heart. Every day I played outside on my rocking horse, and I'd take the dog everywhere with me. Once, I asked if I could take the dog to bed with me to cuddle, but Mum said no – because it was too dirty.

None of us kids went to nursery or school in Iraq. I didn't know school existed until I turned ten. Instead, Dad, no longer working at the college, gave us lessons at home. Being a whizz at maths – I believe he has a PhD in the subject – Dad taught us how to count and do sums and such from an early age. I enjoyed maths but didn't much relish learning to read. There was no equivalent of *The Tiger Who Came to Tea* or *The Gruffalo* or any other fun picture books in our house. No, the only title introduced to us – the one from which I learned how to read – was the Quran. I preferred working outside and being among the animals and nature than our lessons indoors.

Often, Dad, my uncles and Grandpa Babakir would go out to 'patrol the mountains' at night. I was too young to know about the Iran-Iraq war or Saddam Hussein's Anfal campaign, and no one explained why the men had to 'patrol' the mountains, although I believe Dad and Grandpa were in the Peshmerga, the Kurdish branch of the Iraqi Armed Forces. Sometimes, those patrolling missions went on for days, which secretly pleased me as it meant we got a break from home-schooling.

I loved being helpful at home and, from the age of five, I joined in the farm work with Bahman and Kejal. Every morning we'd get up at 5 am and head out to collect the chicken eggs and milk the cows. We would also make butter – by pouring milk into a cowskin bag and shaking it vigorously for what felt like an age. But the muckiest job was shovelling dung out of the horse and cow barns. Yeah, we would mix the smelly mess with straw, then use the manure as fuel for cooking or to heat the house in winter. It was hard work but rewarding too – and we got to play afterwards. We three would meet Miriam, Shanar, Daryan, and Eylo, and we'd go to the river, climb fig and date trees and shake the branches until the fruits fell, or play in the shells of unfinished buildings that lined the rubble-strewn roads. Much as I loved my rocking horse and dog that barely yapped, I honestly didn't want any more toys; I was in my element outside. Even alone, I amused myself by making mud pies or playing with the chickens. I'd feed them worms and chase them around the yard, making clucking noises. I thought they were the cutest, funniest things.

As a child, I never thought playing outside could lead to an act deemed as 'whore behaviour'. Nor did I imagine that playing with my male cousins would soon be discouraged. Admittedly, I knew from an early age that certain deeds were a big no-no for little girls. I knew not to lift my dress over my head or do a roly-poly in front of boys or men, for example. Swimming costumes, shorts, sleeveless dresses – what were they? We wore long dresses over Aladdin pants (trousers elasticated at the ankles) and polo neck jumpers, even in summer. But still, I was a kid. And like all kids, I was curious.

That curiosity ruined my perfect little world.

One day, as I rocked on my wooden horse next to one of the cowsheds, Dad's cousin Rekan appeared in the yard. It wasn't unusual to see Rekan as he lived nearby, and relatives came and went from our house every day. He gave me a nod in his wrap hat, and I smiled and carried on rocking, the sun-baked mud cracking and grinding beneath me. Rekan, who looked to be made from broomsticks and wooden pegs, grew taller as he approached, and, at once, he was less than a foot away from me. As he crouched to fiddle with the bottom lock on the shed door, I couldn't help but notice his weird fingertips, which were crusty and nail-less. They looked fossilised. I slammed my feet to the ground, jumped off the rocking horse, and bent to touch Rekan's hands. He flinched and whipped his hand to his chest as though I'd electrocuted him. 'What are you doing?' he said, his tone slow but steady. I assumed I'd made him jump. He certainly didn't sound angry.

'Oh my God,' I said, 'it's your fingernails. They look so different.' Rekan made no reply but shot me a confused look as he rose. Then he turned and shambled lankily across the yard and into the house. I got back on my rocking horse.

Less than twenty minutes later, Mum's voice walloped around the yard: 'Bek-*hal*, Bek-*hal*, get inside, *now*.' She stood in the kitchen doorway, fists glued to her waist, eyes ablaze. I did what I was told, scuttled over to her, thinking, *why does Mum look and sound so angry?* As I reached the doorway her hands came at me. She grabbed my six-year-old arm in a vice-like hold in one hand and pinched and twisted the top of my ear with the other, then hustled me inside, through the kitchen, shouting, '*Gahba, gah*-ba,' and into the lounge, where Dad was waiting for me, his eyebrows pulled together so tight they made a furry 'X' at the bridge of his nose. His hands were balled in front of his thighs. A length of rope connected his fists. He glowered at me, through me. Was this my dad? He looked as though he was about to murder me. Just then, Mum pushed me towards him and from that moment on, I could barely breathe for screaming and crying and the searing pain that ripped through my entire being.

Dad seized my hands and tied them together, yanking the ends of the rope until my wrists burned like they were on fire. At the same time, whack, Mum slapped the back of my head. Then Dad beat the hell out of me. 'Who the fuck told you to touch his hand?' he yelled. Slap, slap, slapping my face to the rhythm of his words. My whole body shook. I tried to speak, to explain the fingernail thing, but loud sobs came instead as Dad forced me backwards onto the floor, knelt over me and started hitting me all over – on my legs and arms and torso. He grabbed a fistful of my hair and yanked my head from side to side, like a rag doll. 'You're a fucking whore's child. Don't you *ever* touch his hand.' His face glistened with exertion. Spit sprayed from his mouth. Behind him, the twenty-one-beamed golden sunburst on the Kurdish flag blurred to a jaundiced blob. 'How could you do this, you fucking whore? Do you fucking understand what you've done wrong?' Smack.

'Hit her again, she doesn't understand.' That was Mum, standing over Dad, her face a mixture of fury and disgust inside her hijab. The torture continued for about forty minutes, Dad banging his palms against the sides of his head between beating me.

'You're the devil's child,' he spat. 'Whose fucking child are you?'

I turned my face into the rug. 'Please … stop … I'm sorry … I didn't … know…' I choked on my words, drenched the rug with my tears, saliva, and snot. 'Please stop.'

To be fair, Dad did stop hitting me after I begged him for mercy. He untied my hands then, in a flat voice, said: 'Now get to your room. Get out of my sight. You disgust me, whore-child.'

After my first beating, I cried all night. My body ached and stung all over, and my hair was in knotted clumps from being yanked. I lay in a ball on my thin mattress, barely noticing the fizzy hiss of cockroaches, my mind awhirl with dark thoughts. Rekan, in his twenties, must have told Dad that I'd touched his hand. *Why would he do that? What's so bad about touching a man's hand?* Mostly, I was shocked at Mum and Dad's violence. Hours before, they'd cuddled me. Two days ago, Dad had dabbed clove oil on my gums and hugged me tight to his chest while praying over me – because I had a toothache. Now, I felt heartbroken. *They're evil. I hate them.* I didn't want to hate my parents – I loved them.

Looking back, I know Dad's reason for beating me. He assumed I'd made a pass at his then twenty-something-year-old cousin. I mean, what the fuck? I was *six*. From then onwards, I was in a permanent state of fear. I didn't know which actions might get me another beating. Every little thing I said or did or contemplated doing had a question mark hanging over it: Can I go outside with my dress on? Can I answer the door to a guest? Can I sit next to my male cousin? Eventually, trial and error seemed the only way to find out. And I would make many more mistakes.

My next error almost cost me my life. It happened one weekend in spring 1989 when we visited Dad's sister, Baze, and her family, who lived in big army-style wigwams in countryside close to the Tanjaro River in Sulaymaniyah. Uncle Afran, Aunty Alal and their kids joined us, along with Dad's other sister Berzan and her two sons, Dana and Aliker.

Soon after we arrived, Bahman, Dana and Aliker decided to head down to the river to play. I wanted to go too, so I tugged repeatedly at Mum's dress. 'Please, please can I go with them,' I begged, 'Please let me go to the river.' The boys were already walking away from the camp.

'OK,' sighed Mum, then, waggling her finger in my face, added, 'But don't you *dare* go in the water.' I thanked her and hurried along the path to join my brother and cousins. They didn't want me there. Even Bahman laughed and pushed me away when Dana, through a vicious, slimy grin, said: 'This is not a place for girls – you're not welcome, Bekhal.' I tagged along, running to keep up with them.

When we reached the river, the boys gathered sticks and stones and threw them into the water. I stood on the riverbank and watched them having fun. The water foamed and flowed choppily, and the boys' missiles raced downstream before they could pinpoint where they had landed. 'Let's jump on the rocks,' said Dana, already stepping onto a jagged one. Bahman and Aliker followed, and they leapt from rock to rock. Not wanting to be left behind, I did the same, but as I hopped onto rock number three, I slid and banged my head as I plunged, feet-first, into the water.

I was little, and I couldn't swim. I tried to stand up, but my feet didn't reach the bottom and my head went under the water. The current dragged me at speed along the river. Every time I managed to raise my head above water, I went under again. Through the gushing foam I could see my brother and cousins, now back on the riverbank, laughing and throwing sticks at me. I screamed, 'Help,' but again water engulfed me, filling my mouth and nose, and throwing me against rocks. I gasped and grappled at those rocks as I tumbled on, thinking, *I'm going to die*, until, whoosh, the surf hurled me up the shore in front of Bahman, Dana and Aliker. I crawled up the bank, spluttering and panting. 'Help me,' I said again, then I vomited pure water. My brother's laugh was the loudest of the three of them.

Somehow, I managed to get to my feet and follow the boys back to the camp. They took a long route, through fields and over hills, jeering at me every time I croaked, 'Please don't tell Mum I went in the water,' or threw up, or choked. My nose and throat burned. I staggered on, shivering and belching. River water spewed from my nose as I vomited. Luckily, I hadn't lost my ugly, boy's loafers in the river – probably because they were way too small for me. They pinched my feet as I walked. All I wanted was a big cuddle from my mum.

She was waiting for me, my mother, when we reached the camp, striking her fists-on-hips pose I now read to mean: 'You're going to get such a beating.' And she did beat me. After scratching my arm – apparently the white marks her nails left behind proved I'd been in the water – she dragged me into the women's tent and beat me, beat me, beat me with a stick, shouting, 'I told you not to go in the fucking water,' over and over and over again. I wanted to die.

Well, I didn't die but I'd learned yet another lesson: don't go in the fucking water. Life returned to as normal as it could be … for a while, anyway. A few days after we'd returned from Aunty the following happened.

It was early evening, about half-six, seven-ish, and I was outside trying to round up the chickens for the night when I heard Mum's voice above the clucks. 'Bakha, come inside now,' she called. Relieved to hear my nickname, I scooped another two flapping chickens into my arms and ran into the coop. (Rounding up chickens is a tricky job as they'll try their best to escape.) When I came out of the coop Mum was there. 'Come on, Bakha, we're leaving. We need to hurry.'

'What do you mean?' I said. 'Where are we going? I need to put the chickens to bed.'

Mum held her arms wide and put her head on one side. 'Forget the chickens. We're leaving here, Bakha. We're leaving now. All of us are going. We're never coming back.'

I stood there open-mouthed, the chickens hopping and flapping around me. I heard the clunk of stable doors and the donkeys started braying. 'But … the chickens.' I loved my chickens. I didn't want to leave the chickens.

'Come on, Bakha, we really need to get going.'

I nodded, even though I didn't understand what was happening or where on earth we were going. 'Can I take my rocking horse and dog?'

Mum shook her head and motioned towards the kitchen. 'Come on, it's time to go, Bekhal,' she said.

Chapter Two

TROUBLEMAKER

'Keep your head down and scarf over your mouth,' said Mum, packing me into an empty rice sack harnessed over the donkey. Mum's warm breath brushed my face. It smelled of cloves, her signature scent.

'But where are we going?' I asked, still none the wiser since Mum had hurried me away from the chickens. 'Are we really not coming back, ever?' Behind the fleet of grunting donkeys, our mud house, unlit and abandoned, looked like a lump of coal against the navy sky. '*Please* can I take my rocking horse?' Questions, questions, I had so many.

'Shh, be quiet, Bakha.' Mum tucked a men's jamana [scarf] around me inside the sack. 'We must all stay quiet. If we make a noise, we could be in danger. No, Allah. We must not be seen, and we must not be heard. No, Allah, no.'

As Mum rammed in other bits and bobs – figs and dates wrapped in paper, a small bottle of water, more clothes, Aunty Alal did the same on the other side of the harness, where Miriam faced me in another rice sack. If we craned our necks, we could see each other's faces over the donkey's back.

There were sixteen of us, plus at least twenty donkeys, in our convoy. Banaz and Shanar, being about the same age and weight, were also packaged in rice bags over the donkey in front of ours. Payzee was in a sling on Mum's back. The older kids – Bahman, Kejal, Daryan, and Eylo, got to sit on the donkeys' backs, while the grown-ups would walk alongside the animals, who were saddled with parcels of food, bundles of hay, blankets, clothes and a few pots and pans – bare necessities our parents had frantically gathered and packed on our way out of the door. I had on three pairs of Aladdin trousers, two or three polo neck jumpers, two long dresses, a cardigan, and a few scarves. I was snug.

The men, rifles strapped to their fronts, went along the line, connecting the donkeys by rope leads and checking all the parcels and kids were secure, repeating the message Mum had drummed into me: 'Keep your heads down and stay quiet.' And then we were moving, clopping, shuffling, bobbing as one, Grandpa Babakir and Dad at the front, leading us towards the snow-peaked mountains, our home getting smaller and smaller until it vanished.

My sadness at leaving Qalat Dizah momentarily evaporated in the buzz of the occasion. A family donkey trek into the unknown at night was a novelty. It felt secretive, exciting, naughty even. Miriam and I kept poking our heads out of the sack, passing food to each other over the saddle, and giggling every time we heard the *thud-splatter* of poo avalanching from the donkey carrying Banaz and Shanar.

We continued well into the night, cutting cross-country tracks through the mountains, crossing rivers, into dark forests, with only a couple of lanterns and the moon to light the way. The higher we climbed, the colder it got. I remember asking Dad, when he came to check on us little ones, 'Are we there yet?' I was cold and tired, and this didn't feel fun anymore. I wanted to go home to my chickens and rocking horse. At that point, none of us kids knew where we were going, why we had left Iraq, or the risks involved. Only when we heard the grumbling engine of an approaching truck and searchlight beams swiped our heads did things get properly scary.

'Down, get down,' called Grandpa Babakir.

'Everyone *down*,' echoed Dad, and suddenly, we're a panicky tangle, trying to get to the ground through long, frosty grass.

Mum and Aunty Alal gasp loudly, like they're sucking their breath before diving underwater. They breathe out in unison, 'No, Allah, no, Allah,' and scoop Banaz and Shanar out of their pockets on the donkey's back. Payzee cries, the donkeys are hee-hawing like crazy. Our donkey trembles as it brays. Uncle Zoran's hands are big shovels, digging me out of the sack then, swoop, we drop into the grass. Uncle Afran's got Miriam, I think. The boys are trying to get the donkeys to sit but they don't want to go down. Rumble, rumble, the engine's getting nearer. I scrunch my eyes against the blinding, criss-crossing lights, and rattle in Uncle Zoran's arms. Up front, schlick-click, schlick-click, guns at the ready. Save us, Baba and Bapîr? Please, God, let them save us. I'll never be naughty again, I promise. *And…*

Hush, as the sound of the truck chuckled into the distance. The lights went out and, together – the grown-ups, kids, donkeys, grass, mountains, the moon, and the stars – sighed with relief.

Then, we were on the move again.

We journeyed until it was just getting light when we slept in tents the adults made from tree branches, our camp concealed in a forest. Again, we were warned to be quiet, but Grandma Zareen snored like a beast. It poured down too, and the rain seeped through the gaps in the leafy canopy and soaked my blanket. Come nightfall, I was back in my rice sack, drifting in and out of sleep as our weary procession trundled on. *Where are we going?*

Our brush with the truck – I hadn't seen it, but the boys later described it as a 'massive army truck with guns and everything' – was not our only incident. On the second night, as we crossed a narrow bridge, the donkey carrying Banaz and Shanar got scared and began snorting and rearing. As one of the uncles (I forget who) tried to calm the donkey, it jerked some more and Shanar flew out of her pouch and tumbled down the rocky slope below. Oh my God, Aunty Alal screamed like a banshee. Mum did too. Grandma Zareen wheezed. But Shanar's wails confirmed she was alive, at least. I peered over the lip of my pouch, scared to look but equally frightened not to, and watched as Dad, fast as lightning, whipped off his cummerbund and threw it like a rope over the cliff edge and called down to Shanar to grab the other end of the sash while Uncle Zoran held a lantern overhead and Uncle Afran chanted a prayer. Dad lifted Shanar to safety, but her face was covered with blood where she'd cracked her forehead on the rocks. Under normal circumstances, Shanar would have gone to hospital; she probably needed stitches, poor thing. These, however, were not normal circumstances, so a makeshift bandage had to suffice. On we went, and I must have fallen into a deep sleep because I don't recall the rest of the journey.

I woke up huddled in a blanket with Miriam. The floor was cold and hard and vibrated with fast footsteps. Familiar voices jabbered, jabbered, jabbered. Squinting, I sat up to assimilate my surroundings. I was inside a huge cement room housing a bulldozer, digger and other monster construction vehicles. The boys were running around and climbing on the machines. Mum, Kejal and Aunty Alal were a few feet away from me, kneeling on a folded blanket, chatting at speed as they unpacked food parcels and folded clothes. Shanar was slumped over Aunty Alal's lap, Dad's khaki cummerbund wrapped around her wounded head. Grandma sat over the group on a chair, tut-tutting, giving Mum evils. Banaz and Payzee were snoozing alongside Miriam and me. Two little bugs in a rug. There was no sign of the men.

'Bakha, my darling, my love, you're awake,' called Mum, smiling.

I rubbed my eyes. Was this for real? 'Where are we, Mum?'

'We're in Piranshahr,' she said.

I tried to mouth the word. 'Where's that?'

Grandma screwed up her meaty face and shot me a look that screamed, *how dare you*, before turning back to Mum. 'That girl's a troublemaker,' she spat.

'We're in Iran. This is our home now,' Mum said calmly, a steamroller parked behind her.

I asked, 'Is this our house?' and Mum laughed. 'Oh no, Allah. We're just staying here until we move into Grandma and Grandpa's new house, which you're going to love.'

'Oh, OK,' I said.

Just then, Miriam sat up, looked around, and asked, 'Where are we?'

The construction vehicles and warehouse belonged to Grandpa Babakir, and all sixteen of us would live there for at least two weeks. Not that I minded; I thought it was fun. On our first afternoon, me and Miriam played in the courtyard outside, where a few open plastic sacks filled with grey powder were stacked. We got creative, mixing the powder with water to make mud pies, but our mixture went hard before we could do much with it, and our hands were caked in the stuff. Fortunately, Dad walked in on in our play session and whisked Miriam and me across the courtyard to a big metal tank, which had a nozzle coming out of it. Dad fiddled with something and water gushed from that nozzle. I thought it was amazing. However, me and Miriam had to scrub with olive oil soap for ages to rid our hands of the hard clumps of dry clay stuff. How were we to know we'd been playing with cement?

I feared our experiment would cost me a beating, but, surprisingly, Dad didn't as much as shout at me. Instead, once our hands were clean, he took us inside and played on the construction machines with us. Wow, that was so much fun; Dad let me sit on his lap in the cab of the digger while I pretended to operate it. 'What are you building, Bakha?' he teased.

'I'm making a big house for us all to live in,' I said.

Dad laughed then, which made me feel all fuzzy inside. *Nice Dad is back*, I thought.

The grown-ups promised we'd be moving to a new house soon, but as the days rolled by, I began to wonder whether this would ever happen. Then, one boiling afternoon, in a convoy of Toyota pick-up trucks (Dad sold our donkeys), we finally pulled up outside what was to be our new home: Grandpa Babakir's house.

My eyes nearly popped out of my head. Seriously, I thought they were joking. Compared to our mud home in Iraq, this was a palace. It was a proper house made from light brown concrete blocks and set in a quiet residential street. Iron gates taller than Grandpa Babakir led to the back garden, and I spied a few apple and date trees at the roadside that would be great for climbing and picking fruit.

We went inside and wandered around, the adults deciding who would be sleeping in which rooms. I thought, *I'm never going to remember my way around this place.*

The house was L-shaped, composed of two long hallways with rooms off them. Outside, a roof held up by wedding cake-style pillars shielded a patio area. Two steep steps took you from the patio down to a grass garden and a pond sprouting plants and flowers. The toilets were in sheds at the bottom of the garden (indoor toilets are considered unhygienic in Iraq and Iran), but inside, there was a wet room furnished with a water tank (with a piece of hosepipe connected to it as a makeshift tap) and a drain in the floor. This was proper luxury. In Iraq, we had to wash in the river or inside a corrugated metal cubicle in the yard, using water heated on the picnic stove.

'Is this really our house?' I asked Mum.

She squeezed my shoulder. 'Yes, Bakha, this is our home,' she said, then Grandma Zareen lumbered into the hall.

'Behya, the kitchen is in *there*,' she said, jabbing a fat thumb over her shoulder.

My grandparents had their own 'headquarters', comprising a utility room, which opened onto the patio, and a large lounge and bedroom divided by a curtain nailed across a doorway. The lounge also overlooked the garden through ramshackle windows framed by gaudy floral print curtains. *How could I ever forget those curtains?*

Grandma Zareen walked around the house as though she were a queen. Well, she waddled rather than walked, to be honest. She and Grandpa looked odd together: Zareen was only four feet-something, and whereas Grandpa was spindly, Grandma often had to turn sideways to go through doorways. A potato alongside a runner bean. I don't mean to be rude, but Zareen was a heavy lady – with a heavy presence. You couldn't miss Zareen – if only for the extravagant headgear she wore whenever we had visitors. It was a wide bejewelled wrap band with two gold domes on either side of her head. Threaded jewels looped from the domes, and a long white wedding-style veil was attached to the back of the band.

Zareen was constantly belittling my mum and aunties, yet they all fawned over her. She would hold gatherings in her lounge, like mothers' meetings. The same crowd congregated most afternoons in between prayer times: Zareen, Mum, Aunty Alal, Sazan, the meddling woman who lived next door to us, and the village doctor, Lilan, who looked like a witch with her coarse grey hair and pointy features. They'd all sit on the floor, gossiping and chugging shisha through hookah pipes. Zareen's throaty cackle, *He, he, he, ha, ha, ha,* crunched through the walls.

Sometimes, I'd catch snippets of conversation from those meetings as I walked past Grandma Zareen's headquarters. Zareen, to Mum: 'Bekhal is a troublemaker,' or 'you need to control that girl [meaning me].' And I'd think, *Why? I haven't done anything wrong.* Sazan would then interject her opinion, which invariably included the word, 'sinetkirin', but I didn't know the meaning of that word then.

The men's get-togethers happened in their lounge or on the patio, where they too would smoke shisha – or hashish – and drink beer from brown glass bottles. Sometimes they drank a clear liquid that smelled like the antiseptic solution we dabbed on cuts and grazes. But they also spent many nights away from home, patrolling the mountains as they'd done when we lived in Kurdistan. The mystery surrounding their jaunts intrigued me. I would kiss Dad's hand – as is customary in our culture – then watch him leave in his big, wrap hat, AK 47 strapped to his back. And I would wonder, *what, exactly, is this 'patrolling the mountains' business?*

Once, when Dad was preparing to leave for the mountains, he asked me to fetch his coat. Delighted to help, I scuttled along to his bedroom and unhooked his camouflage jacket from a nail on the wall. The coat dropped heavily into my arms, and as I caught it, I heard a sloshing sound and noticed a clear glass bottle in the right outside pocket. I won't lie, I had a snoop. Stuffed inside the pocket alongside the bottle was a few cotton balls and a box containing three or four old-fashioned, straight razor blades. Still intrigued, I unscrewed the bottle and sniffed its contents – a colourless liquid that smelled like antiseptic and the drink the men often sipped. *This must be patrolling equipment*, I thought, and quickly screwed the lid, shoved the bottle back where I'd found it, and folded the coat over my arms – just as I heard footsteps approaching. When I turned, Dad was in the door frame. He glared at the coat, at the neck of the bottle poking out of its pocket. 'No, no, no, no, no,' he said, 'put that one back. Pass me the other coat.' He gestured at a beige jacket hanging behind me. There was no way I would argue with him, so I hung up the camouflage coat and handed him the beige one. Then I kissed his hand, and he kissed my head and off he went to patrol the mountains – without his equipment.

The men's world interested me far more than the women's cackling and chit-chat. After the horrific beating I endured for touching Rekan's hand, you'd think I'd be avoiding Dad, but, no; I followed him everywhere. I became his shadow. If he was doing chores around the home, I'd offer to help. I'd walk hand in hand around the garden with him, begging him to quit smoking cigarettes as I'd heard they could kill you. 'Please, Baba, I don't want you to die,' I'd tell him. I wanted Dad to treat me the same as he did Bahman, who was encouraged to sit with the men and help with cleaning and loading their rifles. So, you can imagine my joy when Dad ushered me into the utility room one afternoon and taught me how to load the magazine into his AK 47.

Back then, I craved Dad's approval. At the same time, I was cautious not to overstep the mark. For example, there were certain questions I knew not to ask Dad, the most burning one being: 'Why did we leave our home in Kurdistan?' I did, however, put this question to Mum one day. I picked the right moment – when she was alone in the kitchen making dolma, singing a Kurdish song while making neat vine-leaf parcels, a wistful smile playing on her lips. I could always tell when Mum was daydreaming about the past.

'Why did we leave the old house?' I asked.

'Bakha, my darling, my love, we *had* to leave,' said Mum.

'But *why*?' I insisted.

Mum sighed and started on a new parcel, her dreamy smile fading. 'Because, Bakha, if we had stayed, then your dad, Grandpa Babakir and Bahman – along with all the other men and boys in this family – would have been sent away to war. Our home might have been destroyed and we would have been taken away to a camp.'

I clapped my hand over my mouth, shocked but also relieved Dad had got us away in time. I didn't want to live in a camp, and I most certainly didn't want my dad, grandpa, brother, or other male relatives risking their lives at war. I pushed that thought to the back of my mind and decided never to question our move to Iran again.

We never celebrated birthdays in our household. So, there were no parties or presents as such. At most, if they remembered, Mum and Dad might give us kids money (the equivalent of two pence) to buy an ice cream, which they did do when I turned seven. Mum gave me the cash. 'Today you're seven,' she said, 'here's some money for an ice cream.' Oh my God, I felt so special. Being seven was good – until my parents forced their religion upon me. I mean, *properly* forced it on me.

The shift was quite sudden. I was used to reading from the Quran, but now I was expected to read and memorise at least thirty pages of the book a day. My elders drummed and drummed into me the teachings of the Prophet Muhammad, the last messenger of Allah and founder of Islam, and Mum would make Kejal and me pray five times a day with her and the other women – while the men prayed separately in their exclusive lounge. Mum also taught us the washing ritual, compulsory before each prayer session, which involved cupping water in your hands, then wetting your face, ears, neck, feet, and arms (from wrist to elbow only). You had to wet your eyebrows and eyelashes and at least seven hairs at the front of your head. This procedure ensured we were ritually pure, Mum said. Honestly, all I heard was Muhammad this, Muhammad that and, 'You won't be allowed into heaven if you're naughty.' *Oh no*, I thought, *I'm screwed*. While I hadn't been told off or beaten in a while, I had become known as 'The Troublemaker', thanks to Grandma Zareen. Plus, Bekhal didn't feature in the Quran, so my name was (definitely) not down on the door to paradise. As that awful thought sunk in, I decided my name should be Fatimah from then on. When I announced this to my family, they all laughed at me.

But there was light. Between the overwhelming religious stuff, worrying that smoking would kill Dad, and fretting about which actions might cost me another beating, we had some fun times in that house. Uncle Zoran made sure of that. Compared to my dad, he was so chilled out. Funny, too, with a heartfelt laugh. Uncle Zoran would fool around and entertain us kids with games and magic tricks, such as pulling coins from behind our ears and making stones disappear beneath cups. He also played a pre-bedtime storytelling game. We would sit in a circle on the lounge floor and watch with excitement when Zoran clasped his hands beneath his chin, pulled a spooky face, and began, 'Once upon a time, long, long ago, a…' then he'd point at one of us to continue the story, and we'd go round the circle, each adding a new line to the tale, until it was Uncle Zoran's turn again, when he'd turn our magical stories about princesses and fairies into dark horror stories. I remember one of his endings went something like this: 'The princess was caught by a hairy monster who chewed her up then spat out her legs.' God, we laughed so much at Uncle Zoran's pranks. He was a breath of fresh air.

Bedtimes were often funny too. I shared a bedroom with Banaz, Kejal and Bahman. Miriam, Shanar, Daryan, and Eylo were also together in a separate room a couple of doors down. Our parents couldn't have considered how noisy we would be when they came up with that arrangement. Me and Banaz were the worst for giggling at night.

Now she was almost five, Banaz and I were becoming properly close. Even at that age, Banaz was the most beautiful out of all us girls, and it was at around this time, soon after our move to Iran, that we nicknamed her Nazca. She was such a pretty little girl, with the daintiest hands and fingers and angelic voice that matched her features. Yeah, Banaz was perfect. I could look at her forever.

Me and Banaz slept side by side in our stitched-together duvet beds on the floor. Although we rarely went straight to sleep, especially after storytelling with Uncle Zoran. Instead, we performed hand shadow puppet shows on the wall, complete with sound effects for our birds or rabbits or cows or the monsters that haunted Uncle Zoran's stories. Banaz's shadows were so tiny next to mine, and her monsters were never scary, bless her, but I would pretend to be terrified all the same. We would laugh and laugh, and Kejal would go, 'Shh, you two, I'm trying to sleep,' from the other side of the room. Which made us giggle even more.

But the funniest bedtime pursuit, I thought, was when I would make loud farting noises with my mouth – then shout, 'That was Banaz,' and she would tremble with laughter, and Kejal would again tell us to hush, or threaten to call for Mum and Dad. I never listened to her though.

After all, I was The Troublemaker, right?

Chapter Three

DEPARTURES AND ARRIVALS

So, I could be naughty at times, like any other curious, excitable, or frustrated kid my age. My actions were not always deliberate. I didn't seek trouble. It had a way of finding me – and my God did I get punished for my misdemeanours and 'whore-child' behaviour. Our parents would warn of the kinds of beatings to expect for being 'naughty'. To further enforce this message, Mum and all the aunties repeated a terrifying story that, now I think about it, was wholly inappropriate for children's ears. To the best of my memory, this is how they told it:

'Say your mum dies, but your dad has two wives…' Are you sitting comfortably? I doubt it, sorry, '…well, your step-mum (your baba's surviving wife), will chop off your dead mum's arm, and wrap it in a special cloth to preserve it. Then, whenever you and your siblings are naughty, she'll beat you with your real mother's arm. As she does so, she will tell you, "You're being beaten by your mother's hand – the hand that helped you to grow. This will help you." And when your Dad marries again, his new wife will do the same with your stepmother's arm when she dies.'

Sometimes they'd tell us the story at bedtime, bookended by other tales featuring Muhammad. I'm not joking. At least Uncle Zoran's monster stories were comical, cartoonish. But this yarn our mothers told – which I believed as true – was off-the-scale disturbing. I was still struggling to come to terms with Reş down the shithole. Seriously, what was it with this family and their gruesome arm stories?

For a brief while, maybe during our first month in Iran, I managed to escape getting even a single beating, and in my seven-year-old mind, I began to question whether Mum and Dad's violence towards me in Iraq had been two isolated incidents. Maybe they hadn't meant to be so hard on me? No such luck. Our move to Iran had merely served as a distraction, an interlude. For Dad, at least. And the older I grew, the more he watched my every move.

At this stage, I was still testing what I could or couldn't do. I was so confused. I'd think, *I'll try this and if I don't get hit, I'll know it's allowed*. I soon discovered that practically everything I attempted came with a big, fat, 'NO' tag. For example, I used to wee standing up instead of squatting over the hole – because I was scared Reş would grab me. When Mum found out about this (Kejal grassed on me), I got a beating. Afterwards, Mum explained her reason for disciplining me: 'Your legs will be splattered with wee and that is dirty. Now pray to Allah – or you will not be accepted into heaven.' So that was another lesson learned: never, ever, take your sister into the shithole with you.

Oh, I got some horrific beatings as a kid, especially from Dad. He whacked me with his belt, a stick, and often tied my hands together with a rope first, just as he'd done to me in Iraq. Mum would sometimes hold me down so Dad could get a good aim, and they would let my siblings watch this happen, too. Imagine that tableau: it was like an evil pantomime in the lounge – and I was frequently centre stage. I could not grasp why Dad punished me in this way. Why not ground me? Or ban me from playing outside for a while? I had never seen Uncle Afran beat his kids like this. *Why. Just, why?* More confusing was how my parents switched from being evil to loving in a flash. I could be walking hand in hand around the garden with Dad in the morning. In the afternoon he might make me ballerina dollies fashioned from poppies. But come the evening, he'd be hitting me for something as innocuous as failing to wash my hands properly after petting a dog, especially, heaven forbid, if that dog had licked me. Dog saliva is generally considered impure and unclean in Islam. According to The Hadith – collected traditions of Muhammad based on his actions and sayings – you must wash seven times after touching a canine, first with soil, then six times with water. The soil part is supposed to cleanse you, and as you wash, you must pray to 'Almighty Allah'. This routine seemed a hell of a faff to me, especially as we didn't have to wash after touching chickens, cows or sheep. Contact with livestock is OK because it's food. That's what Dad told me.

The abuse was frequent; if a few days passed without my being whacked, I wondered what was happening. In the end, I thought, *Fuck it, I should have a little fun – because I'll be battered for something or other today, anyway.* I did most of my naughty stuff with Miriam. Like me, she was an explorative, spontaneous type.

Me and Miriam were like close sisters, playing together and holding hands everywhere we went. Miriam's palm was often wet with sweat and felt like sticky dough against mine, but this didn't bother me because we were best buddies. Once, Miriam had this huge verruca on the fleshy part of her hand, just below her lifeline. The next day, an identical growth appeared in the same spot on my hand. I loved that we had matching verrucae. Me and Miriam were inseparable. With her, I could do all the mischievous things of which Kejal disapproved. Cheeky stuff, like sneaking into the kitchen and nicking homemade sweets and mouthfuls of yoghurt when we were supposed to be fasting during Ramadan. Although occasionally, Miriam and I got a bit too carried away in our quest to have fun. Like that morning in winter 1991, when we wanted to join Dad and Uncle Afran on a drive to Iraq. Our dads made frequent trips across the border after setting up a pick-up and delivery business. We had no idea what they picked up or delivered, but trucking through deep snow along perilous narrow mountain roads seemed an exciting prospect to Miriam and me.

Winters were more fun in Iran than Iraq. I can't recall there being much snowfall when we lived in Qalat Dizah – perhaps a flurry or two which turned to brown slush as soon as it hit the ground. In Piranshahr, it properly *snowed*. Several feet could fall in one day, leaving a giant chef's hat of snow upon the flat roof of our house. That snow would eventually be cleared from the roof and dumped by the roadside, forming a mini mountain for us kids to slide down on sack sledges. We made snowmen, and Dad would make us snow horses to play on, which were like incredible sculptures, built around a wooden frame and always with a detailed face and tail. *Dad at his very best.*

Before leaving for Iraq, Dad and Uncle Afran pottered outside, clearing snow from the road, and preparing the Toyota for their journey, scraping ice from the windscreen, putting chains on the tyres, checking the oil and water, and such. It was bitterly cold, around minus ten, but this didn't deter Miriam and me. We ran outside, dressed in our usual gear – a long dress over Aladdin trousers, teamed with a headscarf and rubbery loafers – and began pestering the men.

'Please, Baba, let us come with you?' I begged, my voice clouding the air, snow soaking the bottoms of my Aladdin trousers.

'Please, we'll be good,' added Miriam. Her hand felt like an ice lolly in mine today.

'Please?' we said in unison.

Dad and Afran exchanged bemused looks and in a hopeful moment, I thought they were going to say yes, but they said nothing and continued inspecting the canvas canopy over the back of the truck. Did their silence mean they were considering our idea? 'You won't know we're there,' I tried again.

'And we'll be really helpful.' Miriam's teeth chattered.

'Not today, Bakha,' said Dad, patting my head.

'Sorry, Miriam,' was Uncle Afran's response. 'Why don't you both run along and play in the snow instead?' Then Dad mentioned something about needing fuel cans, and off they went, boots squeaking in the snow, leaving Miriam and me alone in the driveway with the truck. We watched our dads go into the house, then I squeezed Miriam's hand and we shared a cheeky grin that said, 'Are you thinking what I'm thinking?'

'Quick, let's get in,' I said.

Together, we climbed onto the step and into the vehicle, both in fits of giggles. We crawled into a space between two bench seats and used an old sheet of tarpaulin as a blanket to hide beneath. It was dark and smelled of oil and manure in our makeshift tent, but we were too excited to care. We sat hand in hand, feet pulled in, knees touching our chests, shivering and laughing at the same time. Next, we heard Dad and Uncle Afran outside the truck, their voices fuzzy through the tarpaulin and canvas cover. Then, two metallic thuds. *That'll be the doors.* The truck gently seesawed, left, right, left, and, with a bronchial cough, the engine kicked in.

'Oh my God, we're moving,' I said.

Miriam gasped and hiccupped at the same time. 'Do you think they know we're in here?' Another hiccup. The truck slowed, turned left, then powered forwards.

'I don't think so,' I replied, and we both burst out laughing.

'Oh, Bakha, wait till the boys find out. This is far more daring than anything they've ever done.'

'I know. We must be going to Iraq. We did it,' I said. *I will get such a beating for this,* I thought.

Being stowaways was at first thrilling. We couldn't see where we were going, but we felt all the twists and turns and bumps in the road, heard the engine straining and the chains clunking at steep sections. Me and Miriam were getting joggled around in our hiding space, and we couldn't stop giggling. It felt so good to laugh – for a while.

We stopped after what seemed a good two to three hours into the journey. Me and Miriam were frozen to the bone, our hands iced together. Where had my feet gone? I couldn't feel them. My lips were numb too. I felt weak, dizzy. The truck bounced a couple of times, accompanied by the close thud of boots inside the vehicle. I nudged Miriam then the engine spluttered to life again.

Confused, I threw the tarpaulin back, only to be confronted by two men we'd never seen before.

I dread to think what might have happened to Miriam and me had it not been for those two hitchhikers. We might have died of hypothermia. If our truck had crashed, we might have been catapulted out of it. We pleaded with our fellow passengers in the back, 'Please don't tell them we're here.'

When the hitchhikers did grass on us, about ten minutes after we'd picked them up, I expected Dad to haul me out of the truck by my hair and beat me black and blue. He didn't lay a finger on me. Don't get me wrong, he was cross. Uncle Afran wasn't doing cartwheels in the snow either, but I sensed they were both more relieved and amused. I noticed their moustaches lifting when they told us off. Then we continued our journey into Iraq, with Miriam and me squished between our dads on the front seat. The warmth from the heater felt heavenly.

It was dark when we arrived back in Iran, sleepy after our ten-hour round trip in sub-zero temperatures. Mum and Aunty Alal went apeshit when they saw us. Imagine: they had no idea their daughters had snuck into that Toyota. Neither Dad nor Uncle Afran had been able to contact them because we had no landline or mobile phones. While we trucked to Iraq and back, Mum and Aunty Alal frantically knocked on every door in the neighbourhood, asking, 'Have you seen our daughters?' The Iranian police would not be interested in missing kid reports in those days. Mum and Aunty Alal had been worried sick. Understandably so, too. Aunty Alal slapped Miriam, and Mum smacked my bum a few times, but given the seriousness of our offence, we got off lightly. And when Mum did whack me, it felt laboured compared to the effort she usually gave, which I thought strange. *Maybe she's just too exhausted to bother*, I thought. I didn't know Mum was four months pregnant at the time.

On the day my little sister Ashti was born, Banaz had to go to the hospital after a nasty accident at home. It was my fault, too. God, I felt so awful.

That morning, Banaz and I had been playing on our rope swing in a room at the back of the house, taking turns to push one another. The room also housed our tandoor – the round clay oven in the ground that we used for making flatbread, or cooking big joints of meat – and one window frame with no glass in it that overlooked a vegetable patch. There was a circular hole in the roof, directly above the tandoor (to let the smoke out). Our swing consisted of two lengths of rope attached to a sturdy log resting on the roof over the circle. The two ropes were tied together to make a seat, although we added a pillow for extra comfort.

Banaz was loving her turn in the swing. 'Push me harder, I want to go higher,' she squealed. So, I pushed her a little harder, and she elevated her legs towards the facing window as though she thought that would add more height. Up she went, down she swung, like a little fairy, giggling away. 'More, more,' she cried. I pushed her again, this time with extra force, and Banaz and the swing zoomed through the window. As this happened the rope hit the top of the window frame and swung Banaz even higher. I heard her scream, and the swing dropped back through the window, with no Banaz in it.

I ran through the house and out the front door, tears streaming down my face, shouting, 'Nazca, Nazca … I'm so sorry … I didn't mean it … Nazca…' A crowd had already formed when I reached the vegetable patch at the side of the house. I screamed when I saw Banaz, sitting higgledy-piggledy among the chilli plants, blood gushing from her eye as she sobbed her little heart out. Aunty Alal gathered Banaz in her arms. 'I'll get the truck,' said Uncle Afran. Grandma Zareen glared at me through milky cataracts, her veil fluttering in the breeze. She looked scary. Dad stood beside her, arm over her dumpling shoulder. Mum wasn't there – because she was in hospital 'getting a baby'. 'I'm so sorry, she fell off the swing. I'm so sorry, Nazca.' I said as Aunty Alal pattered away holding Banaz. Then Dad slapped me, once, twice around the head.

'Get out of my sight, you disgust me,' he said.

Banaz had landed on one of the wooden stakes supporting the chilli plants. The pointy end of the stick speared her eyebrow, poor thing. I felt so guilty. Later that day, Banaz returned from hospital. She looked like a little pirate in her Aladdin trousers and big patch over her injured eye. Mum came home too, cradling Ashti, the fifth Mahmod daughter she'd dared to bring into her mother-in-law's house. I asked Mum, 'Did Ashti live in your belly like Banaz and Payzee did?' Fascinated by this concept, I wanted to know more. Like, how did Ashti get inside Mum's belly? Did somebody put her there? But Mum changed her story this time.

'No, the stork delivered Ashti to me in the hospital,' she said.

I believed that story too, even though it didn't explain why Mum grew a huge belly each time a new sister came along.

A few weeks after Ashti arrived, there was another addition to our family: Avin, the teenage daughter of Dad's sister Baze. Aunty Baze's husband, Hamza, had recently passed away, leaving Avin without a father, and Baze had not remarried. Without a father, Avin was labelled an orphan, which was deemed shameful within the Kurdish community. Therefore, the powers that be in the Mahmod clan decided Avin should live with us, and Mum and Dad would become her guardians.

Avin appeared one afternoon. I came in after playing outside, and there she was, sitting in my Grandma's lounge with Mum, Aunty Alal, Sazan, and Lilan. Kejal was there too, eyeing Avin as though she were a beautiful princess. Which was not far from the truth. The last time I had seen Avin was on that nightmare camping trip when I almost drowned in the river. She had resembled one of us girls then, but now, she looked like a woman. Oh my God, that girl looked so, so pretty. A unique beauty, with blueish-green eyes that matched the colour of our mountain rivers in summer. She had light hair too – a blend of caramel and honey tones, which she wore in a long, silky plait down to her bum. 'Bekhal, this is your cousin Avin,' said Grandma. 'She's come from Iraq to live here with us. You could learn a lot from Avin.'

Sazan nodded vigorously at Grandma then, gesturing at Kejal and me in turn, muttered something like, 'When are you going to get those two done?' I hadn't a clue what she meant. And to be honest, I was too mesmerised by Avin's presence to care. I smiled and nodded politely at Avin, in the manner I would greet any female guest, and sat on the floor. I literally could not take my eyes off Avin, but there was something about her that made me feel uneasy, frightened even. I swear to God, I thought, *Something horrible is going to happen to that poor girl.*

Chapter Four

GIRLS' TIME?

Avin was wise as well as beautiful. Being thirteen, she had learned all the rules of how to be a Good Muslim Girl and please our elders. Avin had lived with us for a few months now, and I had not heard Mum and Dad so much as raise their voices at her, let alone beat her. They looked upon Avin as another daughter. Their *favourite* daughter. But this didn't make me jealous of Avin. How could I envy someone so pretty and kind? My cousin was somebody I could look up to. Yeah, Grandma was right, I could learn a lot from Avin.

I was besotted by Avin from the moment I met her. Day after day, I followed her around, noting her mannerisms: how she knelt on her shins, with her back as straight as the wall and her head politely bowed. Sometimes, I'd catch myself dropping into a dream-like trance. I loved watching how her hair glistened in the sunshine and seeing how many tones of brown and blonde I could count. You would pay a colourist a lot of money today for hair like that, but Avin's was one hundred per cent natural.

Mum and Dad made a huge fuss of Avin, as did my grandparents, who let her sleep in their headquarters, away from us noisy kids. Although secretly I didn't envy Avin on that; Grandma's snoring sounded like a freight train crashing.

Avin was polite and so helpful around the home, doing the cleaning and assisting Mum and Aunty Alal in the kitchen. She appeared happy, too, despite all she had been through with losing her dad – and effectively losing her mum in the process. I never saw Avin cry or hear her say that she missed her mum, which I thought odd. Just imagining myself in Avin's situation brought tears to my eyes. Don't get me wrong, I despised Dad when he beat me. But if he were to die? Oh, that would have broken my little heart, literally.

I tried to be like Avin, who did as she was told, I noticed, from helping Grandma in and out of her headdress to praying, reading, remembering, and reciting whole sections of the Quran. But I struggled to emulate Avin's 'pure' ways. While I did my best around the home – I became shit hot at the dishes – being a Good Muslim Girl wasn't for me. Praying five times a day, following strict rules about what and when to eat, wearing a polo neck jumper and hijab in summer, washing my hands seven times after touching a cute dog – there were so many crazy rules.

Everything in our culture seemed so over the top to me. I felt stifled. But equally, this was my world, and I could not imagine a different life outside of it. I didn't go to school and watched little television. When we youngsters were allowed (limited) time in front of our black-and-white TV set, our parents would censor which programmes we viewed. I remember watching cartoons such as *The Racoons*, *Inspector Gadget* and *The Pink Panther Show*, which were all dubbed in Arabic, Persian or Kurdish. We also got, in Arabic, the British animation, *Jimbo and the Jet-Set*. This cartoon, about a talking plane who constantly finds himself in a pickle, fascinated me. I'd seen the occasional plane flying overhead in Iraq and Iran, but I had not been on one. Did people go on planes often? A scene showing Jimbo coming in to land at London Airport features in the opening credits, in which you see animated sheep in patchwork fields singing, 'Jim-*bo*, Jim-*bo*,' clusters of pretty houses with chimneypots, and tall skyscrapers as he nears the runway. This scene alone intrigued me as the word 'London' cropped up a lot in our home. Because London, a 'big city in England', was where Dad's second youngest brother, Ari, lived with his wife Berivan and their children. Whenever Jimbo came on the telly, one of the adults would proudly pipe up: 'Your Uncle Ari lives in London.' Then one afternoon, as we sat on the patio watching another episode of *Jimbo and the Jet-Set*, Dad came up the steps from the garden, stood right between Jimbo and us kids and, thumbs in his sash, chest puffed out, announced: 'Your Uncle Ari, Aunty Berivan, and cousins are coming to stay. They arrive tomorrow, so I want you all to be on your best behaviour.'

Argh, Uncle Ari. Even at that young age his name made me squirm. We used to see a lot of him in Iraq before he took his family to live in London a few months before we fled to Iran. Ari's eldest daughter, Heibat, was the same age as Miriam and me, and Helo was a year younger than Banaz. Most Mahmod family members worshipped the ground Ari walked on. You should have seen Grandma Zareen around Ari; she'd wrap him in a big, doughy hug and kiss his face. 'My darling son, my darling boy,' she'd say, the jewels on her headdress twinkling and chiming. Watching Zareen fawn over her son in this way made me wonder, *Why has she never wrapped her cuddly arms around me?*

Outwardly, Dad adored Ari. Inwardly, I think Dad wished his younger brother was more conservative and traditional in the way he presented himself. Ari was loud and showy and always bragging about his possessions and the businesses he owned. I didn't like Ari then, and today I hate him with every fibre of my being. In *my* culture, Ari is a man-whore. I hope he rots in hell.

After Dad's announcement, the telly went off and it was all hands to the deck. Avin and Kejal helped Mum and Aunty Alal with the cooking and, my God, did that smell good? They made stews and fried rice dishes, huge pots of dolma, soups, meat patties, and desserts such as churros. I also wanted to help with the food, but only the eldest daughters could do so. 'Don't worry, your time will come when you're older, Bakha,' said Mum, beating her ladle in the air to her words. 'You can wash the pots.' So, I stood on my crate next to the sink and started scrubbing, earwigging as Mum and Aunty Alal gossiped about Aunty Berivan. 'I've heard she [Berivan] wears Western clothes,' said Aunty Alal.

'No, Allah,' went Mum, tut-tutting.

Once I'd finished the dishes, I did the housework with Avin, Kejal, and Banaz. We scrubbed the house from top to bottom – then cleaned the outside loos. All this effort was for Uncle Ari's benefit. While we worked, the men sat in their lounge, drinking beer and smoking shisha.

The next day, Uncle Ari arrived at our home looking every inch the dodgy businessman, dressed in clothes I'd never seen on a man in my country before, and carrying a bulging suitcase. Then in his early thirties, he had on a baby-pink, button-down shirt with a stiff collar. His trousers were a shiny navy affair, with two vertical, sharp creases running down the middle of each leg, front and back. He wore glossy, grey slip-on shoes with thin soles, and a big, gold show-off-y watch. Gold rings wreathed his fingers too. But more shocking was the gear that Aunty Berivan rocked up in. I'm not kidding you; she was bare-legged from her knees to her ankles. A pencil skirt covered her thighs, but there wasn't much give in the fabric. Partnering the skirt was an animal-print blouse, the sleeves rolled up to her elbows. She looked half zebra, half woman. Had she forgotten her hijab?

I was equally gobsmacked at Heibat and Helo's outfits: box-pleat skirts with hems skimming their knees and white, calf-length socks. If I were to dress like that, I'd be called a whore. Dad would beat me for ever and a day. But none of the adults commented on my cousins' attire, not even my dad. The girls were free to sit crossed legged in their skirts too. I couldn't believe my eyes.

As soon as Ari was through the door, he started boasting about his world while belittling our Iranian lifestyle. 'Oh, you should see the new electric toothbrushes I bought for me and Berivan,' he gushed to Dad as we all made our way to the patio from our grandparents' headquarters, lugging the suitcase in one hand and swinging his misbaha (prayer beads) in the other. 'They weren't cheap, but you get what you pay for, don't you? We'll never use regular toothbrushes again.' And Dad looked at Ari with wide eyes, palpably impressed. 'Oh, and we've just had a magnificent shagpile carpet laid, all through the house, too,' Ari went on. 'How do you cope in the winter? Those rugs can't keep the heat in, eh.' Ari laughed at his own joke, then parked his suitcase in the centre of the patio and, with a lazy side nod, said: 'There are some old clothes in there – stuff Heibat and Helo have grown out of or don't wear anymore. We thought they might do for your girls. Please, help yourself, we'll only throw them away otherwise.'

Mum and Aunty Alal nodded politely and thanked Uncle Ari, then, once the men had gone back inside, they pounced like magpies on that case. Aunty Berivan smiled smugly into her shoulder as she watched her in-laws unpack its contents. Kejal, Banaz, Miriam, Shanar and I joined in too, grabbing articles of clothing from the case. Much as I didn't like Ari, this was exciting. Inside the case were little dresses with straps rather than sleeves, and pleated skirts, like those Heibat and Helo had on. There were pinafores and check-print, short-sleeved dresses, and floral, patterned nylon tubes – like those tattoo bandages you get. A wispy coral article caught my eye as it slithered over the side of the suitcase. I picked it up, thinking, *what a beautiful colour*. It was one of the dresses with straps, in flimsy chiffon with ruffles cascading from the waist to the hem. I pinned the straps to the front of my shoulders and glanced down, admiring the view. The dress reminded me of one of the flower ballerina dolls that Dad made. I felt pretty. I looked at Mum. 'I like this one,' I said. I wondered whether the dress might be allowed if worn over Aladdin trousers and teamed with a polo neck jumper and hijab. Mum's eyebrows crossed, and her lips turned into a pencilled line. A look that said, No.

'I don't think that's suitable, Bakha,' said Mum. I dropped the dress back into the case.

Truth was, none of the garments were suitable for us. At the time, I thought those clothes looked exotic – a glimpse into the Western world of which I knew little about. It hadn't bothered me that the ruffles on the little coral number were frayed, and how could I have known that those checked dresses and pinafores were school uniform items that Heibat and Helo had outgrown. Miriam and Shanar tussled over a pair of arm tights. Mum and Aunty Alal exchanged worried looks, but both managed a few words of thanks to Berivan. 'Oh, not at all,' she replied, pushing a zebra sleeve further up her arm. 'As Ari said, we'll only end up throwing this lot away. They grow so fast at this age, don't they?' Berivan tilted her head and gazed down at Banaz, who had in her hands a tiny pink dress with a picture of a mermaid on its front.

'Look,' said Banaz, holding the dress up and pointing at the red-haired mermaid. Of course, we'd never heard of the Disney cartoon, *The Little Mermaid*, featuring Ariel, the sexy fish-tailed girl in a purple bra with her bare midriff on display.

'That'll suit you, Banaz,' said Berivan.

Prayer time saved Mum from that awkward moment.

The Eastern–Western divide between Ari's daughters and us girls became even more apparent when we all played together in the garden. 'Where are the rest of your toys?' asked Heibat when we showed her our plastic clacker balls.

'We don't have any other toys,' said Miriam, offering the neon green contraption to Heibat, 'but this one's really good fun.'

Heibat crinkled her nose. 'Are you joking?'

'I used to have a rocking horse *and* a furry dog that yaps,' I said, 'but I had to leave them behind in Iraq.' I thought I'd slip that piece of information in there as I wasn't warming to Heibat's attitude towards Miriam.

Heibat and Helo looked at each other and burst out laughing.

We tried to get along with our guest cousins, inviting them to make mud cakes and climb apple trees with us. It was summer, after all. Heibat and Helo flinched at our suggestions. 'That's dirty,' Helo and Heibat said in unison, then bombarded us with chatter about *Teenage Mutant Ninja Turtles* characters (whomever they were), their 'cool schoolfriends' in London, ice skating and McDonald's Happy Meals. Nobody wanted to ask Heibat or Helo, 'Who's McDonald?'

Ari and his family stayed with us for two weeks. They would come and go from our house as though it were their own home, dressed in their Western clothes. Nobody could get a word in edgeways when Ari was around. He bragged about his cars and house, with a 'toilet that flushes, and a shower and bath'. Drone, drone, drone. He made a big song and dance about all the fun after-school activities that Heibat and Helo enjoyed in London: swimming lessons, dance classes, and I forget what else because I stopped listening to Ari after a while. I was relieved when he and his brood Jimbo-ed it back to England.

Our usual routine resumed. The men seemed to be away from the house more often nowadays. Grandpa was an elusive soul, always out and about, helping people in the Kurdish community. I rarely saw Grandpa. Dad and Uncle Afran were busy trucking back and forth to Iraq – although I still didn't know what they picked up or delivered – and their nocturnal mountain patrol trips with Grandpa Babakir continued.

Between prayer times and doing chores around the home, we kids would play, either indoors, tearing up and down the hallways during games of hide-and-seek, or outside in the trees. Our rope swing in the tandoor room was still in operation, despite Banaz's accident, but often we couldn't use it because the women were in there, sitting on the circular brick wall surrounding the oven, yakking away as they slapped wet dough against the interior tandoor walls to make flatbread. Mum, as always, spent much of her time in the kitchen, but she seemed happy there. Sometimes, Mum would make huge pots – I'm talking three feet in diameter – full of fried rice and stews, which she and Aunty Alal took out to the street to serve portions to neighbours and passers-by. My God, people would queue the entire length of the street for Mum's culinary creations. It warmed my heart to see such an act of kindness.

Mum has always been creative; she taught us girls how to sew and crochet, weave, and embroider fancy pictures of swans. Avin, Kejal, Banaz, Miriam, Shanar and me (Payzee and Ashti were too young), would sit for hours in the lounge, stitching our swan designs onto pillowcases. Grandma, Aunty Alal, Sazan and Lilan would sew with us too. Banaz loved embroidery and her swans were always far more intricate than mine, but I enjoyed those sessions too. They were peaceful, which made for a refreshing change. There were no men or boys around, no angry vibes in the room. No swearing or bitching. Just proper, quiet girls' time. But, as I'd grown to learn, things could never stay peaceful for long in our house. Alongside those pockets of calmness, I suffered more horrendous beatings – usually about three or four a week. I had almost got used to them, and I taught myself how to deal with the pain without screaming my head off with every thrash of Dad's belt, which would invariably prolong my punishment.

Nothing, however, could prepare me for the next round of pain to be inflicted upon me.

One early evening in late summer, just after the men had set off for the mountains, Lilan appeared at our front door, Gladstone bag heavy in her liver-spotted hand. There was nothing unusual about Lilan showing up; she was always at ours, performing weird procedures such as cupping or leech therapy on the women, or just there to socialise. But the atmosphere in the house had shifted. All the women, and Avin, were in Grandma's headquarters, but I couldn't hear the habitual rounds of, *he hes, ha, has, or, no, Allah, no, Allah.* There was no sickly fruit smell of shisha smoke wafting under the closed door to Grandma's lounge. I was in the hallway with Miriam when Grandma waddled past and ushered Lilan in. Grandma kissed Lilan on both cheeks. 'Come through, we're just setting-up,' she said, her voice low and formal. Lilan followed Grandma into her lounge. Miriam and I thought no more of it and ran back to the tandoor room, where the rest of the girls were playing on the swing. The boys were outside, I imagined, and Payzee and Ashti must have been asleep, somewhere.

'Your turn, Bakha,' cried Banaz, sliding off the swing when she saw me. Seriously, Banaz would give you her last penny.

'I'll push,' said Miriam as I climbed into the harness. Kejal stood with her back to the wall, arms folded over her chest, totally disinterested, until Avin walked into the room, when she suddenly sprung to life.

'Avin, are there any chores I can help you with?' she said in a floaty voice. But the situation felt tense.

Avin, our beautiful, princessy cousin who never frowned, knitted her perfect brows, and said, 'Kejal, I need you to come with me to see Grandma Zareen.' She confirmed this statement with three serious little nods, then looked at Banaz and Shanar and told them: 'You two must come too.'

I sat in the swing, gently swaying, feet dangling, thinking, *Am I the only one of all my sisters to not be in trouble for once?* For the way this scene was panning out, I predicted a punishment awaited in Grandma's headquarters. But I couldn't think what Banaz or Shanar had done wrong. Kejal followed the Good Muslim Girl rules and went above and beyond to please our elders. 'What's happening, Avin?' I blurted. I couldn't help myself.

'I'll come back for you and Miriam in a little while,' she replied, still frowning. Kejal followed Avin out of the room. Banaz and Shanar hurried after them, like cygnets keeping up with their mother.

Their footsteps dimmed. A solemn thud of a door closing followed. I looked at Miriam and her almond eyes widened with fear. 'Shall we go outside, see if we can see anything through the window?' she said in a loud whisper.

I jumped off the swing. 'Good idea.'

Grandma's lounge window was closed, but we heard the violent screams from the other side of the garden. We ran across the lawn to the window curtained with gaudy green flowers. There was a gap, about the width of an adult's head, between the drapes, but I had to let go of Miriam's hand so I could reach the window ledge. Now we could hear a child wailing, deep, raw sobs. Gripping the ledge, I hopped up and down, trying to glimpse whatever horrors were occurring inside the room. Being a few inches smaller than me, Miriam couldn't do the same. Another child screamed, but all I could see was the wall and the backs of two hijabed heads. I hopped a few more times, trying to get higher, then Avin's face appeared in the window to the sound of more sobbing, and Avin's words ticker-taped in my mind: *I'll come back for you and Miriam in a little while.*

'Quick, it's Avin, run,' I said. We bolted across the lawn and around the side of the house, panting fast, then cut left into Sazan's garden and ran into the toilet, locking the wooden door behind us. We crouched in the corner behind the shithole, both gasping in the fusty air while trying to remain quiet. It wasn't yet dark out, but it soon would be, although, for once, Reş never crossed my mind. Clacker balls collided inside my chest.

Miriam's voice juddered. 'I'm scared, Bakha … I'm scared.' Wood rattled, then banged, then crashed. There was somebody at the door.

Avin shook the door hard enough to knock the little hook lock open. She powered into the toilet and, in seconds, Avin was lifting us out of there. She flung Miriam over her shoulder and carried me under her arm as I kicked my legs and screamed, 'Put me down, I don't want to go in there.' Into the house, along the hallway, past the tandoor and kitchen, and finally, into the utility room in Grandma's headquarters.

What happened next scarred me for life. Mentally *and* physically. First, Aunty Alal came through from the lounge and picked up her daughter. I heard Miriam's cries for help, and I wanted to run into the lounge and rescue her, but Avin's grip was as strong as a wrestler's. Less than two minutes or so later, Aunty Alal carried Miriam to her bedroom. At the same time, Mum appeared in the utility room, plucked me from Avin's arms and took me into the lounge.

A plastic sheet lay on the floor. Grandma, Lilan and Sazan were kneeling on it, alongside the Gladstone bag, and a clear glass bottle and a box containing blades. The same bottle and box I'd found in Dad's coat pocket. I screamed, 'Don't kill me, please don't kill me,' and kicked my legs in protest as Mum held me tight and knelt on the sheet. Aunty Alal appeared from nowhere and pinned my right leg to the floor. Sazan did the same with my left leg as mum held my arms down. Then somebody – I don't remember who – lifted my dress and pulled down my Aladdin trousers and underwear. When I tried to wriggle free, Mum snapped, 'Keep still, Bekhal. It's important you keep still,' as Grandma knelt over my belly, razor in her not too steady hand, squinting at my private parts while Lilan recited instructions. I heard that word mentioned again, 'sinetkirin', several times, before Grandma lowered the blade and ripped it through the part of my body I knew only as 'privates' or 'thing' or 'that'.

I can't even begin to explain the pain that caused. I had a high pain threshold, I still do today, but this was unimaginable. Blood spurted from between my legs. I saw the part Grandma had cut from me on the sheet, and I apologise for being so graphic, but it was jumping up and down. My vision began to blur. Lilan started pouring alcohol over the place where she'd cut me, and I howled and howled. More blood poured from me, like when you leave a tap on, and all the women started panicking.

'You've cut a nerve,' Lilan told Grandma.

I looked up at Mum. There were two of her. 'How can you let them do this to me?' I croaked.

Somebody yelled, 'Get the lard,' but I must have been drifting in and out of consciousness because I don't remember standing. The women must have lifted me. Mum cupped my armpits as two of the others held my legs wide apart. Then I felt an almighty burning sensation. The last thing I saw was those horrible green flowers on Grandma's curtains.

I woke up in bed, swimming in sweat and shaking uncontrollably. I can't tell you how old I was. The last time I'd been reminded of my birthday was when Mum told me, 'You're seven now.' I think that had been during springtime, which probably meant my eighth birthday had gone unannounced. So, I was seven, or eight … whatever. What those women did to us little girls was barbaric, unforgivable.

I pulled the cover around me and said a silent prayer in my head.

Please God, don't let me die.

Chapter Five

THAT'S WHAT HAPPENS
TO NAUGHTY GIRLS

Sinetkirin. I'd heard the word so often, hissed through exhalations of hookah, slithering venomously through the conversations that wafted from Grandma Zareen's headquarters: *Sinetkirin, Sinetkirin, Sinetkirin.* A term slipped with nonchalance into sentences featuring 'Bekhal', my sisters, and Miriam and Shanar's names. Sinetkirin, I hate that fucking word. It means circumcision, although I would not find this out until much later in life.

My grandmother butchered my genitals. Miriam, Kejal, Banaz, and Shanar underwent the same degrading procedure before me, although they were cut by Lilan, the village doctor. Now, I know this horrific operation as Female Genital Mutilation (FGM), but nobody told us so at the time.

FGM says it all. It's mutilation of the clitoris and, in some instances, a girl's inner and outer labia will be removed too. Sometimes the labia will be stitched together. Females in my culture are put through this heinous experience as children – before they reach puberty. The purpose, of course, is to supress our sexuality, ensure future marriages and, as was the case in our clan, to retain 'family honour'. It would've been a huge coup for Dad once the community knew his three eldest daughters had 'been done'. Same went for Uncle Afran after Miriam and Shanar's genitals were cut. It's sickening beyond belief. FGM is illegal in the UK. The NHS label the crime as child abuse. Some girls die from blood loss or severe infections. But, hey, never mind – because it's all about 'honour', right? Such is the mentality of some of the men in our family.

My FGM, which was supposed to be the standard cut to the clitoris kind, went devastatingly wrong. Grandma Zareen had not, as far as I'm aware, performed this backstreet surgery before she sliced me open. Effectively, I was her dummy to practise on – and I believe she did this out of pure hatred towards me. How could my mother have allowed this to happen? Back then, my grandmother was in her late seventies and, with cataracts in both eyes, her vision was severely poor. She didn't have a steady hand, either, coupled with the fact that she clearly had no idea what she was doing. The razor cut one of my nerve endings, hence the excruciating pain I endured. To rectify Grandma's handiwork and cauterise the area, the women threw scalding vegetable oil over my private parts. Seriously, I could have died. They should have taken me to hospital, but no. Instead, I was bandaged up, put into bed, and, in the days that followed, when I was vomiting and running a raging fever, they told me to eat beetroot – because 'beetroot is a healer'.

Kejal, Banaz, Miriam and Shanar did not suffer the same physical damage as I did after their FGMs. I couldn't walk for days; I couldn't even move. My mum had to re-dress the area and take me to the toilet. Urinating made me scream. The bleeding went on for at least thirty to forty days. I couldn't lay on my front and I had to wear a nappy. When I finally started walking again, I hobbled from side to side like a penguin for weeks – and some of the other kids thought this was hilarious. Banaz, bless her, knew I was unwell and made a fuss of me. I can still see her kneeling next to me on my duvet bed, biting into one of the cubed boiled sweets Mum made from brown sugar, then passing the remainder of the treat to me. 'Here, you can have my sweet, Bakha,' she said, before repeating the process with her next sugar cube.

We girls did discuss what had happened to us, but I would burst into tears whenever I spoke about my experience. 'She [Grandma] cut me so bad,' I told them, 'I thought I was going to die.' Kejal made a face at me, as if to say, 'Don't be so dramatic, Bekhal.' None of us knew why we'd been cut. There had been no warning about it, either. Even when those women pinned us to the floor and pulled our trousers down, there had been no gentle mutterings of, 'Now, this might hurt a bit.' Likewise, our mothers offered no explanation as to why this had happened. We felt violated. Confused, too. Mum had always told us girls to never, ever expose our private parts. 'Nobody ever touches you there,' she would also warn. Why, then, were we being exposed and mutilated in this brutal manner?

A few days after my FGM, Dad returned from the mountains. That was the first time I attempted to walk again. I shambled out of the bedroom, clinging to Mum's arm. As we turned into the hallway, Dad was there. He had on the beige coat again. I kissed his hand. 'Hello, Baba,' I said.

Dad kissed my head, and my eyes brimmed with tears. 'They cut me up, Baba,' I said, and the tears slipped down my face. 'They cut me up, they cut me up, they cut...'

I couldn't speak for crying. Where was my cuddle? Where was the furious, protective dad demanding to know, 'Who the hell hurt my darling daughter?' I looked up at him, searching his face for a flicker of compassion, but instead he tilted his head and raised his eyebrows at Mum as if to say, *What is she on about?* Then Mum mimed a snipping action with her fingers, like scissors, and his expression changed to, *Oh, OK, gotcha, say no more.* He rubbed his moustache, then pulled a coin out of his pocket and handed it to me.

'Here, go and buy yourself an ice-cream or two,' he said, and carried on walking along the hall to his bedroom. Dad knew about the goings on in Grandma's lounge. He had obviously provided the FGM equipment, which he knew I'd seen previously. I could have died, but he didn't want to know. He didn't care. *Go and buy yourself an ice-cream? Really? Do I look as though I can walk to the bloody shop?*

I would lay awake at night wondering why I had been so invasively abused. When my parents beat me, it was usually for a reason. To teach me a lesson, supposedly. But, for this, we were offered no explanation whatsoever. Initially, I concluded their actions had been a bid to tame me – because I was too hyperactive, perhaps. Vivid images of my Grandma hovering over me with the blade woke me from feverish nightmares with a jolt. What disgusted me most was how our parents planned those operations on their girls. They had discussed them, secured the equipment, then cut us one after the other. It was like an assembly line of FGMs. I thought about the part Avin had played in the situation. Grandma had clearly told her to round us kids up, and Avin, being a Good Muslim Girl, had respected her wishes. But I wasn't angry at Avin for this. I knew Avin wouldn't deliberately hurt me. I adored Avin.

Mum didn't comfort me or admit a massive error had been made when I was cut. She didn't give me a hug and say, 'I'm really sorry that went wrong, it wasn't meant to go that way.' So many times I tried to ask her why it had happened even, but she would just shake her head and say, 'No, Allah, not now. I'll tell you later.' I waited six years for that explanation.

The biggest lesson I learned from my FGM was this: *I do not want to be part of this culture; I do not want to follow this religion, these crazy beliefs.* In time I realised that FGM is an evil ploy to control young girls. Just as we were controlled and oppressed in so many other ways. I wasn't allowed an opinion on *anything*. I couldn't even comment on a new cartoon I'd watched on television. Oh yes, the message was loud and clear for girls in our house: shut up and don't be seen or heard. Read the Quran. Pray, pray, pray. Blah, blah, blah. And while I knew nothing other than my religion, I couldn't imagine children lived this way in other countries. Heibat and Helo could dress as they liked in London. They didn't have to pray five times a day either or read the Quran. Heibat had told me as much during their visit. *One day I'll run away*, I thought. *I do not want this life.*

Unfortunately, I did not have much choice in the matter at eight years old.

About a year after Grandma had mutilated me, we moved to a new house in a nearby neighbourhood, just a few streets along from our old house. Sadly, Uncle Zoran didn't come with us as he'd returned to Iraq to 'find a wife'. I was gutted; Uncle Zoran made me laugh with his stories and tricks. There were so many times I'd look at him and think, *I wish you were my dad instead*.

Our new house was smaller and more modern than the old one, with a dial telephone and a hammam bath made of beautiful blue mosaic tiles in the garden. However, the bath would never be filled with water and used as a hot tub. God, no, that's haram, kufre [blasphemous]. Instead, our hammam was used as a fire pit. In summer, Mum used to make me sit by the fire while she stabbed the nit-comb into my head. Wearing a hijab in extreme heat led to outbreaks of nits.

Days after we moved, Dad bought a lamb, a little white one with a black tuft of fur on his head, like a rosette. The lamb was a boy, for sure, but I named him Bakha, after me. Oh, he was the cutest thing, all springy on his feet, with pink ears that looked too big for his face. We kept him in the garden, tied to a walnut tree by a long rope lead, so he could still run around. I fed him chunks of aubergine, slices of apple, courgettes, potato peelings, anything I could lay my hands on. Bakha the lamb had a permanent smile on his face and baaed gratefully when I stroked him under his chin. I would baa back at him and think how lovely his life must be. Bakha the lamb was my new friend and pet. He made me happy.

One sunny afternoon that same week, Mum invited guests from the community over for dinner. I helped serve our visitors, delivering steaming bowls of food from the kitchen to the garden, where the women were kneeling on tablecloths laid on the grass. The men dined separately indoors. Once all our guests had been served, I joined the women. The atmosphere was friendly, people chatting and laughing as they scooped generous handfuls of rice and stewed meat into their mouths. Compliments flowed.

Behya, bless your hand that cooked this meal.

Kiss your hand that cooked this food. (Our guests clambered over one another to kiss Mum's hand.)

Bismillah [in the name of God, the first word in the Quran].

Tamxwes, tamxwes [tasty, tasty].

Mashallah, bless your hand, Mashallah.

I dug into my bowl of stew and savoured the flavours: turmeric, coriander, fresh chili. The meat had that perfect melt-in-your-mouth texture. I ate the lot, then mopped up the soupy sauce with shreds of warm flatbread. *Yum, yum, tamxwes.* Then I had a thought: *I wonder if Bakha the lamb likes flatbread?* Tearing the last of my bread into manageable portions, I diverted my gaze towards the walnut tree and panicked. The rope was still tied to the tree but there was no sign of Bakha. Where had my friend gone? A noise rumbled in my head like I had two empty seashells clamped to my ears. I heard that same whooshing sound whenever Dad was about to beat me. I glanced across the tablecloth at Mum. 'Where's Bakha gone?' I said and she started laughing.

'I'm looking right at her,' she said, and her friends laughed with her.

'No, *Bakha*. My pet lamb. The one who lives over there.' I pointed at the walnut tree over Mum's shoulder, but she didn't even turn to look.

'Oh, Bakha, my darling, my love,' she said, hands clapped to her cheeks, slowly shaking her head. 'You've just eaten the lamb.' Then she erupted into one of her uncontrollable laughing fits, while tears burned my eyes. I felt so guilty. We regularly ate lamb, so I hadn't stopped to think that I could be tucking into my Bakha. Sure, I'd seen my parents kill sheep in Iraq, but I honestly thought Dad had bought us this lamb as a pet.

I missed Bakha so much. It's incredible how much joy that lamb gave me. He'd given me hope, too. In my mind, Bakha, and our new house, had heralded a fresh start, an opportunity for home life to improve in many ways. I foolishly thought my parents might stop beating me, just as they'd ceased doing so for a bit when we first moved to Iran. As it turned out, Bakha's murder seemed to trigger a chain of horror events.

Had Dad killed Bakha because he'd seen me playing with him? Was this another attempt to control me? Probably. Just my being curious about animals was a sign I might have a mind of my own. But, as I said, I was not allowed to voice or show opinions.

Dad became more violent by the day. I thought as I grew older, the beatings would subside, but they became more frequent and sustained. It was like Dad was playing a torture game with me. He found new techniques with which to harm me too. He once tied my hands behind my back and to a pillar in the tandoor room. He forced me into a seated position on the floor, with my knees bent towards my chest, pulled off my sandals, and turned on the picnic gas. Next, he took a metal scraper and heated the blade part in the flame. Then he sat on my knees, with his back facing me, and one by one, lifted my legs and burned the soles of my feet with the scorching scraper. I screamed and cried and kicked my legs, but Dad was too powerful, and the more I protested, the harder he pressed the scraper into my feet. 'Tu ne zarokê min î [you're no child of mine],' he yelled again and again. 'I'm teaching you a lesson, you whore. You're not my child. You can't be my child. You're fucking trouble.' Mum was in the room, but she did not intervene. I don't think I did anything bad or 'whore-like' to warrant that level of cruelty, but I remember Dad shouting, 'Don't you ever ignore me again,' when he stopped burning me some twenty minutes' later, followed by his usual closing words: 'Have you learned your lesson?'

Oh, there were too many 'lessons' to mention, but I would mumble, 'Yes, Baba,' then disappear to the bedroom, out of his sight.

Occasionally, I would misbehave purely for excitement. I'm mostly talking sneaky, kids-being-kids, games such as dialling random numbers on the telephone or knocking on a neighbour's door, then running away before they answered. My siblings and cousins would play pranks with me too. Although, it would invariably be me, The Troublemaker, who would shoulder the blame when we got caught. Which happened a lot, but one such incident left me covered with bruises.

Shanar was my partner in this crime of opportunity. One morning, as we headed outside, we saw our neighbour who lived opposite, Aram, pull up in his black Rover. Aram, a handsome man in his early twenties, worked as a taxi driver, and our parents had become friendly with him and his mum, Ruby, whose husband had recently died. Unlike my Aunty Baze, Ruby, then in her late fifties, had been allowed to keep her son because she was considered too old to remarry.

Aram seemed to be in a hurry. He shot from his taxi to the house and left his driver's door wide open. 'He must be on a toilet break,' I said to Shanar, and we both giggled as we scuttled across the street and climbed into the front seat of Aram's Rover, where we happened upon his money holder comprising vertical columns filled with coins. I'm not proud of what we did next, but it seemed like harmless fun at the time. Without discussion, Shanar pinched a coin from the holder – probably the UK equivalent of twenty pence – then we made a run for it, with me slamming the taxi door as we fled. Big mistake. Unbeknownst to Shanar and me, Aram heard the door slam and had watched us making our getaway along the street from his bathroom window. By the time we reached the sweet shop, Aram was in our house, talking to Dad.

Oh my God, we bought the biggest bag of boiled sweets and scoffed the lot on our way home, careful to throw away the bag and wrappers afterwards. I felt a ripple of adrenaline in my belly, butterflies. Excited to know we'd done something illicit but had gotten away with it. That's what I thought, anyway. We made it home and went into the garden.

'Look casual,' I said to Shanar when Dad and Uncle Afran appeared. They stood, side by side outside the door that led inside to the kitchen, arms folded, glaring at us. Dad's eyebrows were crossed.

'Bekhal, come here, now,' he called.

'You too, Shanar,' parroted Uncle Afran.

'Don't say anything about the money,' I whispered as we made our way across the lawn. That eerie seashell echo flooded my ears.

'OK,' said Shanar.

Surprisingly, Uncle Afran spoke first. Bending from the waist he lowered his face to Shanar's and in a measured tone, asked: 'What did you do, Shanar? Did you go inside Aram's taxi?'

I glanced at Shanar. Her chin and bottom lip wobbled as one. Then, she broke and, jerking her little forearm in my direction, blurted, 'It was Bakha. She took the coin from Aram's car, and we went to the shop and bought sweets.' And what did Uncle Afran say to that? Not much. He gave Shanar a light slap on the back of her neck and told her it was haram to steal. End of. As you will no doubt guess, my punishment was a million times worse.

'Go into the kitchen,' barked Dad. I wanted to run but I didn't dare. He followed me inside, grabbed his trusty length of khaki rope from a nail on the wall, and again forced my arms behind my back and tied them together. I knew by the number of times he tugged and wrapped that rope around my wrists that it was a proper military knot. 'Don't you dare move,' he said and stepped outside for a few moments, then came back in with a section of hosepipe looped twice in his hand. Still holding his hose whip, he pushed me down to the concrete floor, onto my front, then, whack, whack, whack, whack, he whipped my bum with the hose. Over and over and over he hit me, screaming like a lunatic and quoting from the Quran as he did so, '*Gahba* [bitch]. *Qehpik* [whore]. I should cut off your fucking fingers, cut off your hands.' I sobbed and coughed into the concrete. My body ached and burned all over. I wanted the concrete to crack and swallow me whole.

Uncle Afran came running into the kitchen. 'Stop, Mahmod, you're going to kill her. Stop, that's enough.'

But Dad continued, hitting me harder. 'Don't fucking tell me to stop. She's a fucking wayward child. She needs to learn a lesson. I should cut out her tongue for lying...' and so the profanities crescendoed.

Lash, lash, lash.

I can't even remember getting to my feet after Dad thrashed me with the hose. The bruises took an age to heal, but the psychological impact of his violence would stay with me forever. The evil commentary that spluttered from Dad's mouth whenever he hit me, those horrible names he used – whore-child, bitch – made me feel worthless and unloved. Yet still, I would cling to the rare moments when Dad was nice to me.

We girls were not allowed to venture further than our immediate neighbourhood without an adult or responsible other. And if that person were a man, we would have to walk behind him. We rarely visited public places other than mosques. Only essential shopping was allowed, although Grandma, Mum, my aunties, Avin, and sometimes Kejal (because she followed the Good Muslim Girl rules) regularly went to a nearby indoor market. Being The Troublemaker, I never expected to be invited on such expeditions and, to be honest, it wasn't worth my asking as I imagined the answer would be a resounding, no. So, it shocked me when Avin came up to me after morning prayer one day and said I was to go to the market with her. 'What, just the two of us are going?' I said.

'Yes, but we must hurry, or we'll miss the fresh ingredients.'

I grabbed my hijab and sandals.

I felt so grown-up walking alongside Avin. The market was just a twenty-minute walk from our house, but this was *freedom*. Even the hustle and bustle around the stalls thrilled me; to watch and mingle with other people away from my father's tyrannical glare was liberating. I wanted to stop to admire the beautiful Persian rugs and silks, explore the pyramids of exotic fruit and vegetables, dried seeds, and spices. My senses were overwhelmed with smells and colours and haggling voices. I could have spent the entire day at that market, but Avin hurried me from stall to stall, pulling her hijab low over her forehead. She seemed edgy, all twitchy-eyed. At one point, I noticed a group of Kurdish men looking at Avin. They were leering and sniggering and nudging one another. But the weirdest thing happened just before we left the market. She led me to a stall and stopped beside a row of hanging carpets. 'That one is nice,' she said, pointing at a blue Persian rug. As I looked up, I also sensed a tall shape in my peripheral vision. I turned my head in time to see Avin's hand poke from beneath her hijab. Then she pressed a piece of paper, folded into a neat tiny triangle, into the hand of a young man, who quickly pocketed it before passing what looked to be an identical paper triangle back to Avin. I heard him mumble something to Avin, then he disappeared into a crowd thronging a shisha pipe stall.

'Who was that man you were talking to by the carpets?' I asked Avin on our way home.

'Oh, nobody, he just bumped into me,' she said, 'but please don't mention this at home.'

I gave her a big smile that filled my hijab. 'I won't say a word, Avin, I promise.'

God, I was chuffed to be sharing a secret with my beautiful older cousin – or sister as we called her. Suddenly, I'd never seen those paper triangles and I believed Avin's version of events.

Later that week, I woke in the early hours to the sound of shouting and crying. I got up and tiptoed to the bedroom door, careful not to wake the others. I slipped out of the door and stood quietly in the hall, listening to the racket coming from the lounge. This was a risky move; Dad said people got their ears sliced off for eavesdropping. I heard him shouting expletives normally aimed at me: '*Gahba, Qehpik.* You have brought shame on this family.'

Then Mum, shrieking: 'I can't believe what that fucking gahba's done. Get her out,' to the haunting tune of loud, hollow sobs that sounded as though they were coming from deep within a cave.

After a few seconds the sobs dissolved into repeated cries of, 'No, please don't make me go, don't make me go. Min bibore, min bibore [I'm sorry, I'm sorry].' There was a breathy delicateness to the voice that was unmistakable. *That's Avin*, I thought, and my heart turned to jelly.

There were sounds of a struggle amid a shuffling of feet on cement. I went back into the bedroom, where Kejal, Bahman and Banaz were sitting up, squinting, as the sound of a chugging engine floated through the open window. 'What's happening?' said Banaz.

I whispered, 'I don't know,' and pattered over to the window. I knelt and peered over the ledge and swallowed hard. Outside in the street, Avin, hugging the same worn-out rucksack she'd arrived at our old house with, was being frogmarched by Mum and Dad onto a bus. The doors hissed as they closed, then the bus rolled away into the salmon light of dawn. 'Avin's gone,' I said, and began to cry.

As per normal in our stranger-than-fiction household, our parents didn't mention Avin's departure until we asked. 'Avin's been sent back to Iraq to get married,' said Mum. I thought she was joking but her pencil-line mouth expression told us otherwise.

'But she's only fifteen,' I said. Avin had told me her age only a few weeks ago.

Mum shrugged. 'That's what happens to naughty girls, Bakha.'

All of us girls missed Avin. We later found out that she had been caught exchanging love letters with an eighteen-year-old Iranian man whom she had met at the market, which explained the scene I'd witnessed at the carpet stall. Now, to 'teach her a lesson' and restore honour in the Mahmod family, Avin was being forced into a child marriage. I felt so sorry for Avin but, at the same time, I thought, *No way will I let that happen to me*. How could my dad, whom I'd now secretly nicknamed the Evil Punisher, do this to Avin? She wasn't even his real daughter. But listen to this: a few weeks after Dad shoved Avin onto that bus, he played cupid to our Kurdish taxi driver neighbour Aram and his Iranian lover. Oh yes, Aram had fallen in love with an Iranian girl – a girl of his choosing – so Dad spoke to the girl's father and convinced him that his daughter and Aram should be together. Next thing we knew, the wedding had been arranged.

At that age – I think I must have been about nine – I still didn't fully understand why girls in our family were treated so badly, especially by Dad. I couldn't begin to believe there could be another father in this world as cruel as mine. Then two horrific events happened on our doorstep that proved me wrong. First, Sahin, a sixteen-year-old girl who lived a few doors down from the sweet shop, was found burned to death in the family's bathroom. Everybody in the neighbourhood was talking about it. I overheard Mum and Aunty Alal discussing how Sahin died and discovered her dad had scalded her from head to toe with boiling water. 'That's what happens when they don't listen to their fathers,' Mum muttered.

Less than a month after Sahin's murder, a second, similar tragedy happened.

I was in the garden with Miriam, knocking dates and walnuts out of the trees, when we heard piercing screams. We dropped our sticks and followed the noise to the front of the house and across the road, where an agitated crowd had gathered. Women were shouting and crying, 'Help her, somebody help her.' As the crowd parted Miriam and I stopped running, then stumbled forwards then backwards a few steps, too shocked to speak. There in a front of us, was a girl, no older than fourteen, inside a vat filled with steaming tar. Her eyes were glazed, and she was no longer screaming. Then there was a tangle of heads and arms around the barrel as people tried to heave the girl out of the boiling tar. Somebody shouted, 'Call for an ambulance,' just as Mum and Aunty Alal appeared and hurried Miriam and me indoors.

The girl's name was Jhara. She was rushed to hospital, but sadly died. I didn't know Jhara, but when I asked Mum how she ended up in that vat of tar, she planted her fists on her hips, sighed and said: 'Jhara was a naughty girl who didn't listen to her father. That's what happens when people don't listen.' Mum tutted to herself for a moment, then told me to do the dishes.

I went into the kitchen thinking, *I'm naughty. Does that mean my dad will kill me?*

Chapter Six

MORE LESSONS LEARNED

The murders of those two girls disturbed me for weeks. I could not erase the picture of Jhara from my mind: her helpless face, spattered with black, treacly specs, surrounded by rising steam and hair that stuck to the tar like big globs of melted marshmallow. Oh, but those eyes: black as the tarmac, wide open but staring at nothing or nobody. I had a reoccurring nightmare in which I wanted to help Jhara out of the barrel, but I couldn't reach the lip of it, so I tried to tip it over, then suddenly, I would be swept away in a torrent of boiling tar, trying desperately to keep my head above the surface as the barrel sunk into blackness.

The vat of tarmac, outside Ruby's house, remained following the tragedy. Ruby and Aram did not know Jhara or her family and had no connection to the crime. The barrel was there because they were tarmacking their roof. Every time I passed that house a burning heat prickled my skin. The day after Jhara died, I stuck my finger into that barrel of tar – then quickly retracted my hand. It felt like boiling glue, and when I peeled the dried clump of tar off my finger, it ripped off a couple of layers of my skin. That made me think about Jhara, who'd been submerged to her chin in that molten gunk. *Who could do such an evil thing to a young, innocent girl?*

Nobody mentioned the term 'honour killings' at that time. All the information I gleaned on the two murders came from snippets I overheard when the women chit-chatted. Ruby, or Aunty Ruby as we now called her, would come round to ours and sit and smoke shisha with Grandma Zareen, Mum and Aunty Alal. That evil witch of a doctor, Lilan, and her witchy pal Sazan would still visit too. I hated them both.

The gist from the women's conversations was that both Jhara and Sahin had brought shame on their families. One such conversation went something like this:

Mum: The girl down the road [Sahin] had ninety per cent burns. The father burned her to death because he saw her speaking to a man, you know.

Aunty Alal: No, Behya, you've got it all wrong [tut, tut, tut], Sahin ran away from home with a man. But the father and his brothers had been watching her. The brothers found Sahin and brought her home to her father then he…

Aunty Ruby: No, no, no, no, both of you have got it all wrong [tut, puff, exhale, tut]. Sahin's father killed her because she refused to get married.

Lilan: I heard that Jhara's dad killed her because another man raped her.

Sazan: They don't listen to their fathers [cackle, cackle].

Mum: That's what happens when they don't listen.

Grandma Zareen: She brought shame. They both disgraced their families. Their fathers have become heroes in the community, I'm told [wheeze].

A few months after those two dads killed their daughters, we heard another teenage girl had been killed by her father back home in Qalat Dizah. This time, the dad locked his daughter alone in the house, then bombed the building with hand grenades.

What Grandma said, the part about the girls' dads being hailed as heroes, is spot-on. There no doubt would have been celebrations among the men in all three families. Because that's how some of the men in our culture – those who believe in extreme barbaric acts such as 'honour killings' – treat their daughters and women alike. Many of these deaths, like Jhara's, are deliberately staged in public places to attract attention. The perpetrators are proud. In their warped minds they've ended the shame and reinstated their family's honour. It gives them power. In Iraq and Iran men who have committed an honour killing are applauded by their peers. The men will have a party in the street, lift the killer into the air like he's a champion footballer who's scored the winning goal. They'll cheer him, slap him on the back and say, 'Yes, you're a *man*.'

Who will end *their* shame?

Over time, I would hear more cases of 'shameful' girls murdered by their fathers or male relatives – in both Iran and Iraq. But rarely, if ever, were the killers prosecuted. I was astounded that the women gossiped so flippantly about Sahin and Jhara's fathers and their alleged shocking deeds. I thought people who committed terrible crimes in this country were sent to prison or stoned to death. I'd recently heard Dad and Uncle Afran talking about a man who was executed this way in Tehran for 'cheating' on his wife. Honestly, this religion, this culture, the laws of this country … none of it made sense to me. It broke my heart that Sahin and Jhara's lives had been so brutally snuffed out. Both girls could have gone on to live happy lives and have families of their own. What was it with all this talk about 'shame'? I failed to see what Sahin and Jhara had done wrong. I wondered, *what can I do to help?* And that's when I decided: *I'll be a police officer when I grow up – then I can put all the bad fathers in prison.*

Time whizzed by and engendered many changes. Suddenly, our new house didn't feel new anymore. Dad appeared to have a new job or hobby that involved him spending a lot of time at the money exchange in town. I believe he was dabbling in stocks and shares. Then, our family got a green card, which meant we kids could now go to school. That's how I discovered I'd turned ten – because Dad had had to fill in a lot of paperwork for the green card and our school applications. Determined not to miss my birthday again, I confirmed the date with Mum and Dad and made a note of it.

I could not wait to start school. The prospect of making friends, learning new skills, and more about the world outside of our home, filled me with such excitement. A proper education would help in my pursuit to become a police officer, I figured.

Kejal, Banaz, Miriam, Shanar and me were sent to a strict religious all-girls school, while Bahman, Daryan and Eylo went to one for boys. I can't remember the name of my school, but I do recall the fifteen-minute walk there on my first day. As we turned into the pot-holed road that led to the school building, a Toyota truck, like the one Dad and Uncle Afran made their deliveries in, came towards us. When the truck rolled past, I noticed that the driver was wearing a hijab. I stopped, turned, and gaped at the back end of the truck as it bumped into the distance. The other girls walked on behind the boys and Uncle Afran, oblivious to the beautiful moment that had passed them. I stood in the road and waited, hoping the driver would do a U-turn and drive past me again. Seriously, I was blown away. That was the first time I'd ever seen a woman driver. Oh, how I longed to be like that independent lady – minus the hijab. I could not stop thinking about that woman all day.

Our school was a boring utilitarian-looking brown building with a flat roof. Like many other buildings in Iran at that time, it had only a ground floor, and there were no interesting nooks and crannies in which to hide – only an alley that separated our building from the boys' school.

The teachers were strict, but they did not frighten me; a few raps on the palm of my hand with a metre-long wooden ruler felt laughable compared to the beatings I got at home. Although once, I did see a teacher whack one girl's hand so hard that the ruler split open her palm and blood gushed everywhere.

All girls underwent a rigorous inspection every morning. We were made to stand while the headmistress scrutinised us. She would check we were wearing our hijabs correctly. Then we would be asked to place our hands on the table while she examined our fingernails. And if your nails were dirty or too long or your hijab was slightly out of place, the headmistress would beat you with her ruler. Astonishingly, I received the ruler punishment once or twice only. Perhaps all those lessons I'd learned at home were beginning to pay off?

I loved going to school. So much so that I never wanted to leave at the end of each school day. I looked on school as a break away from home, a form of escapism. Our lessons took place in one classroom and included religion (of course), geography, history, and maths, which was my favourite subject. I had a knack for numbers, more so than words, due to Dad's tuition in the subject at home.

Once, one of our teachers – whom I knew only as Miss – asked us to bring photos of ourselves as babies in to school. We were to play a game the following day, she explained, in which we would try to match the little ones in the photos to their older selves. I thought this was an amazing idea. That day after school, I rummaged through our family photographs and found one of me as a chubby eight-month-old baby sitting on Mum's knee. Holding the picture between my fingers I felt overcome with nostalgia. *My parents loved me when I was a baby*, I realised, gulping back tears.

When Miss handed our pictures back to us after the game the following day, she said, 'You were a very sweet baby, Bekhal,' and I beamed with pride. In fairness, Miss had probably said the same to each of my classmates, but I lapped up the compliment because I could not remember the last time a grown-up had made me feel special. Miss's kind words inspired me to dig out some more photographs of myself as a 'sweet' baby. Over the next few weeks, I took in more pictures and bombarded my teachers with them. 'You can keep that one,' I'd say with every image I parted with. Mum was not pleased when she found out what I'd done. Looking back, I think I must have been craving affection.

As I settled into school life and began to make friends, I soon realised many of my classmates had much easier home lives than me. None of the girls I spoke to were made to read thirty pages of the Quran every day, for example. And no one talked of their parents beating them.

A few months into the school term, I met a girl who would become my best friend. I had just turned eleven, according to the scribbled note I'd made of my birthday, but Tia Shirvani was in the year above me and so grown up at twelve-going-on-thirteen. Tia was a not just a pretty girl, but proper drop-dead gorgeous. Picturing Tia today, I would say she looked like a younger version of Marylin Monroe. Tia could have passed for an English girl with her pale skin and long brown sugar hair, which reminded me of Avin's multi-toned tresses. But there was something else unique about Tia: she had breasts. I mean, not just teensy-weensy lumps, but a big set of boobs. I'd say she was a 32C or D cup. During break times I would follow Tia into the alleyway next to the boys' school. Oh my God, she would meet boys in that alley and chat to them. I never joined in; I wouldn't know what to say to those boys even if I dared such an act. I was also terrified Bahman, Daryan or Eylo would see me. So I just waited in the background, looking like a gormless idiot. *If I got caught talking to a boy, I could end up in a barrel of tar like Jhara.*

One break time, as I watched Tia flirt with two boys who spoke in deep, wobbly voices, she fumbled beneath her hijab and produced a white, rectangular pad with two little flaps attached to its long sides. 'You see this,' said Tia, holding the object aloft by its flaps as she popped her hip – that girl knew how to be sexy in a hijab even – 'This is a sanitary towel. I use these when I'm on my *period.* I've been getting my periods for over a year now – because I am a *woman.'*

The boys smiled approvingly at Tia's breasts. 'Cool,' they both said as I pretended to inspect my nails, clueless. Back then, I did not know what puberty meant. I assumed the 'sanitary towel' was a medical dressing of some kind, like the one Mum taped to my leg that time a rusty nail speared my knee in a nasty rope swing accident. What were periods? Did Tia mean our school lessons? They were called periods. Was I missing something here? Did I need one of those towels for the classroom? I hadn't heard the term 'sanitary towel' used at home. Likewise, I was completely unaware of the physical changes that would soon occur to my body, inside and out. I carried on looking at my fingernails while Tia said goodbye to the boys. I was in awe of that girl.

Tia lived in a massive house a few streets away from our home, so she began walking to and from school with me and my sisters and cousins, accompanied by an adult, always. During our walks I got to know my friend well. I hung on to every word that escaped her lips – because I was intrigued. Tia spoke about movies I'd never heard of. '*Dirty Dancing* is my favourite movie ever,' she said, 'don't you just wish you could be like Baby?'

I shot my head over my shoulder, paranoid Kejal or Uncle Afran had heard me engage in a conversation that contained the words *Dirty Dancing*.

'Aha,' I croaked, and on Tia went. What did I make of George Clooney? Did I think he was more handsome than Patrick Swayze? 'Ooh, isn't Leonardo DiCaprio to die for? I mean, swoon or what?' Had I seen the movie, *Stand by Me*? Tia stopped for a moment, pulled a serious face, and shook her head as though to rid it of a terrifying thought. 'Whoa, that film's a tearjerker. Isn't it so tragic what happened to River Phoenix?'

Embarrassed at my naivety and unsure how to respond, I made a hm-mmm noise, then blurted: 'Do you watch *Inspector Gadget*?'

Tia gave a little laugh. 'Yeah, sometimes,' she said, bless her heart.

I quickly changed the subject. 'Tell me about your family.'

Tia said many of her relatives lived in England. 'They're always sending me clothes and other things that you can't get over here,' she said, 'like dresses and stuff.'

'Wow, how sweet of them,' I said, picturing the suitcase of inappropriate garments Uncle Ari had dumped on our patio.'

'Aw, I know,' said Tia, loosening her hijab. She would wear hers in a casual fashion outside of school. 'I have an older cousin in London who sends me make-up and nail varnishes too. She said

Kate Moss and grunge are, like, *so* huge in England just now.'
And Tia was off again: Kurt Cobain, Courtney Love, *Nevermind*,
Nirvana, and the song 'Smells Like Teen Spirit'. 'Hey, Bekhal,'
she finished, 'why don't you come over to my house one day after
school? We can hang out – and I can show you some of my stuff.'

A lump formed in my throat. *Did Tia really just say that? I would
give the world to play at hers and see her stuff.* 'Oh, Tia, I would love to,'
I said, 'but I'll need to check with my Dad first.' A heavy sensation
swelled in my chest. *That'll be another 'No'.*

When Dad said yes to my going to Tia's house, I suspected he'd
undergone secret, transformative surgery of some description. A
personality change, perhaps. *Was such surgery possible?* Although
Tia's dad had called our house to ask Dad's permission. 'OK,' he
said, when he came off the phone, 'you can go but only for an hour
or two – then I'll be there to pick you up.'

I kissed Dad's hand. 'Sipas ji were, gelek sipas, Baba [thank you,
thank you so much, Dad].'

The next day after school, I walked back to Tia's house with
her. My stomach was bubbling with a mixture of excitement and
nerves. Outside our family, I had never been to another kid's house
to 'hang out' before.

Tia's house was as impressive inside as its exterior. Grand,
but homely too, with elaborate furniture in different kinds of
lacquered woods that you could almost see your reflection in.
Some tables and units had curves and legs. Plants in pots adorned
the window ledges and there were paintings in frames on the walls.
As we headed through the long hallway to Tia's bedroom, I met
her dad. 'Hey, you must be Bekhal,' he said with a big smile. Gosh,
he was so friendly. He placed his hand over his heart and bowed
gently. 'It's a pleasure to meet you, Miss Bekhal.'

I smiled back at him, 'You too, agha Shirvani.'

Wow, Mr Shirvani was so laid back compared to my dad. He
didn't belittle Tia, not one bit. He asked us if we'd had a fun day
at school, then said, 'Welcome to our home, Bekhal.'

Stepping into Tia's bedroom was like entering another realm. It was huge, about ten by eight metres square. And she had a double bed. I mean a proper, raised bed dressed in a crisp, white embroidery Anglaise cover and puffy pillows like clouds. Tia pulled off her hijab and slung it over a chair facing a pink marble dressing table loaded with rows of pretty perfume bottles. Also on the dressing table was a bulging floral bag, unzipped and sprouting pencils, plastic boxes, brushes, and tubes. *Tia had make-up.* A funky speech-bubble mirror hung on the wall above the dressing table. *Is Tia a princess?* I thought as my eyes swept the room.

'Have a seat,' said Tia, motioning at the bed. I sat down, amazed at how springy and soft the mattress felt. 'I'll show you my dresses,' Tia added, opening wide the doors to a tall, freestanding cupboard to reveal a row of colourful garments. She flicked through the hangers, humming a song I didn't know, pulling out dresses, and slinging them over the top of the cupboard doors. 'We should have a fashion show. This one would look great on you.' Tia turned, holding a slithery blue oblong attached to a hanger by two stringy straps. 'It's a slip dress. My cousin says it's fashionable to wear a slip dress over a cute little T-shirt.'

I nodded nervously. 'It's beautiful,' I said, 'but it will look far better on you than me.'

'Well, I'll try this one on first, then maybe you could try a different one afterwards?'

Before I could answer, Tia undressed right in front of me. She lifted her dress over her head, threw it to the floor, then yanked down her Aladdin trousers and stepped out of the fabric. 'God, I hate those things,' she said. I bowed my head in shock as Tia stood there in just her bra and knickers. 'What is it, what's wrong, Bekhal?'

'This is haram,' I said.

Tia giggled. 'Aw, come on, it's fine. We're all girls together here. You can't believe all you read in the Quran.'

I didn't take part in the fashion show, but I enjoyed watching Tia model her dresses. I still turned away each time she stripped to her underwear, though. After six or so changes, Tia showed me her perfumes and make-up. 'Help yourself,' said Tia, so I reached for a blue bottle, pulled off its lid, and stared at the nozzle, unsure what to do next. 'You just press that top bit and spray it on your wrists and neck,' Tia explained. I pushed the nozzle and aimed it at my wrist, then flinched when the spray hit my skin. A sweet, almondy smell issued. Tia said that aroma was *LouLou* by Cacharel.

Two hours later, Dad came to pick me up. I could tell he didn't approve of Tia or her dad or their Westernised house. When Mr Shirvani invited Dad into the lounge for a cup of tea, Dad snorted, then shot Tia a look of disgust. 'Bekhal needs to get home for *prayer* time,' he said and hustled me out of the front door before I could properly say goodbye or 'thank you for having me' to my friend or her father. 'You're not going to that whore-family's house ever again,' said Dad as we walked home, 'and I don't want you mixing with that gahba. She's trouble.' I walked behind Dad with my head down, heartbroken that I would never again spend time with Tia in her princessy bedroom. There was so much I wanted to say in protest, but I wouldn't dare answer Dad back. *He can't stop me from seeing Tia at school though.*

Later that week, as we walked into school, Tia invited me to her house again. 'Why don't you come after school today?'

'I'd love to, but my dad won't let me,' I said. 'I'm sorry.'

Tia laughed. 'Oh, just come anyway. Make some excuse – it'll be fine.'

I found myself saying, 'OK.'

After school, I went home as usual, then told Mum I was off to see Aleah, an older girl who lived a few doors down from us. Being a hard-working university student, Mum and Dad never minded me spending time with Aleah. I went to Tia's house instead.

I loved being back in Tia's bedroom. As I again settled on her comfy mattress, I wondered what it must be like for Tia to sleep in this bed, in a room all to herself. 'Hey, can I do your make-up?' Tia asked. 'Black eyeliner would so suit you.'

I recoiled, but Tia was already at her dressing table, rummaging through the floral bag. 'It's just … well … my parents will go mad if they see me wearing make-up.' That was an understatement.

'Are you kidding?' Tia said to my reflection in the speech-bubble mirror.

'Yeah, you see, my dad is very…' The sound of shouting in the hallway told me Mum and Dad had arrived. 'Oh my God, I am going to get such a beating if they find me here.'

'Don't be silly, nobody beats their kids nowadays,' said Tia.

I leapt from the bed. 'I have to go,' I said, and as soon as I stepped out of the bedroom door, Mum pounced, grabbed my wrist, and dragged me to the front door, where Dad was going crazy at poor Mr Shirvani.

'How can you let my child into your house? How irresponsible of you.'

Mum, still clenching my wrist, literally pulled me home. I was half hopping along the road. When we got home, Dad spat in my face, then beat me with a stick. He beat me so hard that the stick snapped in half. I would have laughed out loud if I were not in so much pain. 'You're ignorant,' sneered Dad, dropping his broken stick to the floor. 'Continue behaving this way and I'll send you to one of your aunties in Iraq.'

Packing me off to Iraq was one of Dad's latest threats, and I began to wonder whether he would force me into child marriage, as he had done to Avin, who by now had a baby boy to her husband, a man nearly twice Avin's age whom she detested – so I'd heard through the women's gossip mill.

The 'aunties' to whom Dad referred would have been relatives in his family – possibly even Avin's mum Baze, regardless of the fact he'd forced her to give up her own daughter when her husband passed away.

Occasionally, however, we would go back to Iraq to visit relatives, often those on Mum's side of the family. I would relish those trips as it meant I would see my other grandma – Hadlah, whom I adored. Hadlah lived in the Kurdistan capital city of Hawler, also called Erbil, which is a three-hour drive north-west of Sulaymaniyah. Much like her brother, Grandpa Babakir, Grandma Hadlah had a gentle nature that I found both calming and refreshing. She was tall like Grandpa, too, and she smelled of cloves and freshly washed linen. I had a great relationship with Grandma Hadlah. I used to massage her feet – she loved that. 'You're a kind girl, Bakha,' she'd say, and my heart would glow. Grandma Hadlah was the opposite of Zareen in every form imaginable.

My grandma lived with her late husband's second wife, Halaw, in a massive villa owned by Halaw's son Hemin. Mum's half-brother was married to a lovely woman called Rona, and they had two daughters and a son – Zerya, Yelda and Alaz. Yelda, the youngest of the two girls, was my age and Alaz was about a year younger than us. During the school summer holidays, we returned to Hawler to see them all.

Dad drove us to Iraq in the Toyota pickup, and we arrived in Hawler amid a ferocious sandstorm. Even beneath the canopy in the back of the truck we had to wrap scarves tight around our faces to shield them from the abrasive shower. But the sand didn't bother me – I was too excited. For as soon as we were out of that truck, it would be *bye-bye Dad and hello freedom*. Dad had other plans with his side of the family.

Uncle Hemin's house was something else, with three floors, a basement, and a roof terrace. The villa was fronted by a palm-lined driveway that ended in ornamental electric gates. The outside walls of the house were decorated in fancy Moroccan-style mosaic tiles and the lawns surrounding the property were cut in stripes and bordered by exotic flowerbeds – all maintained by my uncle's gardener. Inside, a wide spiral staircase connected the three floors, and there was a bathroom with a tall toilet you could sit on – plus another contraption I now know to be called a bidet. When I was much younger, I used to play in that bidet, but I soon stopped doing so when Mum explained its purpose.

As a child, I thought it was normal for Grandma and Halaw to live together. They got along well, like sisters almost, but neither Hadlah nor Halaw bonded with Grandpa Ahmed's third wife.

Mum had an amazing relationship with her mother. I loved watching those two together. Mum would plait Hadlah's hair as they laughed and chatted about the old days. They had the same big, full-hearted laugh. Whenever Mum was around Hadlah, she blossomed into the woman I remember from those early photos taken in Kurdistan: the carefree new mother, with wayward curls escaping from beneath her headscarf.

After Dad dropped us at Uncle Hemin's, we kids played around the house, clattering up and down the spiral staircase and chasing in and out of the spacious rooms. I thought this was great fun; it felt good to play and laugh again. If Dad were there, we would not have dared to run around like that, so I made the most of this rare pocket of freedom. The smell of fresh bread baking and sound of relaxed laughter mingled lovingly in the air. And the modern surroundings gave me hope that maybe, just maybe, there might be a better life outside the shackles of our culture as I knew it. My cousin Alaz soon burst that bubble.

Alaz started acting strange during a game of hide-and-seek. He kept following me into rooms when I searched for a spot in which to hide. I caught him staring at me too, like properly looking me up and down and sneering. That felt uncomfortable, but when he started spitting at me, I flipped. It was bad enough that my dad spat in my face, but this was my cousin, who I saw once a year at most. First, Alaz gobbed at me from behind as he chased me into one of the bedrooms. His saliva didn't hit me, but I heard it splatter on the marble floor. As I wheeled round to confront him, he spat at me again. This time, his aim caught the side of my cheek. Alaz stood there and smirked as I wiped his disgusting slaver on my sleeve and yelled, 'What did you do that for, you pig?'

Alaz jutted his chin and tried to inflate his puny chest. 'I can do whatever I want to you – and you can't do anything about it.'

I could hear blood thumping and swirling in my ears. 'Who do you think you're talking to, you animal?'

I went to walk around Alaz then, but he sidestepped and blocked my path. 'I'm talking to *you*, my future wife,' he said. 'I can say anything I wish to you – and you must obey me. If you don't believe me, go downstairs now and ask our mothers.'

I gave him the filthiest look I could muster, then I spat in *his* face. 'I am *not* your future wife.' I stomped past Alaz, banging my shoulder against his as I did so. 'Nobody will tell me who to marry,' I called out as I descended the spiral staircase. 'Never in a million years.'

And I meant every single word.

Chapter Seven

I DON'T

Kejal came into the lounge, cloaked in fabric from her bowed head to her toes. You couldn't hear the shuffle of her slippers for the scuba-diver sound effects through hookah pipes. Slowly, she glided in, as though on rails, elbows tucked at her waist, balancing a loaded tea tray on forearms held at perfect right angles to her chest. Kejal knelt in the centre of the room, before the semicircle of women – Grandma Zareen, Mum, Aunty Alal, Aunty Ruby, and that busybody bitch, Sazan, then carefully lowered the tray to the floor. Besides her hands and features, not one millimetre of her flesh was visible. Shisha exhalations swirled. All eyes were on Kejal.

Me and Miriam were in the corner of the lounge behind the elders, sitting cross-legged on tasselled Egyptian print cushions as we played a game of jacks with pebbles. The women were also cross-legged beneath their long dresses – a pose reserved for relaxed moments like these when there were no men in the house. Kejal was the only one in the formal kneeling position, and she maintained this posture as she served the tea, one hand pressed over her hijab at her collarbone – to ensure that the fabric didn't gape open when she leaned forwards.

As Kejal poured black tea and plopped brown sugar lumps into Moroccan glasses, the women scrutinised her movements – and voiced their thoughts, of course.

'I'll take a baklava, but no sugar in my tea.' Sazan indicated the tray with her hookah, then turned to Mum. 'Surely on Allah's name that girl should be ready by now, Behya. I mean, how many years have I known her six, seven? People will be talking.'

'I would say Kejal is more than ready, Sazan,' Aunty Ruby shot back. 'The girl makes a great lamb stew. I should know – I've sampled it plenty of times. This family is *my* family.'

Sazan made a noise that sounded like she'd burped with her mouth closed. 'Yes, they can all make stew, but can the girl de-feather a chicken and cook it whole from scratch?'

Miriam nudged me and we both started sniggering. Kejal continued with her duties, making dainty clinking noises.

'Of course, she knows how to de-feather and cook a chicken,' said Mum.

Alal tapped Mum's knee. 'And Kejal makes a perfect mastaw [a frothy drink dessert made from handmade yoghurt, water and salt with chopped mint handpicked from the garden].'

Grandma's chins concertinaed. 'Her dolma isn't up to scratch – Behya that's your responsibility. She [Kejal] should know how to make good dolma by now.'

Reaching for the pebbles, Miriam whispered, 'I think Grandma's had enough dolma,' then blew out her cheeks to make her face fat, and I had to look away. Oh God, you know when you find something hysterically funny, but you know you're not allowed to laugh? That was me in that room just then. I kept my head down, fiddling with one of the cushion tassels with one hand, pinching my nose with the other.

'Do you have a husband in mind for Kejal yet, Behya?' asked Aunty Ruby.

Miriam snorted.

Kejal had just turned thirteen and our family was preparing her for marriage. Now I understood why Kejal helped in the kitchen so often – it was so Mum could pass on her culinary expertise and make good wife material of her daughter. Bizarrely, Kejal seemed happy to go along with this. She would act all prim and proper and do everything by the book, eager to please my parents, who would no doubt be conversing with relatives in Iraq, trying to line up a male cousin husband for her. It was a bit wicked of Miriam and me to laugh, but we were not necessarily making fun of Kejal – it was the absurdity of the situation. Seriously, the women were obsessed with arranged marriages, even those outside of our family. 'I can't believe they've not married her off yet,' was a well-used line.

After my cousin Alaz's disgusting attempt to claim me, I was even more determined not to be forced into a marriage. *I will run away from home if Dad tries to marry me off,* I told myself. *Then, when I become a police officer, I'll release all the troubled girls like Avin from their horrible husbands and put an end to forced marriages for ever.*

Ah, growing older, becoming a woman: developing a sense of style, and experimenting with make-up, perfume, nail varnishes and hairstyles; watching pop videos and drooling over famous, unattainable heart-throb boys; flicking through the glossy pages of *Vogue*, *Marie Claire* or *Cosmopolitan* magazine, admiring the latest catwalk fashions and make-up trends and reading problem pages; a pretty first bra? Spa days, movie days, happy days; teary days made better when your Mum cuddles you and explains, 'Don't worry, love, PMT is a bitch from hell.' Oh, if only. The nearest I came to experiencing any of that stuff was on those two occasions I spent in Tia's bedroom. And now, as I approached twelve, I didn't want my parents noticing my transformation into adulthood – because I knew that would trigger only one thought: arranged marriage.

I freaked out when my boobs began to grow. Fortunately, Mum no longer accompanied me to the wet room to help me wash, so she didn't see how my body was changing. And my small breasts went unnoticed beneath my dress and hijab at first. But as the months went by, my boobs became bigger – and they hurt so much too. I resented those cement, puddingy things clinging to my chest. I remember looking down at them in the wet room one night thinking, *Shit, they'll [my parents] have me on the first bus to Iraq if they notice this lot.* So, needs must, I got inventive, and strapped my boobs flat to my chest using big medical bandages I found in a cupboard. Job done.

Much as I tried to resist womanhood, there were so many aspects of it I longed to embrace. Make-up was one of them. Of course, I was not allowed anywhere near the stuff as that would be 'whore behaviour' for a twelve-year-old unmarried girl. However, married women in my society are encouraged to wear make-up so that their husbands will find them attractive. Again, it's all about the men.

Mum, all the aunties, and especially Grandma Zareen, were big fans of mountain clay eyeliner, which they made by grinding lumps of clay that the men brought back from the mountains. The clay has a shimmer to it and is said to be good for your skin. The way women packaged this eyeliner, however, was less glamorous. They would make drawstring bags using thread and the dried skins of (discarded) goat or sheep testicles. The women were never without their little eyeliner pouches, which they kept tucked inside their bras. I could've sat for hours watching Mum as she applied a light charcoal wash of clay over her entire eyelids, then used a toothpick to draw intense black sweeping lines close to her lashes. It was like watching an artist at work; I longed to try painting my own eyes – or Miriam's. Yes, I could picture Miriam's almond eyes rimmed with mountain clay, with the lines winged upwards at the outer edges. And I wondered how difficult it would be to apply lipstick. Tia had shown me lipsticks in varying shades, from frosted pinks to plums and rich reds, but the creamy batons of colour looked too thick to navigate a smooth finish. *How do you stop yourself from going over the edges?* As you will no doubt expect to hear, my inquisitiveness about make-up landed me in deep shit.

Eyebrow threading was also a beauty staple for the women in our house. Their eyebrow therapist was Fareena, a woman who ran a beauty parlour from her house at the end of our road. One day after school, Mum took Miriam and me to her appointment.

Fareena was unlike other older women I knew. Fortyish, with orangey-brown hair that waved in varying lengths about her shoulders, her face was a fanfare of colour. She had rouged cheeks, red lips and emerald eyelids that matched her long flowing dress. Fareena was what you would then describe as a 'modern Iranian woman'. To me, she was an exotic bird of paradise.

While Mum was getting her eyebrows done, Miriam and I were left alone in the next room, which contained a long table topped with make-up and all kinds of lotions and potions. This was carrot-dangling territory at its worst. Miriam was equally curious as me about make-up, so how could we refuse a little snoop at the contents on that table. We opened a compact and brushed the solid beige powder with our fingertips. 'What's this for?' asked Miriam.

'I think you put it on your face,' I said, feeling all worldly. Then we moved on to a row of beautiful lipsticks contained in gold tube cases. I picked one up, took off the lid, and twirled the base to reveal the colour part which, to my astonishment, was green. 'Let's take it,' Miriam urged. Intrigued to know what green lipstick would look like on, I needed no encouragement. I stuffed the lipstick into the pocket of my Aladdin trousers.

'We can return it next time we're here,' I said.

When we got home, I told Mum I was going for a wash. 'OK, Bakha, I'll prepare the room, but don't be too long in there.' Once Mum had laid out my stuff – a washing glove handmade from sheep's wool (one of these will set you back a tenner in Boots nowadays), a bar of universal green olive soap, and a towel to dry on, I went into the wet room and fastened the makeshift lock – a piece of string looped over a hook. Then I undressed at breakneck speed, freed myself of those boob-squishing bandages, and untwirled the green lipstick, marvelling at the glow of the gold case in the early evening light penetrating the frosted window above my head. A happy feeling whirled in my belly: adrenaline. *I'm doing a grown-up thing … in secret.* Peering into the small, jagged piece of mirror glued to the wall, I dragged the lipstick over my lips, expecting my mouth to turn green. But the lipstick left no trace of colour. Confused, I repeated the process, this time pressing harder and drawing all around my lips too. Still nothing, so I went to town with the thing, drawing circles on my cheeks and rubbing the stick over my eyelids, right up to my eyebrows, just how Fareena had done with her emerald eyeshadow. And just as I made a start on my nose, my face began to colour.

My lips and the skin surrounding them burst into chili red, then the abstract circles I'd scribbled on my cheeks made themselves known, followed by the strokes I had made on my eyes and nose. It was like watching a polaroid photo develop, hoping for a nice picture of yourself but instead seeing a clown who'd downed twenty pints before painting her face. *Shit, what have I done?* I turned on the hose nozzle connected to the hot water tank, soaked, and soaped my woollen glove and vigorously rubbed my face with it, but the lipstick marks persisted, and my face reddened further. Breathing hard, I rubbed more soap into the glove. At the same time, I heard Mum's voice, followed by three harsh knocks of her knuckles on the door. 'Bekhal, you've been in there too long. Let me in.'

My skin goosebumped. I squeezed the glove so tight it almost dried in my hand. 'I'm washing, Mum.' My voice sounded as though it were coming from the drain in the floor.

'Open this door, now, Bekhal.' I turned to see the flimsy metal door rattling on its loose hinges. 'I mean it, Bekhal, don't be a gahba, open up.'

'I can't, Mum, I'm not decent. Please, give me five more minutes?' But nothing I said mattered. Mum continued to shake the door, causing the string loop to hop towards the spike of the hook.

'Open it,' she shouted, and with one final push, forced the door open. I slapped my hands to my boobs, but it was too late. Mum had seen them – and the hideous marks on my face. I stepped backwards and watched with terror as Mum's lips pinched and all the colour drained from her face. 'What the fuck have you done to your fucking face?' she growled. Her eyes fell upon the gold lipstick case on the shelf beneath the mirror. 'You gahba!' she yelled, then flicked her foot to her bum and pulled off her slipper.

'I'm sorry ... it was an accident ... I didn't mean...'

Mum's slipper stung my thigh. The onslaught was underway.

Mum hit me all over my naked body with her slipper, then she grabbed a wooden ladle from the bucket on the floor and hit me with that too. I put my head down and cowered and tried to dodge her strokes, but every time I moved, she whacked me harder. In another attempt to escape her blows I stepped onto the tiled platform next to the tank, but as I backed into that area, I scorched my bum on the picnic gas, and my screams echoed in that soulless cement room. 'You shouldn't fucking move when I'm hitting you. Stay the fuck where you are. You're getting more for that.' I sobbed until I was faint and hyperventilating while Mum continued to beat me. When she finally threw her ladle to the floor, she grabbed my wash glove and scrubbed me so hard from head to toe that my skin looked like raw beef. On her way out of the wet room, she plucked my lipstick off the shelf. 'Gahba,' she muttered.

Shit, she knows I've got boobs, I thought. My whole body shrieked with pain.

The lipstick was one of those twenty-four-hour colour-stay affairs. This I learned later in life when I bought one for myself. I should not have stolen that lipstick from Fareena, but I did not deserve to be humiliated and beaten. I kept asking, *Why? What satisfaction do my parents get from beating me up? Are they not frightened they'll hit me too hard and accidentally kill me? Would they be sad if I died?* A few days after the lipstick debacle, I thought that might happen.

To this day, I cannot pinpoint what I did wrong for Dad to inflict this next punishment on me. I do remember Mum getting irate because Kejal and I bickered a lot while Dad was away at the money exchange place. But those arguments would be over petty matters like who had lost the last game of jacks. Sometimes we'd squabble over a pencil, silly stuff. Anyway, on this day, just as I'd finished washing the dishes, Mum and Dad took me into a small storage room and closed the door behind us. Then Dad told me to lie face up on the floor with my arms by my sides, palms down. I looked at Mum. 'Don't be a gahba,' she said, 'listen to your father.' I had no choice. I lay on the cold dusty floor, expecting another beating. Might as well comply and get this over with, I thought. And I assumed Dad would appear overhead wielding his belt or stick or piece of wood or hose or whatever, but that did not happen. Instead, he stood over me, facing forwards with his feet straddling my head. And before I could assimilate what was happening, he dropped to a crouching position, pinned my arms to the floor, then sat, full force, on my face.

I kicked my legs and tried to scream but I couldn't breathe. Dad literally had his butt crack over my mouth and nose, and I couldn't free my arms from his strong grip. Next, Mum started pinching my legs. Her voice was a series of vibrations travelling through deep water to where I lay pinioned to the ocean floor, drowning. That's how I felt: like I was drowning, suffocating. I gulped and shook. My head turned to papier mâché, and as I began to drift away, Dad suddenly rose. I gasped long and hard thinking – *I'm alive* – then, thump, he sat down again, smothering my face with his backside. He did this on and off for about ten minutes and I honestly expected to die. Indeed, I might well have suffocated had I not done what I did next. Somehow, I managed to angle my head so that my mouth faced his left butt cheek. Then I bit through the material of his trousers and into his flesh – as hard as I could. He yelped and shot up like a bullet, clutching his bum, shouting, 'That fucking gahba just bit me,' and Mum started pinching me again.

'No, Allah, the ghaba, the ghaba.'

After that, Dad hit me with the usual torrent of abuse, calling me 'bitch', 'whore', 'rebel child'. 'Continue behaving this way and I'll send you to your aunty in Iraq. You will never be accepted into heaven.' I took no notice. My priority at that moment was to breathe again.

Dad's attacks always left me traumatised, but I noticed I was getting even more emotional after his violent episodes. A flashback of him sitting on my face would cause me to burst into tears. I cried a lot nowadays, but I couldn't think why. Nobody, not even my Mum, had explained hormonal changes to me.

It was summertime and I had on gold Aladdin trousers when my first period arrived. I wasn't expecting it – because I still didn't know what a period was. I remember playing about in the garden with Banaz, Payzee, Shanar and Miriam and feeling a sudden rush of heat surge through my body. I felt crap, exhausted, then Shanar pointed at my ankle and cried, 'Look, you're bleeding,' and when I glanced down, there were a couple of dots of blood on the right inside leg of my pretty trousers. I felt a dampness further up my trouser leg too.

I panicked. 'Oh my God, oh my God, where's it coming from, I'm going to die.' I cried, and ran around the garden like a lunatic. Everybody laughed at me, including Mum, Aunty Alal and Aunty Ruby, who were sitting on the grass, gossiping. I ran into the tandoor room, sat on the floor, and cried my eyes out, thinking, *I'm bleeding, I must be dying.*

The next day, when I walked into the lounge, all the women stared at me. 'How's your period going?' asked Ruby, and then they all started talking about me as though I wasn't there.

'Now she's ready, you can get her married off. There'll be offers flooding in now, you know,' Sazan said.

'Ha, if we can find somebody who will take her.' That was Grandma.

I said, 'What's a period?' and they all started cackling.

'It means you're a woman now,' said Mum, looking chuffed with herself. 'You'll bleed once a month from now on.'

The women wouldn't stop banging on about my period. The aunties told their other female friends, who passed the news on to their pals, and so on until the whole of Iran and Iraq probably knew that Bekhal Mahmod has started her periods and is now available for marriage.

Now I understood what Tia had been talking about when she'd showed her sanitary towel to the boys. Us girls – Kejal, me, and soon Miriam too – were not allowed to use shop-bought towels as they were deemed unhygienic. So, we had to make our pads out of strips of old towels – then boil and wash them after use. We would dry these towels on the heaters in the storage room, hidden beneath other items. If Dad found one of mine or Kejal's washed towels, he would beat us. But that was not my biggest fear; I was more worried about being 'married off'. If I had been forewarned about my periods, I would never have told a soul when it happened. But I guess that was another of my family's twisted games of deceit and control. I continued to bandage my boobs all the same.

How I longed to escape. I would often daydream about what it must be like to live in a liberal country like the UK. Would my parents be allowed to beat me or try to force me into marriage if we lived in England? I began to ask myself these questions. Tia said the fact my dad beat me and stopped me from going to her house proved he must be 'old-fashioned'. She did not know the half of it.

In January 1996, there was big news in our crazy family home that overshadowed periods or arranged marriages or daughters getting killed for being 'naughty'. Grandpa Babakir and Grandma Zareen were to move to London. 'Bahman will go with them,' said Dad. This came as a shock. Secretly, I was over the moon that Zareen was going, but I would miss my brother, even though he could be a bully and we didn't always see eye to eye. I would also be sorry to see Grandpa Babakir go. He was the most placid person in our family. The move must have been in the pipeline for some time, but Dad must only have told us at the last minute because, a few days later, we were saying farewell to my grandparents and brother. Their departure was not without ceremony. Dad bought the fattest lamb I'd ever seen and the whole family gathered in the garden to watch as he and Uncle Afran slaughtered the poor animal by slitting its throat. I stared at my sandals with watery eyes, not wanting to observe the same torture Bakha the lamb suffered in his final moments. Prayers were said: *Bismillah. Oh Allah, the most gracious, most merciful. Allah is the greatest. Oh Allah, from me to you. Oh Allah, accept it from me.* I wanted to shout, *Oh Allah, please get me out of here.*

Afterwards, they hung the dead lamb upside down to drain its blood into a bowl. Then we all chanted more prayers while Dad poured the blood at Grandpa, Grandma and Bahman's feet. This, apparently, would protect them on their journey and new life in the UK. Then the lamb was cut into joints, marinaded in garlic and spices and cooked in the tandoor. The celebrations continued over dinner. Grandma wore one of her fanciest headpieces, which looked more like a crown, and the shisha pipes came out. Neighbours and friends arrived to say goodbye to Babakir and Zareen. Their friends from other cities in Iran travelled to the house too. And when the moment came for Aram to drive Grandma, Grandpa and Bahman to the airport, the street teemed with well-wishers, who waved and cheered as the Rover pulled away, carrying my brother and grandparents into the night and a new life in England.

A Mahmod exodus followed. A few days after the big send-off party, Uncle Afran announced that he too would be moving to the UK – and he'd be taking his whole family with him. Within a week, they were leaving. Oh my God, I was heartbroken. Mum and Aunty Alal had to prise Miriam and me apart; we stood outside the house for at least twenty minutes, crying and hugging one another. 'Oh please, please don't go. Please don't leave me, Miriam,' I sobbed, as the men piled suitcases into Aram's taxi. I crumpled to the ground, buried my face in my hands and cried as the Rover again pulled away. And just like that, my cousin, my partner in crime and best friend in the world, was gone.

Salty water filled my hands and seeped through my fingers. I could have irrigated the whole garden with my tears. And just then, I felt two delicate arms around my torso, and a little voice said, 'I'm sorry, Bakha.'

I dropped my hands into my lap and turned. 'Oh, Nazca,' I said, and she tightened her grip.

It was horrible after my relatives left. The house felt so quiet and sad and abandoned. The beatings became more frequent and severe too. Uncle Afran would occasionally step in and try to calm Dad whenever his violence got out of hand – as he had done when Dad annihilated me with the hosepipe. Now, there was nobody around to stop the Evil Punisher, and I resented him more with every day. So, you can imagine my joy when I discovered that Dad too would be following in Uncle Afran's footsteps. Dad would be leaving for the UK in early February – and he would be gone for a 'considerable amount of time'. I would have offered to pack for him, but I didn't much fancy another beating.

Before Dad left for England, he and Mum returned to Iraq for a few days so he could say goodbye to friends and relatives. Aunty Ruby was left in charge of us kids, but she wasn't strict like Mum and Dad. As soon as our parents were out the front door, a lightness I'd never experienced enveloped me.

Chapter Eight

EAST MEETS WEST

Dad left for the UK the day after he and Mum returned from Iraq. There was no animal slaughtering ceremony or crowds waving him off in the street. Just Mum and us girls, wishing Dad a safe onward journey before Aram drove him to the airport. Mum held back tears, though she would later cry buckets, in private. Ashti, now four, asked Dad, 'When will you be back?' and he scooped her up in his arms and let her grab his moustache, now infused with grey wires.

Dad laughed and wriggled his whiskers, like he would do for me when I was little, when his moustache had been pure black and silky. 'I'll be home soon,' he lied.

I was the last kid to say goodbye to Dad. I kissed his hand and told him to be safe. Then I mumbled, 'I love you,' and watched him walk to the car. My face muscles twitched as I suppressed a smile. The Rover pulled away. *Dad's gone, he's definitely gone.* I wanted to dance a happy dance. Instead, I did the dishes.

I would not see Dad for another two years.

Life was far more chilled in Dad's absence. For the first time in many years, I felt as though I could breathe again. I no longer had to contemplate my actions or fear the wrath of the Evil Punisher.

And my habitual wake-up thoughts of *Will I get a beating today?* Or *how can I avoid a beating today*, vanished. Don't get me wrong, Mum would still hit me from time to time, but her beatings didn't come close to the brutal hidings she gave me when Dad was there. Now, she would just slap me, and once she had finished doing so, I would naively think, *That was OK – didn't hurt much.* I knew Mum missed Dad terribly, but equally, she appeared more relaxed without him around. She didn't shout or pinch her lips as much, and her skin looked smoother, rested.

I realise now that Mum, despite being ridiculously in love with Dad, was dominated by him. And while this does not excuse Mum's malevolent outbursts – the beating she gave me over the lipstick, for example – it does, to some extent, explain her abominable behaviour at times. If Mum did not discipline me according to Dad's standards, she would have failed to keep me in check, which would have reflected badly on Mum's immaculate, good Muslim wife reputation. A year or so later, I would see Dad hit his wife for failing to control me.

Yeah, those two years in Iran were good. I especially enjoyed going to school and chatting with Tia, who regaled me with movie, music, and fashion news. One day in the playground, she said, 'Oh my God, Bakha, have you heard the latest Spice Girls' song?' and I tilted my head in confusion. *Who were the Spice Girls?* I thought Tia might be referring to the women who sat alongside their vendor husbands at the indoor market.

'It's called "Spice Up Your Life",' Tia explained, 'My cousin sent me a VHS recording of the music video. It's so cool. All the girls are in a spaceship – it's so futuristic. Scary Spice is definitely my favourite – she's got her tongue pierced too.'

I asked Tia outright: 'Who are the Spice Girls?' and she filled me in with who was who – Baby, Posh, Ginger and Sporty.

'Each Spice Girl has her own identity,' gushed Tia, then she made a sideways V sign with her index and middle finger. 'It's all about girl power.'

It never failed to amuse me how Tia assumed I knew all this Western stuff. She did not grasp how strict my dad was, either, but to be fair, I played this down a lot out of sheer embarrassment. 'Hey, maybe your dad will bring you back some cool stuff from London?' she frequently asked, to which I'd shrug and say, maybe, then change the subject. I suspected I would be lynched for using the term 'girl power' in front of Dad.

Sometimes, I'd try to picture my relatives' new London surroundings in my mind, based on the photographs Aunty Alal had posted to us. There were a few of Miriam and Shanar, posing in their new pyjamas in the bathroom, pink, synthetic-bristled toothbrushes poised beneath toothy smiles. I had not seen toothbrushes like those before. In Iraq and Iran, we cleaned our teeth with a miswak twig, using our saliva, bicarbonate of soda and lemon juice as toothpaste. I barely recognised my Miriam in those pictures.

Another photo showed the street where they lived in south London. All the houses were made from red bricks or painted white and had two or three levels and pointy, triangular roofs. I noticed there wasn't much space between the houses, and some of them were joined together. I wondered how Bahman was adapting to life in London, and whether he'd made lots of new friends. *Did everybody speak our language in England?* The UK felt like a world away to me.

Coincidentally, a few weeks before Dad returned to Iran, Mum sent Kejal, Banaz, Payzee and me to private English classes with Aleah, the university student who lived in our street. This seemed like a random decision to all of us girls, and we began to wonder whether we too might be moving to England. 'Why else would we be learning English?' Kejal pointed out, but whenever we put this scenario to Mum, she would dismiss the suggestion with a flick of her ladle.

'No, Allah, no. This is our home. Your father just wants you to be educated. Everybody speaks English nowadays.' But it did seem odd to me. First Grandpa and Grandma had taken Bahman to the UK. Then Uncle Afran followed with his family. Recently, Uncle Zoran had moved to London too, taking his new wife Yelda with him. And I didn't know anybody in Iran who spoke English. As Kejal said, why were we going to these classes?

I didn't enjoy learning English because I found it difficult. And I could not grasp this concept of writing from left to right. In Persian Farsi, the language in which we spoke and wrote at school, we write from right to left. As we do in Arabic, too. As I tried to copy the English alphabet letters that Aleah demonstrated, I automatically started writing to the left and my pen dropped off the page before I even got started. We didn't learn much English, only 'hello' and the alphabet, but I hoped I might grasp the language one day, if only so I could better understand what was happening in this Western land where my cousins had settled.

Dad returned in late January 1998, bringing with him sad news from England. Grandpa Babakir was seriously unwell, and we were all to pray for him, said Dad, and his face darkened into an expression I did not recognise. His cheeks hollowed, and I imagined somebody pulling a cord at the back of his head that caused his eyelids and moustache to collapse. He had a faraway look in his tired eyes. Helpless, that's how he looked. Helpless, and sad.

Dad did not say what was wrong with Grandpa, but I overheard him talking to Mum one day about 'cancer', and, oh my God, I was devastated. I knew about cancer – I used to fear Dad would get it in his lungs from smoking too many Marlboro Reds. I hadn't seen much of Grandpa Babakir before he left for England because he would invariably be out doing 'community' work. When he was at home, he rarely emerged from his headquarters. But he was still my favourite grandparent, and I couldn't bear to lose him. Suddenly, I wished I were little again, reaching to touch his fingertips and gazing into his wise old eyes.

Uncle Ari's name cropped up a lot too, much to my annoyance. 'Ari's businesses are doing well,' I heard Dad say to Aram. 'He's thriving in London – and he's highly regarded in the community over there. You should see his house. And he's invested in other properties too – flats, all over London.' Aside from being an arrogant pig, I did not trust Ari. He's that guy who would step over you if you were on fire, or the man who would not help you into the life raft. Ari would leave you to die, for sure. But Dad clearly thought the world of his younger brother who he told us had also 'just won a jackpot in the National Lottery.' I wanted to puke when I heard this. Ari was repulsively materialistic already, let alone as a millionaire, as Dad had implied.

I tried to keep my head down and out of Dad's way. He had been home only a few days, but I feared it would not be long before the old routine and beatings resumed. Although I couldn't help but notice that he and Mum were acting strangely. Dad spent most of his time at the money exchange, and Mum cooked even more food than usual. And when Mum and Dad were together, they'd have secretive conversations in hushed voices. This panicked me. Were they discussing husbands for Kejal and me? Was that the real reason for Dad coming back – to marry us off? Kejal was around the marriageable age mark at fifteen. I was fourteen, and Banaz would soon be twelve, so I was conscious of protecting her from all this crazy marriage business too.

On the fifth night, I could not sleep for worrying. I had convinced myself that Dad had lined up a cousin for me to marry. I got up and tiptoed to the bedroom window, shouldering my blankets. God, it was freezing. Outside, fat flakes of snow swirled in the night sky. There was already a foot of snow on the ground. I cupped my hands at my temples, pressed my little fingers against the glass and lost myself in the hypnotic movement of snowfall for a while. *At least it should be fun walking to school tomorrow*, I thought, then crept back to bed.

Mum woke us up in the middle of the night. At least, it felt like the middle of the night because it was still pitch-black outside. Her slippers sounded panicky. 'Kejal, get up, now. Get dressed, it's time to go. Help your sisters.' Shuffle, shuffle, slap, shuffle at speed.

Then Mum shook my shoulder with her slippered foot, 'Come on, Bakha, we need to leave soon.'

I sat up, squinting at the ceiling light, 'Where are we going? What about school?'

'No, Allah, enough with your questions, Bakha. We'll be late for the bus. Now, get dressed. And wear plenty of clothes – it's cold out.'

Seriously, an hour later, dressed in multiple layers, we were boarding a coach to Tehran. Just us girls and Mum. Dad would join us in the capital the next day, he assured us. We didn't know where we were headed until minutes before Dad packed us onto that coach. 'We're going to live in the UK,' he announced, icicles in his moustache. 'This is best for us all,' he added, eyes darting from child to child. 'It means we'll be close to Grandma and Grandpa; you can be with your brother – and your cousins, of course. This is a great opportunity for us all. We will have a better life in England. And most importantly, you will all get a good education.' I looked at Kejal and her face lifted with joy. The coach arrived at the request stop, its destination sign shouting 'Tehran' in green. It was not yet five a.m.

The coach was crowded and there were not enough free seats for us all to sit together, so Kejal and I sat up the front behind the driver, a stubbled guy in his late teens, and another man who looked slightly younger in a lower seat to the driver's right. Mum settled with Banaz, Payzee and Ashti somewhere towards the back of the coach.

I felt tired but I could not sleep, especially after the bombshell Dad had just dropped. I said to Kejal, 'Are we really moving to England? Is this happening?'

'Yes, isn't it exciting? I told you we would be moving to London when Mum sent us to those English classes with Aleah.' Then Kejal touched my hand. I'd never seen her look so happy. 'Oh, let's practise our English.'

I lifted one shoulder. 'OK,' I said, but the only English word I knew was 'hello'.

As Kejal chatted animatedly about London, my mind was still in Iran. What about Tia and all my other school friends? I hadn't said goodbye to them. Would I never sleep in our bedroom again, or do the dishes in our kitchen? Granted, not all my memories were fond ones, but I had spent the last seven years of my life in Iran, and there were parts of that life I was not ready to let go of. I gazed out of the window at the snowy mountains, imposing yet majestic as they emerged from the night. *Why had Dad left it until the last minute to tell us we were moving? This is so typical of him.*

About an hour into the journey, the guy next to the driver turned and smiled at us. And Kejal must have read his expression as an invitation to chat because she sprung forth to the edge of her seat and burst into dialogue. 'Hi, I'm Kejal. My grandpa is Babakir Mahmod and my dad is Mahmod Babakir Mahmod. You've probably heard of them. They're very well known in Iraq and Iran. Our family has quite a reputation.' I sat there gaping like a fish. This wasn't the Kejal I knew, the Good Muslim Girl who lived by the rules.

The guy in the lower seat scratched his temple. 'Hi, I'm Ervin,' he said, 'and that's my brother Saman.' He gave a sideways nod at the driver, who said, 'Hey, how're you doing?' over his shoulder.

Kejal went on: 'Anyway, we've lived in Iran for many years but – oh, by the way, this is my sister Bekhal [a brief gesture at me] – now we're moving to England. Most of our family already live there and…' I swivelled in my seat to look down the aisle. If Mum saw us talking to these boys, we'd be in deep trouble. Fortunately, I could not see her, which (hopefully) meant she could not see us either. '…We'll be living in London and going to school there and everything.'

'That sounds interesting,' said Saman, glancing at Kejal.

'Yes, we should keep in touch with you both. Why don't you give us your phone numbers and we'll call you from London?'

I could not believe my ears. Kejal was not just chatting to these boys, she was *promising* herself to them.

Ervin grabbed a pen and piece of paper from the glove compartment. 'Good idea,' he said, scribbling away. He handed the paper to Kejal. 'Call us.'

Oh. My. God.

We arrived in Tehran early evening-ish, tired but also goggle-eyed. Until now, I had only seen snapshots of the city on the television, when Dad had the news channel on. But driving through the city seemed unreal, dreamlike. The roads were so smooth it felt as though we were floating along them. There was less snow than there had been back home – just slushy piles at the roadsides, and so many cars and bright lights and tall, glossy buildings. We passed down street after street of glass-fronted shops displaying neon signs in Arabic. The traffic moved at an obedient pace – far slower than in Piranshahr.

The rest of our evening in Tehran is a bit of a blur – probably because we had been travelling for almost twelve hours (including toilet and food breaks) and I had only slept for a couple of hours the previous night. However, I do remember us all sleeping in a big beige room in a B&B and wondering where the hell I was when I woke up the next morning.

Dad must have driven through the night as he arrived in Tehran mid-morning, looking worn out. While he organised our paperwork, Mum took us girls to a kind of cash-and-carry shop that sold everything from food to Iranian dolls, household goods and clothes. She bought us shoulder-padded baggy coats that reached our ankles, boots, hats, more headscarves, and a pair of gloves each. My coat was pigeon grey and looked like it was on loan from *Inspector Gadget*'s wardrobe. Our new clothes, plus the few items Mum had packed into one suitcase, would be the only possessions we would take to the UK from Iran.

Everything happened so fast. That afternoon, we sat in an office at the British embassy while Dad talked to a man and filled in lots of forms. I heard the word asylum used a lot, but I didn't pay much attention to their conversation otherwise – I was still trying to process the fact we were moving to England. We each had our photographs taken and, by the end of the day, our travel documents had been approved. Banaz and I were placed on the same passport, our little pictures side by side on the page. (That passport remains one of my few treasured possessions.)

After our meeting at the embassy, we caught another coach direct to Tehran Mehrabad Airport, where we said goodbye to Dad. He would join us in London in a few weeks' time, he said, 'Once I've sold the house in Piranshahr.' He explained that we would be flying first to Berlin, then on to 'London Heathrow Airport'. Then he walked away, leaving us inside the busy airport and for a moment, Mum closed her eyes as her mouth fell, and she lifted the flowing part of her hijab to cover her eyes. I knew that look. It was Mum wiping her tears without letting on to anybody that she was crying. Payzee and Ashti had ants in their pants, giggling and asking, 'What happens next, when are we going to England?' as travellers criss-crossed in front of us on the marble concourse. I'd never seen such a place – it was madness in there: escalators shuttling people between floors; women behind desks, smiling in their hijabs and full make-up; suited men speaking into handheld phones with long aerials, and a million conversations in different languages weaved in the air. Then a melodic voice sounded over the public address system urging passengers flying to Berlin to 'Please make their way to the departure lounge,' and Mum dropped her hijab and straightened her back.

'No, Allah, that's us,' she said, then looked down at Ashti, tugging at Mum's dress. 'Now, my darling, my love. We're going to England, now.'

Chapter Nine

11 DORSET ROAD

London, England, February 1998

'Bakha, stop staring,' hissed Mum as we entered the arrivals hall at London Heathrow Airport. She tapped my shoulder. 'I said stop it. Don't look that way, look *this* way.' I continued to look *that* way, at the woman running, in long spiky heels, towards a handsome man wielding a massive bunch of red roses. Who could stop me from looking? *I'm in England now.*

The woman, in her early twenties, abandoned her luggage trolley and squealed as she click-clacked past us. She was wearing jeans and a short white jumper that rode up her spine when the man lifted her in a tight hug. She wrapped her legs around his waist and her high blonde ponytail bounced and swished. Still in that position, she raked her fingers into the man's floppy hair and began kissing him in a way that looked like she was eating his lips and tongue. Nobody shouted or told the couple to stop. If anything, their amorous display attracted 'Ah-isn't-that-sweet' looks from people in the crowd. 'I said, stop looking,' said Mum, but I was mesmerised.

How could I not have noticed the canoodling couple? Or the illuminated adverts for fragrances that showed men – and women

– posing in their underwear. From the moment we stepped off the plane, around 7 a.m., I was captivated. I must have looked like a proper freak, gawping at everything and everyone. On entering the terminal building, we'd passed a massive shop with shelves loaded with perfume, make-up, cigarettes, and alcohol, then a smaller store displaying colourful garments made from elasticated triangles in its window (I'd never seen a bikini before). I didn't see one woman walking behind her husband. Many couples strolled hand in hand, I noticed, or the man would drape his arm over the woman's shoulder. Kids sat on loaded trollies with little fingers busy on hand-held electronic games. And when a crowd of female cabin crew members strode past in their fitted skirts, chatting, and laughing and pulling neat wheelie cases, I thought, *Wow, those girls can do whatever they want. They have freedom.*

We joined an interminable queue for immigration control. The snaking line seemed to be at a standstill, and when we did eventually reach the front, immigration officers ushered us into a private room. The uniformed man and woman tried to discuss our documents and asylum details with Mum, but the officers didn't speak Kurdish, and the only three words Mum knew in English were: 'No speak English.' Eventually, an interpreter translated the meeting via telephone. Banaz drew a picture of a bird to keep Ashti entertained, while Payzee nodded off on Kejal's shoulder. I sat there in my polo neck jumper, hijab and *Inspector Gadget* coat, gazing up at the fluorescent strip light and thinking, *What is happening?* To this day, I do not know the full ins and outs of our asylum application, but from what Mum told the officials, our case centred around Grandpa Babakir's devastating prognosis (doctors had given him just six months to live), and the fact most of the Mahmod family now lived in the UK. Mum also spoke about how the UK would provide 'a better life for our children', adding that my brother Bahman would have been forced to join the army had he stayed in Iran.

After the immigration meeting, we were escorted to another building for medical tests. Again, due to the language barrier, none of us had a clue what was going on. The female medic took impressions of my teeth, shone a torch into my eyes and mouth and prodded my ears with a strange, cold instrument. She measured and weighed me – then told me, via mime actions, to strip to my underwear. Oh my God, I was mortified. I had on my one and only, ill-fitting bra – one that Mum forced me to wear. She'd marched me along to the indoor market in Iran to buy the thing, which I did not want – I would rather stick to bandaging my boobs. It was a hideous bra – once a wishy-washy pink but now the colour of a raw prawn, with wide straps and pointy cups. I also had full-on, cave-woman-style armpit and leg fuzz – because we girls were not allowed to shave our body hair. Where I came from, this state of undress in public was forbidden. For the first time in my life, I could not wait to put on my Aladdin trousers, dress, polo neck jumper and hijab.

We spent about six hours at the airport. Customs officers pulled everything out of Mum's suitcase and rigorously searched our bags. One female officer pointed at two see-through bags of saffron, then raised her shoulders as she spread her hands. To which Mum responded, in Kurdish, 'It's hard to get hold of saffron in England. And it's expensive too. In Iran, it grows in our garden.' The woman nodded, seemingly satisfied, despite not understanding a word Mum had said, then waved us on our way into London, England.

Ari was there to greet us in the arrivals hall, looking smug in a wool overcoat, speaking into a phone with a flip-down mouthpiece and long antenna – like the ones I'd seen the suited men using at the airport in Tehran. When Ari spotted us, he stuffed the phone into his pocket and laughed. 'Hey, Behya,' he said, planting his hands on Mum's shoulders. He kissed her forehead. 'Welcome to London.' Then he kissed us girls on the forehead as he gushed, 'Welcome to England. Welcome to the United Kingdom.' He reeked of cologne. A male voice hollered in Kurdish from Ari's coat pocket. 'Ari Mahmod, are you there?'

By the time we left the airport, it was early afternoon and the traffic moved slowly on the motorway. Mum sat quietly in the front passenger seat, listening to Ari go on about his new 'kitchen island' and 'dishwasher'. 'We must get you all over once we've finished, Behya. You'll love cooking in Berivan's kitchen, it's huge – and it has all the mod cons.' In the back seat, squished between Kejal, with Ashti on her lap, the door and Ari's seat, which he'd pushed back as far as it could go, I pressed my nose against the window and watched my ghostly breath vanish in the glass. England crawled along in grey and muddy greens for a while, then we made endless turns into streets packed with shops, petrol garages and several bus stops, and my stomach churned when Ari circled a roundabout three times before picking an exit. 'So, this is Wimbledon,' he said, as the indicator click-clocked us into a road lined with houses, most of them made from red bricks like those I'd seen in the pictures Aunty Alal had sent. Ari pulled up alongside a cottagey, semi-detached house with a slanted tiled roof. A wooden gate flanked by box hedges gave way to a concrete path leading to a black door. 'Here we are, 11 Dorset Road,' added Ari, smiling over his left shoulder at Banaz and Payzee. 'This is your new home in London.'

Kejal jiggled Ashti on her knee and pointed at the house through the window. 'Look, Ashti,' she said. 'That's our new home.'

Ashti giggled but looked confused, bless her. She must have been exhausted after all that travelling and chaos at the airport.

Ari turned to Mum. 'Well, it's not technically *your* home but, still, at least it's a roof over your heads. I must warn you, though, Behya – it's going to be a tight squeeze in there.'

Mum thanked Ari for picking us up from the airport. I felt sorry for Mum then, she looked so tired.

Ari was right. Eleven Dorset Road was not our home, but my grandparents and brother lived there, and we would be staying with them for the time being. We had nowhere else to go.

Waves of emotions hit me as we neared the black door with its brass numerals: excitement, dread, hope and sadness. I could not wait to see Bahman and Grandpa – but I was also scared. Babakir's liver cancer was beyond treatable, Mum had warned. I knew he was dying, but there was a part of me that did not want to see him looking so poorly. At the same time, I thought about the possible opportunities ahead. Would Western society change my parents' views on life? *They can't make us girls continue living by the same strict rules, can they? I mean, this is London, not Iran or Iraq.* Equally, I felt sad about leaving our home in Iran at such short notice. I missed Tia, and all my other schoolfriends, the snow and the mountains. And there was something that unnerved me about this house. Maybe it was the black door or the bitter old woman in the headdress who waited beyond it. Perhaps I was just frightened of the unknown?

I swear to God, I did not recognise Bahman when he answered the door. He'd left Iran as a teenager with stringy arms and legs. Now, he had broad shoulders, and his head brushed the top of the door frame. I couldn't pinpoint Bahman's exact age because, as I explained, we did not celebrate birthdays in our family, but I guessed he must be around seventeen or eighteen. Bahman had Mum's thin lips and expressions, but Dad's height, and his voice had deepened too. My bully-boy brother had become a man. Mum could not stop her tears this time. She hugged Bahman and kissed his face. 'Oh, my Allah, my child, my boy,' she said. 'Oh, look how you've grown. I've missed you so much.'

We took off our shoes and followed Bahman and Ari along the narrow hallway in our oversized coats from Tehran. The carpet felt nice and spongy underfoot. We went into a lounge at the back of the house, and I had to stop myself from gasping aloud when I saw Grandpa Babakir. He was in a hospital bed, propped up by the raised head section and pillows. He had on the traditional clothes he wore at home: a turban hat that looked too heavy for his frail head, and a stone-beige krass (dress shirt) and mraxani (matching jacket). Grandma sat on a green leather-look sofa beside the bed, dabbing her eyes with a big, floral-print handkerchief. 'What is happening to him?' she cried when Mum kissed her hello on both cheeks. When he saw us kids, Grandpa gave a small smile and tried to push himself up.

'Do you want to sit on the sofa, Grandpa?' said Bahman, already helping Grandpa down from the bed. Ari assisted too and we girls politely averted our eyes until Grandpa took his place on the sofa. He looked so drained. His cummerbund had been wrapped multiple times around his middle, and his skin was like yellow cling film covering jagged bones and gnarly veins. It was so upsetting to see Grandpa, the head of our family, a man so strong and dignified, fading before us.

I kissed Grandpa's hand, knelt on the floor next to the sofa, and he asked me about our journey to the UK.

'Oh, it was great,' I said. 'I really enjoyed it – and everything went smoothly too.' I'd had my head stuffed in a sick bag from take-off in Iran to touchdown in London. 'It's so good to see you again, Grandpa.'

'And you too, Bakha,' he said and coughed too loudly for his frail body.

Grandma waved her handkerchief at Grandpa. 'Look at him. What is wrong with him,' she wept.

Grandpa managed to chat with us for half an hour or so before he began to fall asleep, when Bahman and Ari helped him back into his hospital bed. Then Ari left and said he'd be back shortly with the 'rest of the crew'.

As Grandpa slept, Bahman showed us around the house. I thought it strange how there were no stairs inside a two-storey property, so I asked Bahman about this. 'Oh, the stairs are hidden behind there,' he said, pointing at the tiled wall in the bathroom. 'Upstairs is a separate flat.' This concept of hidden stairs felt creepy to me. In fact, the whole house gave me the creeps. Grandma's bedroom, where Mum, Payzee and Ashti would also sleep, was the first room at the front of the house. The lounge where Grandpa slept in his hospital bed backed on to Grandma's room and led to a small, shared garden via two glass doors. Then there was the bathroom, housing an algae green suite equipped with mobility aids, Bahman's boxy bedroom, and a kitchen with a door that opened into an alley at the side of the house. Compared with our home in Iran, where most rooms had doorways leading to the garden, there were few exits from this house. Bahman said Kejal, Banaz and I could sleep in his room, and he would join Grandpa in the lounge.

Despite Ari's earlier 'tight squeeze' quip, there was no such thing as a crowded house in our brood. That evening, the whole UK contingent of the Mahmod family crammed into 11 Dorset Road: Ari returned with Aunty Berivan, Heibat and Helo. Uncle Zoran appeared with his new wife Yelda, who seemed a bit standoffish, and of course, Uncle Afran and Aunty Alal came with Miriam and Shanar. Mum must have been exhausted, but still she rustled up massive pots of dolma, and the aunties brought food they'd made too. Suddenly, the house smelled and sounded like home, especially when Miriam walked into the lounge. I had longed for this moment.

'Oh my God, Bakha!' screeched Miriam.

'Oh my God, Miriam!' I said with equal excitement, and we rocked side to side as we hugged.

Being with Miriam again was so amazing. It felt as though no time had passed since we'd said our teary goodbyes in Iran. She was still the same mischievous Miriam, although she looked Westernised in jeans and a long-sleeved T-shirt. She wore her hair in a stylish long bob that swung when she turned her head. And she wasn't wearing a hijab anymore. Neither was Shanar.

Amid the busyness, nobody noticed when Miriam and I disappeared to Bahman's bedroom. Kejal was helping Mum in the kitchen, and the men were with Grandpa, while Heibat and Helo enthralled my other sisters with their handheld 'digital pets'.

I sat next to Miriam on Bahman's bed, and we chatted for a while, legs outstretched on the comfy mattrass. I asked Miriam what living in London was like and she painted an optimistic picture. 'It's much more relaxed than at home,' she said, 'I'm allowed to do so much more here. I don't have to cover my head or pray all of the time. I'm not allowed to wear make-up yet, but I've got tinted lip balm and, hey, smell this.' Miriam lifted her arm to my face, and I sniffed her inner wrist. The fragrance was sharper and fruitier than Tia's *LouLou* by Cacharel.

'Wow, you're allowed to wear perfume too?'

'Yes, it's called *Exclamation*,' said Miriam, her hair dancing again. 'All the girls in my class wear it.'

My imagination launched into overdrive. 'Do you think I'll be able to stop wearing my hijab soon, too?'

'I don't see why not – after all, it's a free country, right?'

Then we both exploded into giggles, just like old times. 'Oh, I've missed you so much, Miriam,' I said.

The days drifted on, each one the same as the last. We didn't leave the house – unless a stroll around the shared garden counted as an outing? Bahman, who attended a nearby college (I still don't know where or what he was studying), would bring shopping home for us all, and occasionally Ari would give him or Grandma a lift to the supermarket. Ari never asked whether Mum or we girls would like to tag along.

Mum cooked a lot, and I spent my days cleaning the house. Grandma could barely walk unaided nowadays, let alone get on her hands and knees to scrub the skirting boards. I sanitised the kitchen, pulling out the cooker and fridge and washing machine so I could scrub away all the gunk that had accumulated behind them, and as I worked, I daydreamed about hijab-free days, tinted lip balm, and the smell of *Exclamation*.

Grandma had aged a great deal in the last two years. She was still a big lady, but the sumo wrestler firmness of her body had slackened, and she'd shrunk in height a fair bit too. But while Zareen's body had weakened and softened, her face remained hard and her tongue as sharp as the razor she almost killed me with six years ago. I had recently asked Mum: 'Why were we [my sisters, cousins and I] cut?'

'Oh, Allah, every girl is cut,' she said dismissively. 'It will help you resist haram acts in the future.' And that was the explanation I waited six years to hear. Mum's answer could not have been more unclear, but whenever I pushed for further information or asked why I was the only girl cut by Grandma, Mum would say, 'It was for your own good. Now, that's enough, Bakha.'

I knew Grandma Zareen still hated me. Whenever I crossed her in the hall, she'd lean on her walking stick, squint at me, and say, 'Get out of my way, you troublesome child.' Yet Zareen was happy for her troublesome granddaughter to clean her house and help to wash and dress her. Every morning, Mum, Kejal, and I bathed Grandma, which was quite a task. Mum would help Grandma up the mobility steps and into the algae tub, which was a quarter filled with hot water mixed with a cap of Dettol disinfectant. Grandma would huff and puff and groan with exertion before she finally plunged, backside first, into the bath, causing the water to rise to the brim – an oversized dumpling dropped in a stew. Once Grandma had washed her front, Kejal and I would clean her back and sides, which involved one of us lifting a layer of flab while the other sponged beneath it. We would repeat this process until every lardy fold of skin had been cleaned, using Dove soap and a sheep's wool glove from Iran. Then, we would help Grandma out of the bath and into her clothes and headdress.

Although we were yet to venture outside, I began to discover fascinating aspects of Western life indoors. I was amazed to see two-litre plastic bottles of Coca-Cola, for example, as I'd only ever encountered the small glass ones in Iran. But my first love was Fairy washing-up liquid. I never knew such stuff existed. When I asked Grandma where she kept her bar of olive soap – so I could wash the dishes – she gave her best woman-possessed laugh and pointed at the white squeezy bottle next to the sink. 'He, he, he, he, he,' she went, 'we don't use solid soap for the dishes here.' I could not read the word 'Fairy', but I liked the picture of the baby on the side of the bottle. I unclipped the red cap and poured the green liquid into the sink, then added some water and watched the rainbow bubbles form and glisten. Honestly, I thought, *Thank God for the genius who created this amazing product.*

English-speaking television was a huge novelty for me, and luckily, there was a set in Bahman's bedroom. Mum said we could only watch programmes on the other television in Grandma's lounge, under her supervision, but I found a way around this rule. Because Mum was so preoccupied looking after Grandma and Grandpa or cooking or speaking to Dad on the push-button telephone, it was easy to slip into Bahman's room and catch a few scenes of a programme here and there. And if Mum were to catch me in the act, I could say I was trying to learn English ahead of starting school. I enjoyed flicking through the channels, despite not understanding the language. There was one show I adored that featured a group of six beautiful-looking friends, three men and three women, who seemed always to be happy. Many scenes took place in a coffee shop and, every thirty seconds or so, one of the characters would say something that prompted the studio audience to laugh out loud. I would chuckle along with the canned laughter, and picture myself in that coffee shop, sharing jokes and hugs with close pals, women and men alike. Unbeknownst to me then, I was laughing at punchlines delivered by Chandler, Joey, Phoebe, Monica, Ross, and Rachel, on the set of the cult American sitcom, *Friends*.

Those stolen moments in front of the television were pure escapism. Sometimes Banaz watched shows with me, although she would usually be the one guarding the door while I sat inches away from the screen, my finger hovering over the on/off button on the remote. 'Quick, Bakha, somebody's coming,' Banaz would say. I'd switch off the telly, and we would look at each other for a few taut seconds, then fall about laughing when we realised there was nobody at the door.

Two weeks had passed, and still, we had not ventured beyond the front door of 11 Dorset Road. We were all living on top of one another in cramped, intense conditions, enveloped in the heart-breaking sadness of Grandpa's imminent death. Grandpa mostly slept, and he didn't eat much. I made him salads with fresh vegetables and fruits, which I chopped into teensy manageable pieces, much to Grandma's disdain. You should have seen the look she gave me whenever I collected Grandpa's empty salad bowl from his bedside. Her chalky eyes would bore holes in me as I left the room. Then I would hear her wailing as I did the dishes. 'What's happening to him? Why does he look like that?'

In many ways, life in London was no different from how we lived in Iran: we still had to pray five times a day; we ate traditional food and wore oppressive clothes, and the women would gossip about arranged marriages. The house phone in Grandma's lounge rang continuously – calls from relatives here in London, but also from family members and friends back home. A few times I heard Grandma mention Kejal and me while speaking to various aunties in Iraq. 'The eldest one is ready – and the younger one is not far off,' she'd say, but I ignored her comments. *She can't marry me off. I live in England now.*

One morning, not long after we'd bathed and dressed Grandma, the phone trilled again. I was in the kitchen with Banaz and Kejal, preparing black tea for Grandma and Mum, when a long, wobbling cry made us jump. We looked at one another, then dashed across the hall and into Grandma's room.

Mum was kneeling on the floor, covering her eyes with the hem of her hijab and muttering, 'Return her to Allah, return her to Allah.' Grandma sat on the bed, her feet on a stool beneath her. She was crying. I knelt on the floor between Banaz and Kejal. Fortunately, Payzee and Ashti were in Bahman's room and would not hear Mum's tragic words. Readjusting her hijab, Mum looked up at us girls, her eyes brimming with mountain clay-infused tears. 'No, Allah,' she said slowly, 'we've received some very sad news from Iraq.' Grandma's shoulders heaved as she wheezed. I looked at Banaz, who was nervously picking at the hairline scar on her right index finger, and my heart shook. 'It's Avin. She killed herself in the early hours of this morning.'

'No, please no,' I said, covering my mouth. My chest convulsed as I sobbed. Banaz and Kejal burst into tears too.

'She went on to the roof of their house and shot herself in the head,' added Mum. 'Return her to Allah, return her to Allah.'

Banaz put her head on my shoulder, and I took her hand and held it tightly in my lap, while Kejal winged her arm over us both.

'Poor Avin,' cried Banaz, 'our beautiful sister.'

'She must have been so unhappy,' I said. In my mind I could still see Mum and Dad marching Avin onto that bus to Iraq. Beautiful Avin: sent away in shame for falling in love with a man she met at the indoor market in Iran. Beautiful Avin, forced to marry a man she did not know. And now, our Avin was dead, at nineteen, leaving behind a beautiful toddler son and baby daughter.

'Return her to Allah,' Mum went on.

Grandma sighed. 'Well, I suppose Avin didn't follow the rules.'

The day continued. Another day inside the house, quiet and mournful. We girls got on with our chores: cleaning, helping with the cooking, doing the laundry and dishes and looking after Grandpa. We cried a lot, grieving for Avin, the girl we Mahmod sisters had so admired and adored. As I washed the algae bath, I remembered something Grandma had said to me in the days when she'd lauded Avin as a Good Muslim Girl. *You could learn a lot from Avin, Bekhal.* I shivered all over.

That evening, as we sat on a plastic tablecloth eating dinner, Mum made another announcement. 'Your father called today,' she said, passing a bowl of her perfect fried rice to Kejal. 'It's good news. He's sold our house in Iran.' God, my heart dropped. 'He'll arrive in England in a few days. Oh Allah, this is just what we need – a fresh start in a new country, surrounded by our loving family. At last, we can all be together again.'

Chapter Ten

RETURN OF THE EVIL PUNISHER

I never thought I'd say this, but I was relieved when Dad arrived in London. Well, for a while, at least. The atmosphere inside 11 Dorset Road became less fraught; Grandma's mood brightened beyond recognition once her eldest son was back in the fold. Gone were her aches and pains and various other ailments she routinely bemoaned. The old witch hobbled at reasonable speed with her stick, and swung around in the kitchen, panting like an excitable child. And whenever Dad bent to kiss Grandma, she'd clamp her patty hands on the sides of his head, pull his face close to hers, and kiss him all over his forehead and cheeks. Grandma would never greet a female family member this way. I can't recall Grandma ever smiling at me even.

Now that Dad was back, our relatives visited more often, which also meant more sneaky TV viewings in the bedroom with Miriam, who would explain the programmes to me. And to be fair, this is how I began to pick up some English words and phrases. Miriam taught me how to say, 'How you doin'?', which, I'd learned, was Joey's catchphrase in *Friends*. But my favourite show of all was *Baywatch*. The first time I watched the opening titles, I didn't blink once, I swear. There were up-close shots of women running on golden sand, naked except for tiny bikinis. *Where in the world were women allowed to run around like that?* Another shot showed a red rescue helicopter swooping over the sparkling sea. Then six lifeguards sprinted in a line through the surf, three women in high-legged red swimsuits, and the men wearing flimsy red shorts only. They all looked so beautiful and full of energy. *Such freedom.* *Baywatch* was my occasional portal into a forbidden world, where people could be themselves, and go to the beach and swim in the sea. I never knew people went to beaches until now. *If Dad catches me watching this, he'll kill me,* I thought. Still, I watched it, when I could.

Another good thing about Dad's return was that we could finally go out. Looking back, I reckon Dad must have banned Mum from leaving the house while he was still in Iran. Of course, Dad did not take us to see the Tower of London or Big Ben or Buckingham Palace, but he did introduce us to the shops in Wimbledon and nearby Colliers Wood, an experience that captivated and confused me in equal measure. I loved how the big supermarkets sold clothes as well as food – and that those garments were all brand new. Most of my clothes, apart from dresses Mum made on her sewing machine, were hand-me-downs. In one supermarket, I watched as one girl, probably the same age as Banaz, sifted through a rail of denim dresses until she found one in her size. Then the girl's mum plucked the dress from her daughter's hands, said something cheery, and dropped it into her shopping trolley. Mum told me to stop staring. Everywhere we went, I was told to 'look down' or 'look away' from people, especially boys and men. 'Don't speak to anybody,' Dad warned. After two years in London, Dad knew some English, but still, he struggled to communicate with people. I wanted to understand English so much. Dad said we kids would be starting school in two weeks' time. How would I make new friends if I couldn't speak their language?

Alas, we girls were not allowed to pick clothes for ourselves. Instead, Dad took us to charity shops, where he chose items for each of us among the racks of people's unwanted stuff. Now, I don't mean to sound ungrateful; I love charity shops – and there were some beautiful Western clothes on display in those stores, but the gear Dad picked for us? Honestly, I'm not kidding, I walked away with a tatty black backpack and navy Fila trainers – both meant for boys – and a peach, old ladies-style anorak that made my *Inspector Gadget* coat look like haute couture. Granted, I didn't have a clue about the latest fashions, but I would have loved a pretty pair of girls' shoes, like the ones I'd seen my cousins wearing.

Our shopping excursion was my only outing while living in Dorset Road. Dad was too busy looking after Grandpa and organising our move to new accommodation to take us out again – and we were not allowed to leave the house without him. Occasionally, Mum and Dad would take Grandpa out in his wheelchair. They would go for afternoon walks, or, sometimes, Uncle Ari would take them for a drive or back to his house for a few hours. While they were gone, we kids stayed at home with Grandma, who, conveniently for us, would drop into a deep and loud sleep on the green sofa in the main lounge. As soon as Grandma started snoring, the television would go on. We'd watch *Neighbours*, *Home and Away*, *A Country Practice* and game shows. Our grandparents had a satellite dish too, so there were plenty of channels to hop between. Some afternoons, me and Kejal would sneak into Grandma's bedroom and use her push button telephone to call Ervin and Saman, the boys we'd met on the bus to Tehran. At the time, those calls were hilarious. Kejal and I would snatch the receiver from one another, each trying to impress the boys with talk of our new life in London while Grandma snored in the next room. I remember our first call to Iran. 'London is so much fun,' gushed Kejal, giggling. 'We've been out every day – there's so much to see and do, and…'

I grabbed the phone. 'How you doin'?' I said in a thick, Kurdish accent. I didn't know anything about chat-up lines then – I just thought 'How you doin'?' was a cool thing to say. 'How is life in Iran?' I asked Ervin, but Kejal wrestled the phone from me before he could reply.

'My family is so well known in London,' she said and gave me an expectant look with a series of little nods that said, *back me up on this one.* I laughed. I never knew this rebellious streak existed in Kejal's Good Muslim Girl DNA.

Ten days later, we finally left 11 Dorset Road and moved into a bed-and-breakfast in West London. Dad said this was a temporary measure until the council gave us a house.

The B&B, Barry House, was in a terraced, stucco-fronted, period building on Sussex Place, between Paddington and Bayswater, which looked to be a lovely part of London. We stayed in bedroom number 20, which had an en suite bathroom and adjoining kitchen area. There were two bunk beds and a double bed in our room, so Bahman got the big bed and me, Kejal, Banaz and Payzee slept in the bunks. Ashti joined Mum and Dad in their room in the attic. However, Mum and Dad would stay in our room from morning until bedtime, except occasional days when they'd go to their room for an afternoon nap.

Initially, I enjoyed living at the B&B. It was cosy inside, with blue carpets patterned with little amber crowns throughout. And there was a dining room in the basement where we went for breakfast, which I thought was the most incredible thing ever. You could help yourself to cereals and fruit and orange or apple juice, tea and coffee, and if you wanted a cooked breakfast, a staff member would prepare the food in the kitchen and deliver it to your table. We couldn't eat sausages or bacon, but the scrambled eggs on toast were a real treat. There was a television on the dining room wall, too, and I would eat as slowly as possible so we could stay longer and watch *GMTV.* Again, I didn't understand a word, but I loved the visuals – the presenters' Western outfits, and the London skyline behind the colourful sofa.

About two weeks into our stay at Barry House, Dad summoned Kejal, Banaz and me to kneel at his feet while he sat on Bahman's double bed. 'Tomorrow, you will start school,' he said, and I looked at the threadbare blue carpet thinking, *Yes, escape!* We had been holed in this room for an eternity. Mum and Dad would not let us girls out of their sight. The only time I got to myself was during my ten-minute shower slot, which would invariably be cut short when Mum rapped on the door, screaming, *Get out, you're taking too long*. Just as she would do in Iran. 'This will not be your permanent school,' continued Dad, 'but you must work hard. And no matter what the other children are wearing, you must wear your hijabs. You will *not* bring shame on this family.'

'No, Allah, no shame,' echoed Mum. Bang went my notion that Dad might relax a bit, but at least school would get me out of this claustrophobic room during the week.

At first, Dad escorted us on the mile-long walk to North Westminster Community School. Sometimes, if we were running late, we'd catch the bus, which was a performance and a half. If there were no seats available, Dad would make Kejal, Banaz and me stand squished together while he faced us and elbowed every boy or man out of the way. If somebody in outlandish or provocative clothes got on, Dad would smile at them and mutter, 'Mizir ker,' which means 'fucking donkey' in Kurdish.

On my first day at school, I felt like an outcast. All the other girls sported uniforms comprising short skirts teamed with a blazer, black tights, or thigh-length white socks. They shouldered stylish handbags and wore make-up – skilfully applied eyeliner, bronzer and sugary pink lipsticks – and made dramatic gestures when they spoke. They would play with their hair or stick their hands on their hips or wag an index finger in the air. I watched their mouths as they spoke, trying to decipher what they were saying, but the only words I grasped, which the girls repeated in many conversations, were, 'Fuck you.' Some girls caught me watching them and cast me dirty looks that screamed, 'Who are you, and what *are* you wearing?' Seriously, I could not have looked more incongruous if I'd tried. I had on black baggy trousers, a polo neck, long black dress, hijab and that disgusting peach anorak and boys' trainers. *Why won't that horrible bastard let me wear girls' shoes? Why, why, why?*

I had no idea what the teachers were saying during classes, so I was delighted when the headteacher assigned an Iranian girl to sit next to me in lessons and help me with my English. Ester came from Tehran, but she dressed the same as the other girls. I followed Ester around like a lost sheep, hoping she'd be my first London schoolfriend. Sadly, that friendship wasn't to be. I think Ester, sweet as she was, felt socially embarrassed by me – because of how I looked. Whenever I invited her (in Farsi) to the canteen at lunchtime, she would make an excuse. As soon as a lesson ended, she would leap from her seat and rush out of the room, laughing with the other girls, and I would be left with nobody to talk to.

After a few weeks, Dad stopped escorting us to and from school every day. He gave us bus fare money and strict instructions to always walk together and come straight back to the B&B after school. I was stunned, but secretly thrilled. All three of us were. Some days, we would leave for school extra early so we could walk and save our bus money, which Kejal and I spent on calls to Ervin and Saman from the payphone in the B&B. We would do this whenever Mum and Dad went for their afternoon naps, then return to our room, giggling and feeling like women of the world after those calls that lasted no more than a minute or two.

Oh my God, I needed some outlet for my frustration and misery. We were cooped up in that room, eating every meal and praying together in there. I had no schoolfriends as such, and I still didn't speak the language, aside from a few words and phrases. The 'fuck you' saying seemed popular; I heard that everywhere I went – on the bus, in the street. An angry man had shouted 'Fuck you' at a traffic warden outside our B&B one morning, so I knew it to be an expression said with fury. Kejal and Banaz had picked up on 'fuck you' too, so we'd walk to school, saying 'fuck you' to one another, not knowing we were swearing.

I desperately wanted to fit in with the other girls at school, but Dad would never let me dress like them. In the P.E. changing rooms, my classmates chatted and laughed as they paraded in their underwear, the air heady with a cocktail of their deodorants and perfumes. The thought of undressing in front of those girls horrified me; no way would I let them see my ugly raw prawn bra and hairy legs and armpits. None of those girls had body hair like mine and I wondered how they kept their skin so smooth. They had much thinner, neater-shaped eyebrows than me, too. The more disparities I noticed between my Western classmates and me, the more I wanted to experiment. I wanted to wear make-up, shave my legs, pluck my eyebrows and hang out in coffee shops like the characters from *Friends*. Opposite the reception desk in our B&B was a stand packed with flyers advertising fun and interesting things to do in London: galleries, theatres, museums. All of these cultural places were deemed haram by my father. As Dad kept saying, he'd moved us to London for the opportunities available in this country. But how could I make the most of those chances if I couldn't embrace the culture or integrate with people? I thought, *How is Dad giving me a 'better life' if I've got no freedom? I'm fourteen, and I can't even walk to the shop on my own.* Dad's suffocating behaviour led me into temptation.

Before long, we began to find ways to enjoy some freedom after school. We could get away with being forty-five minutes or so late back to the B&B due to a 'delayed bus' or a 'class that ran over', so we used this to our advantage – especially when we discovered Whiteleys Shopping Centre on Queensway.

Oh wow, that place was heavenly – a monumental white building with marble floors I wanted to skate over in my socks. There was a beautiful black, sweeping staircase in the atrium and Corinthian columns separated tiers packed with shops. Whiteleys was halfway between our school and the B&B; we could be at the centre in less than ten minutes if we hurried. Sometimes we jogged there. Kejal, like me, was intrigued about make-up and beauty routines, and Banaz was beginning to show an interest too – although she knew it was forbidden at home. 'I like how the girls at school contour their faces with colours,' she said one day as we scuttled into Whiteleys in our hijabs. 'How do they do that?'

'Yeah, I know, right,' I said. 'It looks so pretty but I don't know how they do it – I think it's coloured powders. But don't ever mention this stuff in front of Mum and Dad, Nazca.'

'I know that,' she said and pointed at The Body Shop. 'Let's go in there.'

We three sisters browsed the beauty aisles in as many shops as possible. Often, I would wander off on my own to look at another aisle or counter. And I'm so ashamed to admit this now, but in those moments, when I spied pyramids of beautifully packaged make-up and perfumes and hair and body products, all shimmering beneath the bright store lights, I began to help myself to a few things. I'd pretend to look at an eye pencil, and the next second, that pencil would have found its way into the waistband of my ugly trousers, hidden beneath my hijab. I took only items I wanted to experiment with: eyelash curlers, tweezers, a packet of razors, an eyeshadow or two, lip pencils, mascara and lip glosses. I never bothered with foundation or face powder because, as I'd told Banaz, I didn't have a clue what to do with them. Stealing a few beauty items gave me an adrenaline buzz, a secret happiness that nobody could demolish. You see, I couldn't buy these products. The only money Mum and Dad ever gave us was our bus fare, and that was either spent on the bus itself or our clandestine calls to the boys in Iran. If I were to ask Mum or Dad for lipstick, or clear lip gloss even, they would beat me. That was the harsh truth of my stifling existence. I'm not proud of what I did, and I swear, I did not steal those items out of spite or because I felt a burning need to commit a criminal act. I did it because I was curious, and I wanted to feel feminine and fit in with my schoolfriends. For God's sake, I just wanted to be *happy*. Once again, my curiosity landed me in trouble.

I was stupid. There I'd been, preaching to Nazca about never mentioning our love for make-up to Mum and Dad, and I couldn't even keep my beauty experiments a secret. I thought I was being careful. I hid my haul of products in a small pedal bin liner which I tied and hooked to some railings outside the bathroom window in the B&B. During my shower slot, I would retrieve my bag of goodies, pick one item to try, then tie the bag to the railings again.

The first time I did this, I chose tweezers, and peering into the mirrored wall cabinet, began to pluck my right eyebrow, starting from the bridge of my nose and working towards the outer corner of my eye. I felt no pain, just a tingling sensation that travelled to my nose and made me want to sneeze. Excited was how I felt. Excited and womanly. Already, my right eye looked bigger, wide awake. Now I could see my browbone and I thought about which colour of eyeshadow would best suit me. Although eyeshadow would have to wait, for any second soon, Mum would rap on that door, guaranteed. I popped my tweezers in the bag, shut the window, and jumped in the shower before my allotted time ended.

That bathroom became my sanctuary, its locked door a temporary barrier between me and my parents. One morning, as I showered before school, I decided to shave my legs and armpits. I was nervous as I didn't know how to do it. Would it hurt? Since my FGM I was fearful of all blades. But I wanted out of the gorilla suit of which I was rapidly growing into. So, I grabbed my razor and, beneath the hot needles of water, made a start on shaving my legs, scraping the blade in all directions over my shins and marvelling at how fast my hair came away. I continued shaving, stopping occasionally to rinse the clogged razor, then just as I dragged the clean blade across my knee, *bang, bang, bang*, went the door. My concentration slipped and I cut my knee with the razor. Shit, I'd lost track of time. 'Bekhal, you've been in there too long. Get out, now.'

'I'm coming, Mum,' I shouted back, 'I'm just washing my hair.' I crouched in the cubicle and began fishing black bristles out of the water. My leg hair was everywhere – and blocking the drain.

'Open this door, now,' yelled Mum, thumping harder.

I stood up and turned off the shower. 'Two minutes, I'm…'

Mum was in the room. *How did she get in?* I retreated to the corner of the shower, one arm over my boobs, the other covering my groin, nervously watching through steamed glass as Mum advanced like a wild beast emerging from the fog. She yanked open the door, snarled at the plastic razor floating in the hairy water, then at the jagged line of blood trickling from my knee, and powered forth, reaching into the cubicle and slapping me all over. 'Where did you get that razor, you fucking gahba?' On and on and on. Nothing had changed. After she'd hit me, Mum stayed in the bathroom and waited for me to dress. 'Wait till you father hears about this,' she said. Dad was out. He'd left early that morning to visit Grandma and Grandpa. I went to school and lost myself in foreign voices, fearing the clang of the home-time bell.

We didn't go to Whiteleys after school that day. That would have been far too risky, an idiotic move. By now, I'd resigned myself to the knowledge that I would get a second beating from Dad the moment I stepped into that bedroom. *Hopefully he'll just slap me a few times and spit in my face. I can handle that. Surely, he can't be too aggressive in a B&B – other guests might hear the commotion and report it to the manager?* Such were my crazy thoughts as I climbed the blue carpeted trail up the stairs, and through the door to bedroom 20.

The room was a bombsite, with clothes and emptied bags strewn across the floor. Somebody had stripped the covers off of my bunk and left them in a messy pile on the mattress. Drawers had been pulled out and emptied. Payzee knelt on the floor with Ashti, watching a kids' programme blaring from the television, which was odd. I didn't think we were allowed to watch stuff like that at this time of the day. Mum and Dad sat side by side on the edge of the bed, but Mum got up after Kejal, Banaz and I walked in. Bahman wasn't there, as usual. He could come and go as he pleased.

'All you girls are coming with me to our room upstairs,' Mum announced, 'except you, Bekhal. You stay here.' She indicated for me to kneel at Dad's feet. Kejal smirked down at me as she led the younger girls out of the room. Then it was just Dad, me, and an English-speaking badger in the room. The badger, a puppet on the television screen above the bed, was wearing a red beret and spoke like a man. *Why was the volume so loud?*

'Get up,' said Dad, his tone surprisingly calm. As I rose, he patted the bed. 'Come, sit down,' he said, smiling. Confused, I did as he told me to do and sat on the shiny, padded cover. 'I found this.' I gulped hard as Dad reached behind him and produced my little pedal bin bag. Then he tipped it upside down and my make-up, tweezers, razors and eyelash curlers – all my secret stuff – clattered over the floor. The badger laughed. Tears filled my eyes through a shuddering intake of breath, and before I could lift my head, Dad grabbed my shoulders and threw me backwards on the bed. He pinned my arm to the mattrass with his knee, slammed his hand over my mouth and nose, and whacked my body with his other hand. When I tried to move my face, he hit me hard around the head. The room began to spin. I couldn't breathe. I attempted to raise my free arm but Dad slapped it down. His assault continued until the end of the badger programme, when he finally lifted his hand from my mouth. 'You fucking qehpik,' he said as I gasped for air. Twice, he spat in my face. He then wiped his mouth and turned his back to me as he stood. 'Now go to bed,' he sneered. I heard my beautiful eyelash curlers snap as the Evil Punisher stamped on them. 'I said, go to bed, qehpik.'

Battered and bruised, I climbed the ladder to my bunk, remade the bed, crawled under the duvet and buried my head beneath the pillow. A heavy pulse throbbed in my right ear where Dad had hit me there. Mum and the girls returned but I was forced to stay in bed while they all chatted and ate dinner, the aroma of Mum's fried rice filling the room. I didn't care, I wasn't hungry. Dad chose to make a big announcement while I could not join in the conversation. 'Good news,' he said. 'We have been offered a house – thanks to our Kurdish connections. The house is close to Grandpa and Grandma, and we can move in next week.' A chorus of cheery mashallas followed. I wanted to be sick. Curling into a tight foetal position I pulled the pillow tight around my ears. The Evil Punisher could stick his house and his promise of a better life for us in England.

'One day, I'll escape,' I whispered.

That day could not come soon enough.

Chapter Eleven

WORDS DON'T KILL YOU

A week later and true to his word, Dad moved us out of the B&B and into a council house in Mitcham, South London. Dad's brothers, Ari and Zoran, drove us to 225 Morden Road, a whitewashed semi, whose walls would witness a catalogue of abuse, sadness and an inhumane act of unthinkable violence.

It was springtime, the first spring I'd seen in England, and I remember Banaz commenting on the daffodils huddled on the narrow grass verge outside our new home. 'Ah, jwana [pretty],' she said, crouching to admire the flowers with their yellow petals and orange trumpets.

I joined Banaz for a moment while the men unloaded the cars and Mum and Kejal took the little ones into the house. 'They're beautiful, Nazca,' I said, and her face broke into a huge smile as she brushed her knuckles against the tip of her nose – one of Banaz's little habits. 'Daffodils are a sign of hope, too.'

Banaz lightly touched the daffodils. 'I love flowers, Bakha. Yellow and orange are my favourite colours. Jwana, jwana.'

I smiled. *I'll never forget what Nazca's favourite colours are now.*

'No English is to be spoken here. No, no English in this house.' Those were Dad's first words once we'd crossed the threshold of

225 Morden Road. 'We are from Iraqi Kurdistan, so we will speak only Kurdish.' I almost laughed. I mean, excuse my language but, surely, he was taking the piss? Dad wanted us to do well at school, he said. How did he expect us to thrive and pass exams and get this 'good education' if we could not speak English at home?

Although it was a fresh, sunny day, it felt chilly and echoey inside the house. There was no furniture, curtains or carpets in the rooms, but the house did have an upstairs with three bedrooms, a bathroom, and a separate room housing the toilet. Dad gave Bahman a bedroom to himself – a box room above the front door, and I would be sharing the second bedroom, also at the front of the house, with Kejal. Banaz, Payzee and Ashti were to share the biggest room overlooking the back garden bordered by wooden fences. Secretly, I was gutted not to be sharing with Banaz, but, on a brighter note, at least Mum and Dad would not be sleeping near me. The downstairs dining room would double as their bedroom, Dad said.

We all slept on the floor for the first few nights, which I enjoyed as it reminded me of our makeshift duvet beds in Iraq and Iran. But gradually, the bare house began to look more like a home. First, a blood-red carpet was fitted throughout the entire house. The rug had the same gold crown motif I remembered from the Bayswater B&B. Then our beds arrived – single divans with drawers in their bases. Dad wallpapered the lounge and his downstairs bedroom in a magnolia vinyl print. A push-button phone, identical to the one at Grandma and Grandpa's house, was installed. And finally, we took delivery of a burgundy leather sofa and big box television – hand-me-downs from Ari.

With the new house came a new school, which I detested from day one. I started at Bishopsford Community School, along with Banaz and Kejal, at the beginning of the summer term, around May 1998. I went into Year Nine, Banaz was in the year below me, and Kejal in Year Ten. Our younger sisters went to a separate primary school – and consequently picked up English far quicker than us older girls.

School uniform was mandatory at Bishopsford, but Dad still made us wear our hijabs. He bought me a regulation, logoed jumper whose sleeves ended just past my fingertips, which I wore with my oversized black trousers, white shirt and black-and-red striped tie, my Fila boys' trainers, peach anorak, and old backpack from the charity shop in Wimbledon. Just like the girls at my Westminster school, my new female classmates wore short skirts and make-up and carried pretty bags. I felt so ugly next to them, and I was bullied from the moment I walked through those green gates. My English was still poor, but I recognised some of the remarks those horrible kids made.

Walking between classes on my first day, a group circled me in the corridor. One of them, a boy with blond stripes in his hair and big wet lips, got right up in my face. 'Oi, you, suicide bomber,' he sneered, then looked at his mates for encouragement. 'Why don't you go back to your own fucking country?' His friends – two other boys and a girl who glared at me through black, clogged lashes – laughed. The girl looked me up and down, then pointed at my shoes, and also used the word 'bomber'. A burning heat prickled my neck. I'd heard 'suicide bomber' mentioned on the news programmes that Dad watched. Suicide bombers were terrorists who blew themselves up with the intention of killing other innocent people. Why would they label me a suicide bomber? What a cruel thing to say, and I hadn't done anything to antagonise them. The boy with the sloppy mouth jutted his chin. He looked like some ugly deep-sea creature. 'Go back to where you came from, bomber,' he spat. I curled my lips between my teeth and balled my fists in the sleeves of jumper. *How dare they. I've been bullied my whole life by my dad. They're not going to hurt me too.* 'Fuck you,' I said and stomped past those bastards in my Filas. By now I'd learned that 'fuck you' was offensive language.

But the bullying didn't end there. Kids abused me daily with more chants of 'suicide bomber', or they'd say things I didn't understand about Saddam Hussein. In lessons, pupils threw burst ink cartridges and the inner sections of pens at me. I'd find lumps of tissue congealed with spit stuck to the back of my jumper, accompanying Post-it notes saying 'kick me', 'hit me' or 'I'm a suicide bomber'.

It would take me a while before I made any proper friends at Bishopsford. Again, I couldn't understand half of what was going on around me. Although, as the weeks went by, I did try to interact with my classmates. In the changing rooms, girls spoke about Boyzone or S Club 7 or the latest episode of *Sunset Beach*, the American soap opera I'd caught snippets of when we lived in Dorset Road. One day after P.E., two girls I knew, Gemma and Alison, were chatting away as they stood by the mirrors over the sinks, doing their hair and make-up. I was sitting on a bench next to them, waiting for one of the toilets to be free so I could change out of my tracksuit bottoms. Much of what Gemma and Alison were saying went over my head because they were talking too fast – until I heard the Spice Girls mentioned. Oh, I swear a small bird started flapping in my chest. I shot to my feet. 'Girl power,' I blurted, remembering my conversation with Tia in Iran. The two girls fell silent for a few seconds, looked at me, looked at each other, then put their heads down and laughed into their make-up bags. They at least tried to conceal their amusement, to be fair. I sat down and pretended to look for something in my backpack. *Nope, no cleansing wipes, perfume or make-up in there.* God, I missed Tia.

As my English improved towards the end of the summer term, I felt even more alienated at school. I even handed pictures of me as a baby to my teachers, as I'd done so at school in Iran. It sounds crazy, I know, but those photos gave me comfort; they reminded me of how perfect my life had been for a short while. Sharing my pictures with teachers confirmed those happy memories existed, somehow.

I watched with envy, boiling in my hijab, as the trendy kids swapped VHS tapes, including a box set of *Friends*, knowing that if they were to offer those tapes to me, I would not be able to take them home. My dad would probably set fire to that *Friends* box set and beat me. And now I understood whole sentences, the bullies' comments drove me to the verge of fury and despair.

The boy with the big mouth and highlights was the worst. His name was Dean, but in my head, I called him Bastard Bully. I couldn't avoid Dean as he was in my form class and his desk was directly in front of mine. He was one of the pupils who would throw pens at me in other classes, too. During registration he'd turn in his seat and narrow his piggish eyes at me. 'Why did you come over here?' he'd ask. 'Why are your parents in *our* country, stealing our houses and jobs? Why don't you go back to your own country?'

'Fuck you,' I'd say, raging. I wanted to rearrange his slobbering face. His remarks also made me think about our family's situation in England. Dad didn't work, so he hadn't stolen anyone's job. As far as I knew, Dad was on benefits. *And just for the record, Bastard Bully, I would love to go back to 'my own country' right now – because I'm given no freedom to live like a normal teenager in* your *country.*

When I told Dad about the other kids bullying me, he did nothing. 'Just keep your mouth shut and ignore it all, Bakha,' he said with a stern face.

'But they say we should go back to our country, that we're stealing their homes and jobs. They call me suicide bomber.'

'Ignore them – it's only words. Words don't kill you.' Again, my father, the man who was supposed to protect me, was not interested in fighting my corner. Dad had plenty of opportunities to flag the issue as he routinely turned up at Bishopsford to speak with our teachers. He demanded to know why his daughters had to participate in P.E. classes. The school overruled him on that matter, but teachers accepted Dad's request that we should not, under any circumstances, receive sex education. Not once did Dad ask those teachers, 'What are you going to do about the kids who bully my daughter?'

Dad was always there, at the gates, waiting, watching like a hawk for us girls at the end of each school day. One scorching June afternoon I walked out with Leyla, a black girl I'd got talking to in the canteen that day. I liked Leyla a lot; she seemed so open-minded and friendly compared to the girls who made fun of me in P.E. She wore her long hair in beautifully crafted cornrows decorated with colourful beads, which fascinated me. I wanted to learn more about her culture. *I've got a friend*, I thought, as we neared the gate, concentrating hard to understand every word Leyla said, sweating in my jumper and headgear. When Dad spotted me with Leyla, he marched towards us, eyebrows crossed. Sweat soaked my hijab. Dad didn't lay a finger on me in the playground, but his threats in Kurdish, through a fake smile beneath his moustache, confirmed an imminent beating. Leyla tilted her chin and shaded her eyes with her hand. 'Hi,' she said to Dad, who shot my potential friend an evil look.

'Don't speak to my daughter again,' he said, and I couldn't even mouth a 'sorry' or 'bye' to Leyla because Dad's eyes were on me. I was so embarrassed. When we got home, Dad beat me.

Our home life was regimented and tedious. We didn't get to take part in after-school activities. Miriam, Shanar, Heibat, and Helo would enthuse about dance classes and outings with their friends while we girls had no semblance of social life under Dad's strict regime. After school, Kejal would help Mum with the cooking while Banaz and I cleaned the entire house before dinner. Then we would do our homework and go to bed. Occasionally, Dad would allow us to watch television, provided we'd finished our homework. However, we were only allowed to watch 'educational' programmes, such as documentaries or the news, which we were not allowed to discuss in English. The adverts shown between programmes intrigued me most, especially the one for Childline, which I understood to be a help service for kids suffering abuse at home. I'd also noticed billboards in the street advertising for Refuge, a charity that campaigns against domestic violence. This was all new to me. *Could these organisations help me?*

Ashti had just turned seven, yet there were no toys in her bedroom. Posters on bedroom walls were a definite no-no for all of us, and meeting friends at weekends was also out of the question for my sisters and me. Bahman, however, could socialise with friends as he pleased. He was rarely home and got up to all kinds of mischief, including drinking alcohol and smoking. So, when opportunities arose for us girls to rebel, we grabbed them.

Most Saturday and Sunday mornings, Mum and Dad went to the farmers' market in Wimbledon. They would take Payzee and Ashti with them, leaving us older ones home alone for a couple of hours. We wouldn't dare leave the house, but we found other ways to entertain ourselves indoors. For example, Kejal and I called Ervin and Saman in Tehran on the house phone, like, several times. Oblivious to the price of those calls, we could spend hour-long sessions talking to the boys about nothing of great note. Kejal continued her pretence, listing things she'd done in London, from 'shopping on Oxford Street' to films she'd allegedly watched at the cinema: *Sliding Doors*, *The Wedding Singer* and *The Object of My Affection* starring 'Rachel from *Friends*'. It saddened me to know Kejal based her list on activities enjoyed only by our cousins and classmates. I too acted as though everything was fine and giggled when Ervin said, 'Dooset daram, Bekhal,' which means 'I like you a lot, Bekhal' in Farsi. Saman said the same to Kejal. 'When can we visit you in London?' the boys asked.

'Soon,' we promised.

Imagine?

I relished those rare moments without Mum and Dad in the house. I remember one drizzly Saturday, just after they'd left for the market, when Banaz revealed a secret stash of make-up. Unbeknownst to our parents, Banaz had struck up a friendship with her classmate, Sara, a trendy, permed Westerner who smoked cigarettes. Sara had gifted Banaz some of her old make-up. 'She said it's stuff she doesn't use anymore,' explained Banaz as she emptied the contents of a pink drawstring bag on the carpet in our front bedroom. 'Look, there are brushes,' Banaz said, raking her fingers through the assortment of cosmetics and applicators. The soft, clickety-clack of plastic was like music to my ears. 'And Sara gave me these face wipes that remove make-up too.' Banaz placed the pack of wipes to one side. *Sara is an angel.*

We all gathered around the pile of make-up. I picked up a pot of gold Barry M glitter eyeshadow. 'Oh, Nazca, this is too good to be true. How kind of your friend.'

'Yes, and now that I have this make-up, I can share it with you both,' said Banaz, plucking a lipstick and handing it to me. 'Hey, Bakha, can you put this one on for me?'

'Let's do Nazca's make-up,' said Kejal. 'She can be our model.'

Banaz's face lit up. 'Oh yes, let's try it. Can you do contouring? And I want, like, the big red lips.' She indicated her mouth with her slim fingers.

'OK,' said Kejal, 'but you'll need to scrub it all off before Mum and Dad get back.'

Banaz nodded, opened a compact containing shimmery bronzer and gave a little gasp. 'Oh, jwana, jwana.'

Banaz had the perfect face on which to practice our make-up skills. Almost thirteen, she was already a proper beauty with her high cheekbones, wide eyes and long, arched eyebrows. Her bone structure made contouring easy because the definition was naturally there. Oh, we had so much fun. Kejal did Banaz's eyebrows, accentuating her arches with a soft, brown pencil. We shaded her eyelids in peach and gold tones that complemented her skin tone, applied black eyeliner and silky mascara that almost doubled the length of her already long lashes. After bronzing and highlighting to achieve Banaz's desired 'contoured look', we gave her heavy rosy cheeks and full-on red lipstick. As we worked, Banaz struck little pouty poses, and checked our progress in a small compact mirror. 'Oh, I love it,' she said in her soft voice, 'I look so different. Can you make my lips redder and more defined?' Bless Banaz: she loved the cheeks and lips best.

'OK, sit still then,' I said and found a brighter shade and a slender brush, but as I painted Banaz's lips, she wouldn't stop giggling. 'It tickles, Bakha,' she said every time I touched the brush to her mouth, which made us all laugh. We lost track of time –

until we heard the heavy clunk of the bottom lock turning in the front door. Banaz inhaled sharply. 'It's them.' A lighter, sticky sound of another key entering the top lock travelled up the stairs. Banaz grabbed the packet of wipes and bolted into the bathroom while Kejal and I quickly stuffed all the tubes and compacts and utensils back into Banaz's pink bag, which we hid in a corner recess of our fitted wardrobe. Fortunately, me and Kejal managed to distract Mum and Dad while Banaz removed her make-up. We helped them unpack the fruit and vegetables, made black tea, and asked about Grandma and Grandpa, who we'd be visiting that afternoon. Poor Grandpa Babakir. That evil disease had now spread to other parts of his body. He could barely speak, and the cancer nurses were at the house every day. Grandma cried and cried and cried.

Banaz appeared in the kitchen some fifteen minutes later. She'd done a remarkable job removing the layers of make-up we'd slapped on her. From then on, we continued to hone our make-up artistry skills on Banaz, making the most of those weekend mornings while Mum and Dad were out. There were many repeated scenarios of Banaz dashing to the bathroom just as the front door went, but, incredibly, we got away with our beauty sessions. Alas, Kejal and I were not so lucky when the first British Telecom bill skidded across the plastic carpet protector in the hallway.

It happened in late July, at the start of the school summer holidays. It was a weekday morning, and I was in the shower, softly humming along to the chorus of 'The Boy Is Mine', by American singers Brandy & Monica. I loved that song. Leyla had let me listen to it on her Walkman at school. Despite Dad's hostility at the gates that day, Leyla had become my best friend, although I kept this quiet at home. As I stepped out of the shower, I heard Dad, shouting and swearing in the hallway. I couldn't catch all he was saying through the bathroom door, but I did hear him yell, in Kurdish: 'Fucking. Five. Hundred. Pounds!' as he slammed the front door.

I dressed quickly and went down to the living room, where Mum was pacing back and forth, repeatedly thumping her palms against her temples as she chanted 'no, Allah; no, Allah; no, Allah.' On the coffee table – the only table in our house – red chiffon fabric flowed from Mum's sewing machine. That would be another traditional dress for one of us girls to wear to the next Kurdish community event, where we'd be introduced to prospective husbands. My innards curdled at the thought. Just then, Kejal walked in. 'What's wrong, Mum?'

'Allah is knowing of all things,' said Mum, then she told us about the five-hundred-pound phone bill that had just landed. 'There are numbers on the bill that we don't recognise,' she explained. 'Calls made to Tehran. Your father is on his way to your grandparents' house with Uncle Ari and Uncle Afran. They're going to check the numbers. No, Allah, five hundred pounds? No, Allah, this can't be so.' I looked at Kejal and her eyes momentarily disappeared into her forehead.

This is what happened behind the scenes. The bright idea to check the numbers on our phone bill against calls made from 11 Dorset Road had been Ari's. Bingo, the same Tehran number also appeared on my grandparents' previous bill. The dates on which those calls were logged coincided with when we were living at the address. Smug Ari then told Dad to call the number in Tehran, which he did do. Ervin and Saman confirmed Kejal and I had called them several times. They even told Dad they were hoping to come to London. Ervin spoke of his wish to marry me, and Saman felt the same about Kejal. Ari then told Dad: 'Your daughters have brought shame upon this family.'

Oh my God, Dad interrogated Kejal and me for two hours and beat us with his belt and shoes. He made Kejal kneel in the dining room (Mum and Dad's bedroom), and I was told to stay in the lounge. He shut the door that separated the two rooms and cross-examined Kejal first. Mum was in the room with them. 'Answer your father, gahba,' she snapped at Kejal, who was sobbing her heart out. Kejal never got into trouble like this. Tears streamed down my face too as Dad's voice boomed between cracks of his belt. The house trembled, causing the unfinished red dress on Mum's sewing machine to flinch and flutter with fear.

Dad thundered on. 'We don't even know their families. Where did you think this would go? Do you think it's acceptable to speak to men, even? What will people think?' I tried to listen to Kejal's answers through the cacophony of shouting, sobbing and physical violence.

The Evil Punisher started on me next. 'Were you ever going to tell us that you're in love with this person, whore-child?' he demanded. 'Did you look at him and like him?'

'No, he's from a good family. They have a good reputation,' I said. Physical attraction to a stranger? No, you can't have that in my culture. Throughout his tirade, Dad forced me backwards on the blood-red carpet, and battered me non-stop for about fifteen minutes, first with his belt, then with his shoe.

'Don't you get it?' Dad yelled, hammering my legs with the sole of his shoe. His face glistened with sweat. 'Now you're in the UK, you're a meal ticket for men from our country who want to marry you to gain citizenship in England.'

Oh, the hypocrisy. Dad was already trying to marry me and Kejal off to our cousins in Iraq. This, I was sure of. I'd overheard Dad's conversations with Ari in the dining room. Ari saying, 'You need to find husbands for your eldest daughters. Bekhal will be the one to dishonour this family if you don't act soon, Mahmod.' The evil son of a bitch.

I felt bad about the phone bill, and I would have paid every penny back to Dad if I could. Had we known the cost of those calls, Kejal and I wouldn't have made them. I certainly had no intentions of marrying Ervin. Those calls were just a bit of fun – until we got caught.

The school summer holidays dragged on – as did our punishment for dialling Tehran. We weren't allowed to watch any television, not even 'educational' programmes, and Dad turned over our bedroom, searching for more evidence relating to those bloody phone calls. Of course, none of us girls could meet friends. The only time we left the house during the holidays was to visit Grandpa (with Mum and Dad) or for family gatherings.

Ari organised a few family picnics in Hyde Park, which turned into the Ari Show each time. Grandpa, riddled with cancer, was in excruciating pain. Yet Ari insisted a day out in his wheelchair was just what the doctor ordered for his father. It broke my heart to see Grandpa in his wheelchair, so frail and blanketed to his neck despite the heat, a faraway look in his yellowed eyes. We'd all bring food and blankets and cushions to sit on but Ari, of course, rocked up with posh, padded sunbeds and huge umbrellas, and laughed at the rest of us, slumming it on the grass. All you could hear was Ari's voice, bragging about his house and garden and businesses, while Grandpa sat there, slowly dying. I remember Ari talking about 'visas' he'd created for male family members in Iraq – and the properties he was 'doing-up' for those men to live in once they arrived in the UK. 'I'm bringing Dana Amin over next,' he said, 'I'll get him working in my Wimbledon shop.' My stomach turned when I heard Dana's name mentioned. Dana is my horrible older cousin – the one who had jeered when I almost drowned in the Tanjaro River in Sulaymaniyah years ago. Other names Ari mentioned were my cousin Mohammed Ali and Mohamad Hama, who the men nicknamed 'Sor' (red or redness) and 'Little Sor' respectively – because they both have reddish skin, and Hama is the shortest of the two. 'I'll get them decorating the flats,' Ari said like he was saving the bloody world. I noticed Grandpa's arm twitching beneath his blanket – as though in protest to what Ari was saying. How I wish Grandpa could have voiced his concern.

I had just started Year Ten when Dad got the call from St George's Hospital in Tooting. Grandpa had been admitted to hospital a few days ago, when doctors warned us to prepare for the worst. That time had now come. The whole family gathered in Grandpa Babakir's hospital room. The man lying in the bed didn't look like Grandpa. As soon as I saw him, I wanted to scream, 'Come back

Grandpa Babakir.' His cheeks and eye sockets were hollow. He couldn't speak, but he rolled his head on the pillow and glanced at Dad, sitting at Grandpa's side, and Dad sobbed as he squeezed Grandpa's right shoulder. 'Baba, don't go. Please don't go. Baba, no.' Dad pinched the bridge of his ballooned nose and squeezed his eyes, allowing tears to cascade down his face, through his moustache. This was the first time I'd seen Dad cry, and it moved me. There was something human about Dad in this moment. The Evil Punisher was now feeling pain himself. I actually felt compassion towards him.

Grandma was on the other side of the bed, holding Grandpa's hand, praying through sobs. Dad's brothers – Ari, Afran and Zoran, sat in a line along the right-hand side of the bed. I stood on Grandma's side with my sisters and Mum. We girls were in floods of tears, listening to Grandpa's breath. Slow, with long pauses between each intake of air. Then he gasped, before letting out a long, shuddering sigh. Grandpa Babakir, head of the Mahmod family, the kind man who was once a face in a tall tree, had gone.

Dad cried, 'No, Baba, no,' and kissed Grandpa's forehead and face. Grandma rocked back and forth, still clutching Grandpa's hand. Me and Banaz hugged each other as we wailed and wailed, and Ari turned and stared at us, chin tilted towards the ceiling so we could see his big hairy nostrils. The look he gave Banaz and me was one of utter contempt, as though we were overreacting to our grandpa's death.

From that moment on, Ari would overpower and destroy our family with his narcissism and acts of pure evil.

Chapter Twelve

ASHES TO ASHES

Seeing Dad break down at Grandpa's bedside sparked a battle of emotions within me. First, a fleeting feeling of love for my father, one I had not experienced since I was a small child. 'Xushm aweit, Baba [I love you, Dad],' he'd said, kissing Grandpa's forehead for the final time, his voice raw but gentle, and I'd wanted to throw my arms around Dad at that point. For all the pain he'd inflicted upon me, I still couldn't bear to see him cry. Dad had worshipped the ground Grandpa walked on, and I felt his irreparable grief. But as I stood there sobbing with my sisters, and the prayers started, interspersed with Dad's repeated cries of 'xushm aweit, Baba,' I suddenly realised, *Dad hasn't said, 'I love you, Bakha' since I was four or five*, and my empathy dissolved to resentment.

Grandpa's passing did not soften Dad as I'd hoped it might do. He didn't cuddle us kids and say, 'Grandpa loved you very much and he's in a better place now.' If anything, Dad's angry outbursts became more frequent and pronounced after Grandpa Babakir died. Grief fuelled his fury, causing him to lash out at anything and everything. If he heard us kids speaking English at home, he'd launch into a tyrannical rant. He caught me, Kejal, Banaz and Payzee, doing so one evening. We were all in the front bedroom when Dad stormed in, yelling, 'Shûraî [disgraceful]. No English.

I told you, no English will be spoken in this house. All of you, downstairs, now.' Dad didn't beat us this time, but he separated us, forcing Banaz and Payzee to sit in the dining room, while Kejal and I were locked in the lounge. 'I don't want to hear one word of English,' Dad warned before slamming the door.

Still, we girls were not allowed to socialise with friends outside of school or dress how we wished. Dad would inspect our bedrooms, rifling through our wardrobes and pulling out the drawers beneath our beds, hunting for haram items such as make-up or Western clothes. Luckily, he never found Banaz's make-up stash. Likewise, he didn't find her Kenzo perfume, another gift from her friend Sara. Banaz, bless her, hid her 'haram' belongings in a secret space where the fitted wardrobe turned a corner.

Kejal, who had become ultra-submissive to Dad since he beat us over the phone bill, fell victim to another of his violent episodes when he caught her wearing a V-neck jumper – a sweater mum had bought for her from a charity shop, which we were expected to wear over a polo neck. We (Dad, Banaz and me) were watching the BBC six o'clock news when Kejal walked into the lounge, carrying our plastic tablecloth. She'd been cooking our dinner with Mum, as per usual. As she knelt to lay the tablecloth in front of the sofa, where Dad was sitting, Banaz and I remained glued to the news item about the then Prime Minister, Tony Blair. The tablecloth rustled behind us as Kejal unfolded it, and all was calm until Dad shouted, 'Qehpik,' and a sharp, stinging clap drowned the newsreader's voice, causing Banaz and me to jump and turn in time to see Kejal topple sideways on her knees from the force of Dad's blow. Her breath caught in her throat as she covered her face with one hand and returned to her kneeling position, trembling from her waist upwards. 'Behya, get in here, now,' Dad called, jabbing the off button on the remote control. Banaz and I sat there, still as two herons, watching this painful scene unfold. Mum flew into the room, almost tripping in her slippers. With her came heat from the kitchen and a comforting smell of cloves and coriander. Dad sat on the edge of the sofa, shot Mum a look of disgust, then flung forth his hands in a shooing motion above Kejal's head. 'Look at your whore of a daughter. Why the fuck is she wearing that jumper?' The long-sleeved, terracotta jumper Kejal had on was made from heavy wool, the V-neck just grazing her collarbone.

Mum nudged Kejal with her foot. 'Get up, ghaba.' Sniffing, Kejal rose and walked backwards out of the room so as not to turn her back on Dad. Mum followed and gave Kejal another telling off in the hall. 'You look like a whore. Go upstairs and change, now – then come back down and show your father.'

Such incidences became a daily routine at home, especially for me. Once, Dad noticed that the top button of my school shirt was undone. For that offence, he grabbed my hair bun and yanked my head backwards, so I was staring at the ceiling. He spat in my face, called me a whore, then pushed me against the wall and smacked me hard around the head a few times. This was Dad's latest modus operandi for punishing me – pulling my hair, spitting in my face and slapping my head. He did this to me so frequently that I began to suffer crippling headaches. I couldn't go a day without taking at least four paracetamols. Dad frightened me. I was a skinny fifteen-year-old girl, and he a powerfully built six-foot man. All the same, I'd had enough of his abuse and all-consuming cultural beliefs. I was sick of being told what to wear in a country where other girls my age got to dress like Scary, Sporty, Baby or Posh Spice. Don't get me wrong, I did not aspire to wear a miniskirt or high heels or anything too revealing. I just wanted some choices in life. Our house felt like a prison, not a home, and the more violent Dad became, the more I rebelled. The way I saw my situation was thus: he (Dad) beats me almost every day over trivial matters, so I might as well make some big mistakes. *I'll get a beating, anyway.*

I first tried smoking on the day of Grandpa Babakir's funeral, which was a huge, manly event. More than a hundred people – family and Kurdish community friends attended the service at Morden Cemetery. The men shovelled earth into Grandpa's grave, then joined hands and stamped on the mound. I cried buckets, and when we left the cemetery, I felt guilty for walking away and leaving Grandpa alone in that dirt-filled hole.

After the burial, the guests went back to Grandma's. My God, the house heaved with people, inside and out. Many of the women sat in Grandma's lounge, while Dad and his brothers and other male relatives I did not recognise gathered in the room where Grandpa once slept in his hospital bed. More men sat in the garden, smoking shisha. Iraqi music, whiny and depressing, played on the stereo, while women served trays of Kurdish food and drink to all of the guests. Dad had bought a few 200-packs of Sovereign cigarettes to cater for the male smokers at the wake. Cigarette cartons occupied tables, counters in Grandma's kitchen and window ledges throughout the house. I found a full packet of Sovereigns in the algae bathroom even. Temptation was everywhere. As I transported trays back and forth from the kitchen, I managed to steal a few packets of cigarettes. My cousin Shanar, already a secret smoker, did the same, and, among the frantic toing and froing and outpourings of emotion, Shanar and I escaped via the alleyway and headed to the Abbey Recreation Play Area, which was a ten-minute walk from Grandma's house.

We sat on a grass spot secluded by wild bushes and trees, then Shanar passed me a cigarette and told me to put the tan filter end between my lips and cup my hands around its tip. 'I've only got a few matches left,' she said as she also instructed me to 'take the smoke into your lungs.' She lit the cigarette, which I held between my index finger and thumb while Shanar also sparked up. 'You need to smoke it, Bakha,' she said. Truth was, I didn't know what to do with the thing. I watched Shanar take her first puff, noting how she closed her eyes and sucked the filter like a straw, then I tried to copy her. But instead of inhaling, I tried to swallow my mouthful of smoke, which made me gag and cough.

'Argh, this is disgusting,' I spluttered before clamping my lips around the filter again. After a few more puffs, I began to feel light-headed. My face and scalp tingled as nicotine hit my brain.

Soon, that whirly, relaxed sensation outweighed the ashy taste. I felt relaxed, liberated. 'I'm buzzing. I'm drunk,' I said, exhaling a stream of grey mist.

'Oh my God, Bakha, don't be silly, you've only had one puff.' Shanar's laugh morphed into a cough. I puffed away, determined to nail this smoking business, and before I knew it, Shanar was handing me a second cigarette, which she lit off the one she was smoking.

I inhaled, then exhaled. 'Oh, this feels *so* good,' I said through an undercurrent of nausea.

Shanar laughed. 'Yeah, let's just stay here for a while and smoke loads of fags.'

An hour later, me and Shanar returned to Grandpa's wake. We were both a bit dizzy after chain-smoking in the park but kept our cool as we walked into the packed garden and resumed our tray-collecting duties. I lost count of the number of fags I smoked that day, but I do remember how I felt afterwards: sick, spaced-out, but excited to have done something of my choosing without violent consequences. Nobody noticed Shanar and I had left Grandma's house.

Years ago, I'd walked hand in hand with Dad around our garden in Iran, begging him to quit smoking. He continued to smoke but eventually quit once Grandpa became ill. Now, after preaching about the dangers of smoking cigarettes, I was also hooked on the filthy habit. Adding to this irony, I didn't even like the taste or smell of tobacco; I started smoking to rebel against Dad, to fit in at school, and for the head-rushes that sent me to a happy place for a fleeting moment.

After a while, Dad stopped walking us to and from school, which seemed strange given his strict attitude concerning every other facet of his daughters' lives. I made the most of this freedom. Back then, you could buy a pack of ten cigarettes for around £1.50. We didn't receive pocket money but occasionally, Dad would give us each some coins for bus fare and lunches, so I spent my loose change on fags.

School became more bearable after I took up smoking. Instead of feeling like a social pariah, I could now mix with the kids who sneaked behind the bike sheds for cigarettes during break times. My best friend Leyla introduced me to her circle of friends, who, like us, were from diverse cultural backgrounds. My new friends called me Becky, which I loved – this nickname name made me feel accepted in the Western world. Besides my sisters, there were no other Kurds in my school, but I became friends with a Turkish girl, Nehir, who did me a huge favour. Nehir was also friendly with Dean, who still bullied me. He really was a horrible little shit with his constant 'suicide bomber' and 'get back to your own country' taunts. When I confided in Nehir about this, she had a word with her 'friend' and, overnight, Dean stopped bullying me. As they say, it's not what you know, it's who you know.

At home, Dad continued his evil campaign of intimidation and control. He became obsessed with the notion I was bringing the family name into disrepute as I began to challenge his power.

Occasionally, I bunked off school in the mornings. It was easy; I would show up to registration, flee via the gates before the first lesson, then return for afternoon registration. Around this time, I became pals with Banaz's friend Sara, who would also skip morning lessons. We would go to the nearby Watermeads Nature Reserve and hide in the fire-charred remains of an old cottage, where Sara introduced me to weed. Oh my God, I loved smoking joints. Getting stoned was my escapism. It numbed my senses yet, somehow, I could think with clarity while high on weed. This drug would soon become my crutch.

I got away with my truancy for several weeks – until the teachers noticed my absence in classes and wrote a letter to Mum and Dad outlining their concerns. Dad beat me senseless, of course.

The more I rebelled, so life at home became intolerable. Beating followed beating followed beating. One of my worst whippings happened when Mum and Dad discovered I smoked. Until now, I had been careful to conceal my habit. I kept my cigarettes and lighter tucked in either side of my bra and always carried a mint breath-freshening spray and deodorant to eradicate the smell of smoke. But one time, Mum and Dad did smell smoke on me. That's what they claimed. I didn't know then that my dad and Ari had ordered Kurdish men, including my relatives, to spy on me. I walked into the house after school to find Mum and Dad in the hall. Before I could take off my shoes, Dad thwacked me around the head. 'You've been smoking, you gahba.' The next half hour was one of the most excruciating, degrading moments of my life. My parents dragged me upstairs and into the bathroom, where Mum stripped me to my underwear, found my secret cigarettes and forced me to stand in the bath as she screamed obscenities. Then she threw a bucket of cold water over me and watched as Dad whacked me all over with his bare hands. The water served as an extra weapon, because wet slaps hurt more. I was fifteen, and practically naked. *What the fuck is this animal doing to me?*

The worst was yet to come.

Towards the end of Year Ten I landed a part time job in a local supermarket. I was so thrilled; the manageress, Kim, offered me the role because I'd impressed her while on a work experience placement at the store. 'You're a credit to our team, Bekhal,' said Kim and my face broke into a huge smile. I felt worthy for once. I worked every Saturday and two or three evenings in the week after school, serving behind the deli counter or stacking shelves. What I loved most, more than my wages, was interacting with people, customers and colleagues alike. That supermarket became my haven away from home.

Dad soon ruined this.

Money was the only reason Dad let me take that job. Cash had also been his motive when Kejal got her part-time position at a mobile phone store a few months previously. Ahead of my first pay packet, Dad took me to the Abbey National Building Society to open an account. And every month when payday arrived, that horrible bastard would walk me to the cash machine and stand over me as I checked my balance. Then he'd make me draw out every single penny of my hard-earned wages, my blood, sweat and tears, and hand the cash to him. Dad would give me fifty pounds and pocket the rest. He did the same with Kejal's wages. 'This is your contribution to our household expenses,' he told us. 'Providing for a family of eight is not cheap.' This riled me. Why didn't he get a job? All Dad did, besides controlling us girls, was socialise with his Kurdish community friends and relatives.

On a few occasions, I managed to withdraw part of my wages before Dad escorted me to the cash machine. Then he found my wage slips and beat the crap out of me. Again, I began to rebel. I would lie about my work hours to get out of the house, and I spent my fifty pounds a month on treats for myself. I'd buy cigarettes, weed, Western clothes, make-up, curling tongs, a bottle of Baileys here and there – and I'd hide all of my purchases in my locker at work.

I began to style my hair differently, inspired by my black friends' amazing updos. I'd twist my long hair into a big high bun, leaving tendrils free at the front and sides to slick with gel and tong into telephone wire curls. Leggings became my favourite fashion item, which I wore to work beneath a long dress instead of my usual baggy trousers. It goes without saying, the Evil Punisher went mental at my transformation.

Dad hated my new hairstyle and snakeskin-patterned leggings with a passion, and I endured the same brutal routine over and over. Every time I tried to sneak out of the house to go to work, he intercepted me. 'Look at the fucking state of you,' he'd sneer, eyeing my hair. 'You look like you've just come out of your mother.' His next move would be to grab my bun and shake, shake, shake my head until my hair came undone, and the room wobbled in wavy lines. Then he'd wrestle me to the floor on my front, kneel on my kidneys, and pinch my legs all over, including my inner thighs, shouting, 'Mizir Qehpik [fucking whore], look how tight they are. Look, you can't even grab these whore trousers.' I'd press my face into the blood-red carpet, trying not to scream, waiting for the torture to end. Finally, he'd haul me to my feet, grab my hair again, march me to the front door, spit in my face, and literally kick me onto the street. 'There, you look really nice now,' he'd say, 'now go to work.'

Even when I was working, I could not escape the Evil Punisher. He gave me a pay-as-you-go mobile phone – Kejal's former handset (she got a new one) – merely to keep tabs on me. He showed up at the supermarket, wandering the aisles with his basket, spying on me. If he saw me talking to a male colleague, he'd approach us and start cussing me in Kurdish, with a faux friendly smile on his face.

I remained defiant, determined not to be broken by my father's reign of abuse. *It's my face, my hair, my body, my life*, I'd remind myself. But soon I plunged into a deep depression. I smoked more weed and drank Baileys concealed in a Tango bottle at school, just to numb my pain and help me through the days. My legs and arms were indigo with bruises – injuries sustained during Dad's attacks. I hated my life, hated myself, and most of all, I hated my father. My friends appeared to have loving parents. They talked about going clothes shopping with their mums or laughed about the embarrassing things their dads did or said. Leyla knew my dad was strict, but I had not told her about the beatings. How could I? I was too embarrassed to share this information with my new friends. I'd cry myself to sleep at night thinking about Dad's violence. *Why bring me into this world, into this country, if you won't let me live my life?*

I reached my lowest ebb one morning in art class during the final term of Year Ten. Art was my favourite subject, as I loved to draw and paint and be creative. My teacher, Miss Evans, often praised my work. One of my pieces – an old boot on which I painted Picasso-inspired designs – was displayed in the headmaster's office. Today's lesson was about the human form. 'I'd like you all to draw or paint something figurative,' said Miss Evans. 'Be as creative and abstract as you like.' I took a sheet of A3 paper, a black marker pen and began to draw a woman's eye, filling the whole page. Working from memory following our make-up sessions on Banaz, I gave my woman long, silky lashes and sleek winged liner, and two tears, spilling from the outer corner of her eye. But my heart wasn't in my work. I cried silent tears with my imaginary woman, smudging her eyeliner as the page drank my sadness. Morbid thoughts crept in. *I don't want to be here, in this world, anymore. I can end it all. Dad can't hurt me if I'm dead. I have a full pack of paracetamol in my bag.*

Wiping my eyes, I pushed back my chair, motioned to Miss Evans that I needed to leave, and hurried into the corridor cradling my rucksack. I ran to the girls' toilets, locked myself in a cubicle, and swallowed one pill after another until I'd emptied both blister strips. I waited fifteen minutes or so, then, paracetamol packet in hand, I unlocked the door – and bumped into the cleaner.

I remember only fragments of that day. The cleaner saw the empty paracetamol packet and asked, 'Did you just take all of those tablets?' and I stared through her, wondering why the sinks were floating towards the ceiling. Miss Evans appeared – a jellyfish in the bathroom, mumbling sounds I could not decipher until I heard the word, 'ambulance'.

'No ambulance … Dad can't find out … no ambulance, no ambulance, no ambulance…' Slumped on the linoleum, I drifted away.

Miss Evans was at my bedside in St Helier Hospital. I don't recall the ambulance ride, or the stomach pump the medics performed on me. The doctors carried out tests on my liver (to check for damage), then discharged me a few hours later. 'Your father said he can't pick you up, Miss Mahmod,' said the nurse.

I gulped. It was like swallowing razor blades. 'OK,' I said. 'Did he sound angry?'

The nurse gave me a pitying smile. 'No, your father just said he couldn't come. I guess he's a busy man.' My eyes filled with tears. Dad wasn't busy. He had recently bought a car too – a red second-hand Vauxhall Cavalier. My supermarket wages helped towards the cost of that motor. I had just tried to kill myself at school. The hospital was a ten-minute drive from our house, but Mum and Dad would not collect me – and that said it all to me.

Miss Evans drove me home. I wanted to stay for ever in her red Mini, its back seat choc-a-block with paint pots and brushes.

'Would you like me to come in with you?' she asked when we pulled up outside 225 Morden Road. It was gone 9.30 p.m., but all windows at the front of the house were aglow besides Bahman's room. *He'll be out again.*

'No, no,' I said. 'I'm fine.' I thanked Miss Evans and opened the passenger door. The house loomed like a giant illuminated tombstone. I did not want to go in.

Dad reacted to my suicide attempt by pinning me to the wall, pulling my hair (again), spitting in my face (again), and shouting: 'How dare you dishonour this family. How dare you draw attention to yourself in this way. What fucking problems do you have in life to do such a thing?' then he smacked me around the head (again). 'You disgust me. Go to bed, gahba.'

Kejal was sitting up in bed. 'Why must you make things so difficult for us?' she said, then turned off her bedside lamp. I climbed into bed, feeling like a failure. *I can't even try to kill myself without getting a beating. Where did I go wrong? Why am I even back here?*

I drenched the pillow with my tears.

Chapter Thirteen

RUN, BAKHA, RUN

My suicide attempt was never again mentioned in our home, and my usual school/work/smoke weed/get beaten routine continued.

When I returned to school the next day, my form teacher, Miss Davies, took me into a private room for a one-to-one chat. 'Is there anything you'd like to speak about, Bekhal? she said softly. 'What made you do what you did yesterday? Can we help in any way?'

'I'm fine,' I lied. 'I'm just having a few problems at home right now.' Truth was, I didn't know where to start. No offence to Miss Davies, but had I explained our warped culture, she would not have understood.

'What kind of problems, Bekhal?'

'Oh, it's OK. My dad just beats me from time to time. He gets angry at stuff that I do.'

'I see,' said Miss Davies. 'Do you want to talk about this?'

I shook my head. What was the point? Miss Davies couldn't do anything to tame the Evil Punisher. Nobody could. I left the room, went to maths class and life carried on.

Secretly, I was relieved my overdose had failed. In retrospect, I didn't want to die that day. My suicide bid was a cry for help – an opportunity to escape from life for a while.

But dreams of an easier existence in London would never come true while I remained in the Mahmod fold, I realised. My childhood aspirations of becoming a police officer were dead in the water too. A career wasn't an option for a woman in my family unless I were to become a doctor or a rocket scientist, or something equally high-flying and well paid. Even then, I would still be expected to marry a cousin or be forced into a marriage with a stranger from our 'tribe'. We girls were forced to go to Kurdish community parties in traditional dresses made by Mum. Dad would 'present' me to potential suitors' families. 'She's a good Muslim girl. She cooks and cleans well. She's got a good head on her shoulders…' Yada, yada, yada. *Fuck off. No, just, No.*

While there were rumblings about marrying Kejal off, the focus shifted to me, the troublemaker. Dad was under pressure from Ari – and the rest of the family – to fix me up with a husband before I further discredited the family's reputation with my 'shame'. Total bullshit.

Since Grandpa's death, Ari had effectively established himself as head of the Mahmod family – a role expected of Dad as the eldest son. In the eyes of the Kurdish community, Dad had failed to control his wayward daughter, which put even more pressure on him to restore the family's 'honour'. Ari had eyes on all the Mahmod girls – except for his 'angel' daughters.

A few weeks after my paracetamol overdose, Miriam invited me to a sleepover at her house. Mum and Dad were reluctant to let me go, but relented when Aunty Alal and Uncle Afran okayed the idea. 'It's the school holidays, Behya,' said Aunty Alal. I was relieved to get out of our house. Miriam and I chatted well into the night, giggling and reminiscing about our days in Iran. We relived our stowaway tale and all the nonsense we used to get up to, and, for a while, I was able to switch off from my troubles. I slept better at Miriam's than I had done in months at home.

The next day, Miriam and I went to meet her male schoolfriend, Faizan, for a short walk in Tooting. I don't think there was anything romantic between Miriam and Faizan, but they clearly enjoyed each other's company. We met near Tooting Broadway Tube station, then wandered down a back street, where me and Miriam sat on the curb between two parked cars to smoke while Faizan stood, also smoking. Then, out of the blue, a madman on a scooter came speeding along the pavement towards Faizan. All three of us dropped our cigarettes as the man, clad in a leather jacket and jeans, jumped off his bike, pulled off his helmet and threw it at Faizan, who sidestepped the missile with a microsecond to spare. 'What the fuck are you doing with my sister and cousin?' the man yelled. I grabbed Miriam and we shot to our feet and backed against a wall, while Miriam's brother, Eylo, completely lost his shit. He charged at Faizan, shoved him, whacked him around the head and showered him in a spray of spit. 'Don't you understand our fucking culture? How dare you speak to my sister and cousin.'

Poor Faizan tried to block Eylo's blows. 'I've not done anything, you've made a mistake, I don't even know them.' As Eylo advanced, Faizan stepped backwards, until his legs touched the bonnet of one of the parked cars.

'Stay away from my fucking sister and cousin – or I'll go and see *your* sister,' Eylo finished. He stood in front of Faizan, breathing hard and giving him a maniacal stare. 'Don't you fucking dare go near my sister or cousin again.' Eylo's gums and teeth sweated spittle.

Faizan wiped Eylo's saliva off his face with his sleeve, took two shaky steps sideways, onto the pavement, and slowly walked away. Eylo's eyes trailed Faizan's hunched shoulders around the corner, while Miriam and I remained glued to the wall, holding hands. Then Eylo trained his evil glare upon us.

'Let's go,' Miriam said under her breath. Moving as one unit, just as we used to do as kids, we inched towards the middle of the pavement, Eylo still staring at us, his leather chest rising and falling at speed. After a few stumbling steps backwards, we turned and ran. I felt Eylo's eyes burning through my coat as we pounded past houses and normal people, going about their normal days. We ran all the way to Tooting Broadway Tube station, where we caught our breath and kissed goodbye.

'I'm going to get such a bollocking for this,' Miriam said, her wet palms pressed to her chest.

'You haven't done anything wrong, Miriam,' I said. 'It's our fucked-up culture that's to blame.' We hugged and kissed again, then I scuttled into the clogged throat of the Tube station and caught the train to Morden, at the end of the black Northern line.

By the time I reached home, Eylo had told the whole family what he'd witnessed that morning in Tooting. Dad summoned me to the lounge. His tone was stern but not aggressive as usual. I thought he might beat me but instead he listened to my version of events. I told him that Miriam had bumped into a schoolfriend – a boy whom I did not know. 'Honestly, Baba,' I said, 'I've never met him before in my life.'

'But you've been seen with this boy. You've put yourself in this shit – and now everybody, including Ari, is going to blame *you* for this drama.'

'What's it got to do with Ari? His daughters have lots of boys as friends. I know so.' This was true – Heibat and Helo had told me as much.

Dad thumped his tea glass on the coffee table. 'Oh, get out of my sight. You disgust me.'

That evening, at around 9 p.m., Uncle Ari and Uncle Afran came to our house. The men debated in Dad's bedroom for ten minutes. I was told to wait in the back bedroom with my sisters, who were all fishing for information. Again, Kejal was not happy. 'Why can't you just do what you're told, Bekhal? You're making life unbearable for the rest of us with your dramas.'

I glared at Kejal. *How dare she take Dad's side.* 'I've done nothing wrong,' I said. 'We're treated like prisoners in this house. None of us girls deserve to be…' The heavy thud of three brothers' feet climbing the stairs silenced me. My heart stopped as the footsteps travelled along the landing, towards the front of the house. A door closed. I looked at Banaz, sitting on the edge of her bed, wringing her hands on her knees. Then our door opened.

'Bekhal, come now. Your father and uncles want to speak to you,' said Mum.

Oh my God, it was like a big fuck-off Ari stage show – and for what? Sharing the same air as another human being? For sharing the same pavement space as a boy whom I'd known less than ten minutes? Really? I walked into the front bedroom to find Dad and Ari sitting on Kejal's bed, and Uncle Afran opposite them on my bed. Ari, in his shiny trousers and shirt unbuttoned below his collarbone, had one foot crossed over his opposite knee and a look on his face that screamed, *Look at me, I'm king of the fucking castle.* I knelt on the floor beside Mum, facing Ari and Dad, and stared at my hands, folded in my lap (you're not allowed to look up unless you're asked a question). For a minute, nobody spoke. Noises filled that space: a car engine starting outside; the teasing sound of next door's television. Ari exhaled hard, air rustling through the thickets of his nasal hair.

'What the fuck is all this nonsense you're saying about my kids?' he began.

I looked up, thinking, *God, he's ugly.* 'I've only repeated stuff that they've told me,' I said. Dad hunched his shoulders. *Not the big man now, eh?*

'I know the lies you're spreading about my daughters. You fucking whore-child.'

'Well, when I said that to Baba, I meant…'

'You have no fucking right to talk about my kids.' Ari's voice bore through me like a pneumatic drill. 'They've done nothing wrong. They're good girls, better than you. Look at what you've done with your life. You are scum.' On and on went Ari, lecturing me on how 'respected' our family was, and how I was 'dishonouring' the Mahmod name, while my dad sat with his head down, taking all this bullshit. Tears burned my eyes. I wasn't sure what hurt me most – Ari's vile rant or Dad's lack of words. Ari stopped speaking for a moment and I bowed my head again. My chest shuddered as I cried, then Ari was off again. 'Look at me when I'm speaking to you, gahba.'

When I lifted my head he shot forwards, digging his elbow into the crook of his crossed leg. 'All you do is bring shame on this family, and your dad hasn't got the balls to do anything about it. Now, he may be a weak man, but I am *not*. Even the police are beneath me.' I looked at Dad, tears streaming down my face. *Why won't he say something?* Ari smirked and beat his raised foot up and down. 'Listen,' he said, pushing his face further towards mine, his breath garlicky. 'I will not put up with this bullshit. I will put an end to this shame. If I had my way –and your father had listened to *me* – if you were my daughter, you'd be turning to ashes by now.'

I gulped, then gagged on my tears and snot. Dad sat there, silent. Afran, the man who'd intervened many times when Dad had beaten me in Iran, also said nothing. Mum, who had just heard her brother-in-law speak of his wish to have me killed, had no words.

'That's all,' Ari finished, and I stood, out of respect – because that's what we're told to do in our culture. Ari got up too. 'Wipe your tears,' he said casually, and lifted his hand for me to kiss it. Reluctantly, I did as Ari told me to do. Sickness swirled in my stomach. I wanted to vomit over his hand – and trousers and feet. Sadly, I didn't do that. 'Now behave yourself,' he added. 'Stop getting into trouble.'

Ari left the room. Dad and Afran followed him. Ari's words looped in my mind like a warped nursery rhyme: *If I had my way, you'd be turning to ashes by now.* Once the men were downstairs, I turned to Mum, wishing, praying she would wrap me in her arms and say, *Shh, Bakha, my darling, my love, everything will be OK. I won't let anybody hurt you.* All I wanted was a cuddle. Was that too much to ask? I felt exhausted. My body and mind ached from years of abuse. Uncle Ari had sat in *my* bedroom, the space where I sleep, labelled me scum, and said he would burn me to death. He had not been joking, either. 'Can you believe what he [Ari] just said?' I asked Mum. 'Would you and Dad really let that happen to me? Would you let my uncle turn me to ashes?'

Mum folded her arms, made a squiggly line with her mouth, then sighed. 'No, Allah, you bring all this shit onto yourself. You get involved in these situations, then wonder why you're in trouble? Had you been good and not gone out with Miriam, Ari would have no reason to be here. But you just can't help yourself, can you?' Mum shuffled out of my room and went downstairs. I counted a 'No, Allah' for each step. I didn't get my cuddle.

I went straight to bed, hoping to escape into a deep, numb sleep, but Ari's voice haunted me into the early hours:

You're scum.

Look at what you've done with your life.

Even the police are beneath me.

If I had my way, you'd be turning to ashes by now.

Behave yourself.

Kejal had a go at me for keeping her awake with my tossing and turning and sniffing. 'Ari sat on your bed tonight and said to me: "If I had my way, you'd be turning to ashes by now". Would *you* be able to sleep if he'd said this to you?' I snapped back.

'Oh, please, stop being so dramatic, Bakha.'

'I'm telling you, Kejal, that man is evil. I would not put anything past Ari. He is out to destroy us. Mark my words.'

'Goodnight, Bakha.'

When I finally fell asleep, I dreamed about work and Avin. In this dream, Avin approached the deli counter where I was pulling a wire through a block of cheese. She looked the same as when she'd first arrived at our house in Iran, but had on a bright, red Western-style dress with thin straps, and matching red lipstick. Her hair, with its gorgeous honey and caramel highlights, fell loose to her waist. She'd lost her hijab. 'Oh my God, Avin, I thought you were dead,' I said in my dream.

Avin's face darkened. 'Bâz-dân la, Bakha [run away, Bakha], bâz-dân la,' she whispered.

I woke up crying.

A few days after Ari's twisted theatrics in my bedroom, I answered a call on our house phone. It was my aunt, Mum's sister Sercan, calling from Iraq. 'Oh, hello Aunty, it's Bekhal,' I said, although I had met the woman only a handful of times when we lived in Iraq. Aunty Sercan's voice trilled down the line. 'Oh, Bekhal, my daughter-in-law, how are you?'

My guts turned to water. I almost cracked the receiver in my hand. 'What are you talking about. I'm not your daughter-in-law.'

Aunty Sercan laughed. She sounded just like Mum. 'Oh, you will be soon, my darling, my love. I'm so pleased you and Akam are getting married. And soon you'll be back here in Iraq. Mashalla, mashalla, my dear.'

Mashalla, my arse. Akam was Sercan's son, my cousin. He was almost twice my age. A recent picture of him, sent to our house, showed a balding man who looked much older than his years. I threw the receiver on the floor and called Mum.

Perched on the top stair, I listened to Mum and Aunty Sercan, laughing away together. They thought my stroppy response funny. I stomped to my bedroom, raging.

The call came at around 7 p.m. on a Saturday. This I remember because I was not long in from work when I'd answered the phone. An hour later, as I sat on my bed studying my Kurdish-English dictionary, trying to ignore Kejal's barrage of questions concerning my alleged impending marriage to Akam, Mum barged in, her face all flushed. 'Bekhal, your father wants to speak to you,' she said, hands on hips. 'Come downstairs now.'

'No,' I said, 'I'm not coming.'

'Oh my God,' went Kejal.

'Bekhal, on Allah's name, you must come now. I'm sick of the shame you're bringing to this family.' Mum's voice wobbled, as though she were about to cry.

'I said, *no*. I know what this is about. I'm not getting married – and you can't make me.'

'Behya, get that gahba downstairs, now.' That was Dad, throwing his voice from the hallway. And then I had no choice. If I didn't go, Dad would only come upstairs and beat me.

'Fine,' I said, 'but you're not marrying me off.'

Downstairs, in Mum and Dad's bedroom, I found myself in the familiar kneeling position at Dad's feet, Mum next to me. It all kicked off.

'Why did you say you're not marrying Akam?' said Dad from the edge of his bed.

'Because I don't want to marry my blood cousin,' I said, crying. 'Please, Baba, if I marry one day, I want to marry someone I love, somebody of my choosing.'

Dad got up then, bent over Mum, grasped her shoulders, shook her and slapped her face. 'Did you hear what that gahba just said,' he yelled. 'Do you see what you've created? It's your fault she's turned out this way.'

Mum lowered her head. This was the first time I'd known Dad to hit Mum. I wanted her to retaliate, but she remained submissive as always. Dad breathed deeply, hands on his head.

'We don't marry for love in our culture, Bekhal,' he said with a demonic snigger. 'Your mother and I didn't love each other when we first met, but we grew to love each other over time. What makes you think you have the right to *choose* a husband?' He sat on the edge of the bed again, his eyes, heavy with purpling bags, fixed on Mum.

I pushed my tongue to the roof of my mouth, took a deep breath through my nose, planted my fists in the blood-red carpet and, slowly, stood up. 'It's my life,' I said. 'Not yours.'

'Mizir Qehpik, sit down, show some respect,' screamed Mum. She reached up, grappling at my hand. 'Sit down, now, let's talk about this.' Mum was trying to regain control of the situation before Dad lost *all* respect for her.

'No,' I said, 'I'm not getting married.' I shook off Mum's hand and, for the first time in my life, turned my back on Dad. I went to walk towards the door, but he was too fast. One, two seconds, and I'm flying backwards.

He's grabbed my hair bun and shoulder and, thump, I go down. My kidneys, already sore from previous attacks, throb on impact. Crack goes my neck as he claws my hair bun and bangs my head off the floor. 'Qehpik [whore], you don't get to choose, you don't get to choose a fucking husband.'

I try to get up but he's over me like a rabid dog, and each time I move a limb, he pins it to the floor with his knee or arm, a punch or a slap. Catarrh crackles in his throat, then lands in my right eye. He shakes my head again and I get blurry flashes of Mum's face and the vinyl walls, who look as though they're sweating. I scream, 'Please God, no, please God, no.'

Mum screams too, 'Who's your fucking God? Allah's your God. Say his name, you gahba. Say his name.'

Dad pulls my hair hard towards the ceiling, stretching my scalp so it feels it might split. 'Disgusting gahba.' He lowers his face to mine and his features distort behind a grey, flickering mesh. It's like I have bugs in my eyes. 'You don't get to choose a husband, whore-child.' Another glob of phlegm splats my face.

Slam, my head hits the floor. I mean nothing to Dad, nothing.

Bâz-dân la, Bakha, bâz-dân la.

Negotiating the stairs after Dad's attack was like climbing a descending escalator in the dark – with a severe migraine. 'What happened to your hair?' said Kejal when I limped into the bedroom. I crawled into bed, too exhausted to reply. 'So, are you going to marry Akam now?'

'No way,' I said.

I couldn't sleep for churning thoughts. *If I had my way, you'd be turning to ashes by now.* A colossal fear engulfed me. Ari had meant what he'd said. I believed he *would* have me killed. *If I stay here, in this family, and continue to fight for my freedom, that could happen. I might not see sixteen.* I thought about the horrific deaths of those poor girls, Jhara and Sahin, in Iran. 'Jhara was a naughty girl who didn't listen to her father. That's what happens when people don't listen,'

Mum had told me. And our beautiful Avin, forced into a marriage that drove her to suicide. *If I don't leave this house, I will never have a life.* Bâz-dân la, Bakha, bâz-dân la. *Run away, run away, run away.*

Night stretched into day. I heard Dad yawning as he came upstairs and went into the bathroom. Voices next door told me my sisters were awake. I recited a prayer in my head, 'Please God, please look after my sisters when I'm gone. Please keep my sisters safe.' Kejal threw back her duvet, mumbled something about washing her hair. Everything felt normal – so far.

My moment of opportunity came later that morning, when Mum and Dad went to the farmers' market. Banaz, Payzee and Ashti joined them. Banaz would normally stay at home with Kejal and me, but Payzee begged her to go. She and Banaz were becoming even closer as they grew older. Before they all left for the market, Dad cornered me in the hall. 'I'll be speaking to you when I get home,' he said. 'You do not get to choose. You will not dishonour this family. You sicken me.'

I kissed Dad's hand. It sickened me.

After they'd left, I paced up and down in the hallway, thinking. As usual, Bahman wasn't home, but Kejal was here, which posed a problem. If Kejal knew about my plan to leave, she would try to stop me – or tell Mum and Dad of my intentions. Right now, Kejal was in the kitchen, cleaning the fridge, a job I knew would take at least an hour. And the kitchen was at the back of the house, so she would not see me leave if I went out the front way. If I was to run away, now was the time to do so.

I crept upstairs, dug from the wardrobe our holdall from Iran, and shoved just a few items into it – clothes, a hairbrush, work uniform, my purse and Abbey National cash card and, finally, the Motorola phone Dad gave to me. Then, I put on the long leather coat I'd recently bought – Dad liked it because it came down to my ankles – opened the bedroom window and dropped out my bag. Next, I climbed backwards out of the window, holding the ledge until my feet found the flat roof over the front door below. I performed the same manoeuvre from this platform to the ground, praying that nobody was watching. Then I picked up my holdall, pulled the leather hood tight around my face, turned left and walked along Morden Road. After fifty yards, I cut a left onto the path that runs alongside the Wandle River, and ran all the way into Ravensbury Park. The sun was shining, and the air tasted of pollen and freedom. I kept on running, laughing and crying and panting at once.

Bâz-dân la, Bakha, bâz-dân la.

Chapter Fourteen

IS THIS HOW FREEDOM FEELS?

'Oh my God, Becky, you must go to the police, now. If you don't call them, I will.' Leyla grabbed her mobile phone from the bedside cabinet. 'He could've killed you. Why would your dad beat you up – I mean, what the actual fuck? You can do him for GBH, at least.'

'No, please don't call the police,' I cried. 'It'll put me in more danger if the police get involved. Seriously, Leyla, please don't. Please, just let me stay here with you for a while. Please, please, Leyla, please let me stay.' I covered my face and sobbed through chattering teeth. It was a hot August day, but I'd not stopped shivering since I left Ravensbury Park over an hour ago. I'd run most of the way to Leyla's house which was some distance, face down, hiding in my heavy leather hood, terrified, convinced even, that Kurdish men were following me.

Leyla put down her phone and wrapped me in a tight hug on her bed. She kissed my head as I trembled in her arms, watching the digital graph on Leyla's hi-fi oscillate in green to the sound of US rapper Missy Elliott. I recognised the album – *Da Real World* – as I had it in my locker at work, along with the portable CD player I'd bought but could never take home. Another wave of sadness engulfed me. How was it possible for a human to shed so many tears? My head banged from last night's beating and my constant crying. I pulled the last tissue from the box next to me and blew my nose. 'I'm sorry. I'm so, so sorry. I'm frightened, Leyla.' My hands blurred in my lap, needly fingers worrying at the soaking tissue. I didn't recognise my bony wrists. How had I become so thin?

I had told Leyla only one part of my story so far – the bit where Dad repeatedly shook me by the hair and smashed my head against the floor. Once I was able to speak again, I told her everything. Tears spilled down my face when I recounted some of the beatings Dad had given me over the years. 'I was six when my dad first beat me,' I said. 'He tied my hands together with rope, threw me to the floor, beat me all over, called me a whore and spat in my face – all because I'd touched my male relative's fingers.' I told Leyla about all the abuse I'd survived in Iran, and how I'd seen Jhara, a teenage girl, burned to death in a barrel of boiling tarmac. 'She was killed by her father because she did not "listen" to him. That's what my mum told me.'

'Oh my God, that's horrendous,' said Leyla, but I continued. Somehow, purging myself of all this misery and tragedy was a little cathartic. I relived the terrifying moment in my bedroom, when Ari had said to me, 'If I had my way, you'd be turning to ashes by now,' and the subsequent call from my aunty in Iraq. 'She called me her daughter-in-law,' I said. 'My parents were trying to marry me off to her son, my cousin. When I told them that I didn't want to do this, Dad beat me.'

'Jesus, Becky, that's sick,' Leyla's hair beads clacked as she jerked back her head.

'That's how it is in our culture. Women can't have love marriages or choose whom they marry, even. To do so would be classed as shameful, a dishonour to the family name. And with dishonour comes a price. Dishonour can cost you your life in my culture.'

I gave Leyla an apologetic smile and she looked at the ceiling, biting her bottom lip.

'What the hell,' she said after a few seconds. 'Does this shit really go on? Even here, in London?' This would later become a recurring reaction whenever I tried to explain the dynamics of the Iraqi-Kurdish culture to some people: shock, disgust but also abject disbelief.

'I know, it sounds like I'm making all this up, but I swear to God…' I jumped as my mobile phone rang.

'Don't answer it,' said Leyla.

My stomach tightened as the phone rang out. *That'll be Kejal, calling because she's noticed I'm missing. Or maybe Mum and Dad are back from the market?* I looked at Leyla. 'I'm frightened,' I said and burst into tears again.

The calls continued all afternoon and into the evening. First, Dad called from the house phone, then Kejal's number appeared on my mobile screen, and when I didn't answer those calls, Dad rang on a withheld number. He left messages. 'OK, this is enough, Bekhal. You come home, now. You cannot do this to our family. Let's sort this out,' he said in his first voicemail. In his next message, I heard him say, 'It's gone silent. It's not ringing.' He said, 'Call us back. How can you do this to us – you're shaming us all,' in his final voicemail of the day. I ignored every call and message.

I stayed at Leyla's house for two nights. Her parents, Marsha and Darren, were chilled people, and they made me feel so welcome in their home. On that Sunday, Marsha made the most incredible roast beef dinner, with macaroni cheese, Yorkshire puddings, roasted vegetables and gravy. Oh my God, that meal was amazing.

However, neither Leyla nor I revealed to her parents my reasons for being there. If they knew, they might call the police or my parents, and I did not want to endanger Marsha and Darren. I also feared they might stop Leyla and me from seeing one another if they found out about my messed-up home life. So, Leyla asked her mum if I could stay for a couple of nights, and Marsha said, 'Yeah, sure, if that's OK with Becky's parents?' Of course, it's OK, I assured Marsha. My parents had never met Marsha and Darren, and they had no idea where they lived. And neither Mahmod nor Behya would report their daughter missing to the police. This much I knew.

Leyla, her family, and weed got me through those first two nights. At bedtime, Leyla and I would sneak out onto the roof of their extension, just below her bedroom window, and smoke joints. Getting stoned calmed me. Without it, I don't think I would have slept. When the effects of marijuana wore off, fear ravaged me to the core. *Seriously, is this how freedom feels?*

But if I were to remain on the run from home, I needed to seek help. I was due to go to work on Thursday. The new school term started at the end of the following week. I'd be going into year eleven, which would end with my GCSE exams. So, on the Tuesday morning, I called the Southall Black Sisters (SBS). The organisation, whose number I found listed in the phone book, appealed to me as it supports women from ethnic minorities who've experienced gender-based violence. I spoke to a lovely woman with a calming voice. She said they could help me but, because I wanted to remain close to my school and workplace, it would be best to seek refuge in my local area. So, the kind woman gave me a number for a confidential service run by my local council.

My memory is a little fuzzy regarding the meeting I attended at the council that afternoon. I could not think straight for fear and all the weed I'd smoked with Leyla. But as a result of that meeting, in which I talked about the abuse I'd suffered at home, the council gave me a room in a nearby women's refuge. As far as I'm aware, social services officials did not visit my parents to investigate my claims.

By Tuesday evening, I was alone in a bedroom of an ex-council flat. My room overlooked a communal green area where signs warned of 'No Ball Games'. I sat on the pine bed and switched on my phone. As expected, there were multiple missed calls, mostly from withheld numbers. Dad had left more angry voicemails, reminding me of the 'shame' I'd caused the family. That night, I slept with the light on.

The next week was unbearable. Although I'd escaped 225 Morden Road, I could not avoid Dad. He turned up at my work, waiting for me outside the supermarket. 'You're coming home with me, gahba,' he'd say in Kurdish with his creepy smile. 'Don't you realise what you've done, you fucking whore? Everybody in this family is talking about you.' And so on. I'd walk away from him, but Dad would follow me, shouting obscenities in Kurdish. Eventually, I broke down and told my manageress, Kim, about my situation. She was horrified but extremely supportive. She banned Dad from entering the store, but this did not stop him trawling the car park in his red cavalier. When my shift ended, I would hide in a colleague's car, curled in the back seat beneath a blanket as they drove me out through the lorry entrance at the back of the store. Then my colleague would drive around for a while before dropping me in a random location, where I'd catch a bus back to the refuge. I changed my route each time, knowing by now that Ari and Dad would have an army of Kurdish men on my case. If one of those men succeeded in delivering me back home to Dad, that man would be hailed as a hero by certain members of our family and the Kurdish community at large. I'd seen and heard Kurdish lads loitering outside the Greggs shop close to the refuge. I only had to hear an Iraqi accent in a store, and I'd drop my shopping and run for my life.

If I had my way, you'd be turning to ashes by now.

Returning to school was a nightmare too – because, of course, Dad would be there at the gates, performing the same show he'd put on outside my work. 'Look at the state of you,' he'd sneer. 'Where do you live now, in a whorehouse? You look like a fucking prostitute.' I'd stopped wearing my hijab and wore a little make-up to school nowadays. Again, he'd follow me, so I'd go direct to work after school. At least he couldn't follow me into the store's locker room – and I could leave via the back entrance. Hiding and running and panicking and crying. That was how I spent my days. This was my new life, my so-called freedom.

The teachers at my school knew I'd moved to a refuge but, honestly, they did not seem concerned about my situation. They didn't sit me down for a chat or suggest a meeting with Mum and

Dad. I didn't give this much thought at the time but, looking back, I think the school failed me.

I missed my siblings so much. I even missed my mum. When I first bumped into Kejal, Banaz and Payzee in the school canteen, my heart slowed to a hard, painful pulse. My chest ached. I wanted to hug them all but was wary of creating a scene in front of the other pupils. Banaz's eyes watered, and her lips began to quiver. 'Oh, Bakha, please come home,' she said. 'We all miss you. Mum misses you. She cries so much.'

I held back my tears. 'I'm sorry, Nazca. I miss you too, but I had to get away. I don't want to marry my cousin. We don't have to live by our cultural rules in this country. I'm sick of being beaten for doing no wrong. Ari said I would be turning to ashes by now if he had his way.' Banaz and Payzee looked at each other with a sadness that split my thudding heart in two.

'Are you OK, Bakha?' said Payzee, who had just joined Bishopsford school.

I gave her a small smile and nodded. 'I'm fine. I'm sorry for leaving you.' Then I looked at Kejal. 'Is that true? Does Mum miss me?'

'Well, Dad has banned us from saying your name in the house,' said Kejal, 'but when he's not around, Mum cries every time your name is mentioned.'

'Really?' That was the only word I could manage. I did not want to cry in the school canteen. *Mum cries for me. Does this mean she loves me?*

Kejal raised one shoulder. 'Yeah. You should come home, Bakha. It's really selfish of you to run away. You're making Mum ill – and causing grief for us girls. We can't do anything now. Nothing. Dad is raging.'

'I'm sorry,' I said again. 'I must go.'

Over the next week, my sisters approached me several times at school and begged me to go home. They brought me gifts: Iraqi chewing gum, made from the sap harvested from pistachio trees in the mountains of Kurdistan (God, I adore that stuff), and home-made churros. One day, Banaz cornered me as I left the canteen. 'Bakha, I have something for you,' she said, unzipping her oversized rucksack. Oh, her voice, so gentle and sincere. It broke me, every time. The smell of Mum and home and my childhood hit me as soon as Banaz opened her bag: warm, spicy, sweet and woody. It was the aroma of cloves. 'Here, these are from home,' she said, passing me a polythene bag. Inside the bag was a sêva mêxekrêj, a clove-nailed apple, and a qenefil, a traditional Kurdish necklace. The apple, said to be a symbol of love and peace, is entirely studded with the dried flower buds, then used as an air freshener. It smells divine – and can last for a century after the apple dries. I lifted the necklace – made by threading soaked cloves and beads together – out of the bag and held it to my nose.

'It's beautiful. Thank you, Nazca,' I said and gave her a hug. I knew how much Banaz loved her clove necklaces.

'Please come home. Mum keeps crying for you. She's very upset. We all miss you, Bakha.'

'I can't,' I said, 'but I do miss you, too, Nazca.'

I hated myself for going against Banaz's wish. I felt scared and vulnerable and craved a cuddle from my mum. But I could not go back to that house, back to the abuse, then back to Iraq to marry my cousin. No way.

I placed my clove apple on the chest of drawers in my room at the refuge and wore my qenefil to bed. The smell was comforting – the nearest equivalent to a cuddle from Mum.

Initially, I didn't speak to many other girls at the refuge, but I wondered what troubles had brought them there. The place was pleasant enough inside, with a communal kitchen furnished with a table and chairs. Not long into my stay, I met a lovely girl called Chelsea: a mixed-race girl with beautiful spiral-curled hair. She was at least five-foot-ten and almost seventeen. We got chatting in the kitchen one Sunday morning, and I warmed to her immediately. Like me, Chelsea had run away from home, although her circumstances sounded less complicated than mine. 'Oh, I had to get away from that house, man,' she said, pulling out a chair and straddling it backwards. As she spoke, she pulled a tobacco pouch from the pocket of her leather jacket and began rolling a cigarette. 'I'm not shitting you – my parents are mental. They drive me crazy, man.'

'Tell me about it,' I said. 'I know that feeling. Do you mind me asking what happened?'

Chelsea licked the Rizla. 'Uh-uh, not at all.' Then she launched into an angry tirade about her parents. 'Argh, they're constantly arguing,' she said, waving her unlit fag. 'But these are full-on shouting and swearing matches that go on for ever, you know? My mum threw a vase at my dad the other night – I think he's been playing away from home, if you know what I mean.'

I made an agreeable noise. 'Sounds awful,' I said, and I know this is a terrible thing to say, but I found myself thinking, *I wish I had Chelsea's problems instead of mine.*

'Anyway, I'm sick of the arguments, so I left. What about you, can I ask why you're here?'

'Oh, cultural stuff, mainly,' I said, 'but I'd rather not talk about it just now.' Oh my God, that was such a lie. I wanted to tell Chelsea my problems, but I was frightened she wouldn't want to be my friend if I did. My situation was so extreme and scary compared to hers.

'Fair enough,' said Chelsea, rising. God, she was tall. 'Listen, sorry, I need to shoot. I'm supposed to be in the West End in, like, an hour.'

My ears pricked. 'I'll come,' I said.

Chelsea laughed. 'Yeah, all right then.'

I latched on to Chelsea like a kid with a new toy. Having a friend in the refuge eased my terror a little. I felt less vulnerable. Chelsea and I sat in each other's rooms chatting, went food shopping together, smoked weed, and cooked meals for one another – when we remembered to eat, that is. Whenever Chelsea said she was going out, I'd be like, 'Please, can I come with you?' and she never said no, bless her. We'd take the Tube into town and mingle with tourists in Leicester Square or walk along the South Bank or Oxford Street – places I would never dare to explore alone. Chelsea became my security blanket.

Then, a few weeks later, on a Friday morning, Chelsea knocked on my door. 'Becky, it's me, I need to talk to you.' I opened the door to find Chelsea – with two canvas holdalls by her feet. One bag was daffodil yellow, the other bright orange. *Ah, Nazca's favourite colours*, I thought.

'Hey, come in,' I said, even though I was already running late for school. But Chelsea remained in the corridor. She pulled an apologetic face as she leaned her shoulder against the door frame and crossed her feet. Chelsea had on her chunky platform trainers that made her look even taller. I stuck the rubber wedge under the door with my foot.

'I'm so sorry, Becky,' said Chelsea and my throat tightened. I knew what was coming next. 'I've made-up with Mum and Dad. I'm going home. Mum's picking me up – she'll be here any second.'

I gave a few nods, then looked up at Chelsea. 'I'm glad you worked things out with your parents,' I said, diverting my gaze to the coarse blue carpet. I didn't want Chelsea to see my tears at a time when I was supposed to be happy for her.

'Aw, Becks, come here.' Chelsea stepped into my room, and I fell into her outstretched arms. 'I promise I'll keep in touch. I've got your number – we can still hang out and stuff.'

'Oh, I would love that,' I said, feeling brighter. 'Let's definitely keep in touch.'

We hugged a few more times, then Chelsea picked up her bags and left.

'Say hi to your parents from me, Chelsea,' I called along the corridor. 'I'll phone you tonight.' How I wished Chelsea could take me home with her. I never spoke to or saw Chelsea again, but wherever she is now, I hope she is happy and safe and well.

The Saturday after Chelsea left, I was supposed to be working but had taken a day's holiday – to avoid seeing Dad. Although banned from the supermarket, he would still try to get in – or wait outside in his car.

Knowing I would feel lonely without Chelsea, I had arranged to visit Leyla. Her mum and dad were out all day, which meant we could sit on the extension and smoke weed. 'I've got some good gear,' Leyla had told me over the phone the previous night. I couldn't wait to get out and see my friend, although I would need to consider which route to take. A few days ago, I'd spotted two Kurdish-looking men in a black Volvo, both of them staring out of the window at me as they slowly drove past. That had happened as I walked to work after school. I'd become a nervous wreck, chain-smoking and barely eating, but I was determined not to let Dad's stalking ruin my day. I got out of bed, grabbed my towel, razor and bodywash, and headed to the bathroom for a shower. *Live your life, Becky, live your life.*

I returned to my room to find more than twenty missed calls and a voicemail message on my phone. Many of the calls were from withheld numbers, presumably from Dad, but there were also a few 0208 numbers. The last number on the list was from Leyla's landline, so I assumed she had left the voicemail. Wrapped in a towel, I sat on my bed and pressed number one on my handset to play the recording. Dad's voice stabbed my ear, Kurdish, loud, lethal. 'Bekhal, Miss, you fucking whore-child, you *gahba*. Come home now or you're dead.' My entire body hollowed. I could not feel my arms or legs or the phone in my shaking hand.

Mum wailed in the background, pleading with me. *'Bakha, my darling, my love, please listen to your father. Come home now.'*

'I mean it, Bekhal. Gahba, qehpik, I have people on you, watching you. I have paid for them. They will bring you to me, alive or in a body bag.'

'Please, Bakha, please. He will do this. Your father means what he is saying. Come home.'

'They will detach your head. Come home now or you're dead. Don't make me ask again, Miss. They will bring you to me – even if it's only your head.'

Bakha, my darling, my love, please. Mum let out one final, tortured cry, cut off mid-wail as the phone smashed into its cradle.

My breath came in short, sharp bursts. I dropped the phone and clasped my chest. *I can't breathe, I can't breathe, I can't breathe.* The blue carpet seesawed, the ceiling dropped, and my head turned to helium.

My Baba will pay to have me killed. Baba will have me beheaded.
I can't breathe.

Chapter Fifteen

MY HOME, MY PRISON

I tried to stand but my legs did not belong to me. I literally could not put one foot in front of the other, and the room jolted left to right, left to right – a wonky slide show mirroring my desperation. Chest heaving, I dropped back onto the bed. *Breathe, Bakha, breathe.*

An hour passed. Or maybe two hours? I wasn't sure, I didn't care. My father, who gave me my life, the man who's supposed to love and protect me at all costs, said he would have me beheaded? I believed the Evil Punisher would kill me. He might not murder me with his hands, but he would instruct my relatives to do his dirty work for him. Beheading is a common method for honour killings, especially in Iraq, along with stoning, strangulation or burning the victim to death. Hence Ari's comment about turning me to ashes. As far as Dad and Ari and their scores of male minions were concerned, I had dishonoured our family.

My so-called crimes ranged from 'whore behaviour' – tonging my hair and wearing leggings, to running away from home and my refusal to enter into an arranged marriage with my cousin Akam. And for all this, I had become the target of an honour killing. My family wanted me dead. End of.

I listened to the message again, then played it over and over until I knew it by heart.

Come home now or you're dead. So, I had two choices: go back to 225 Morden Road and live under Dad's evil dictatorship, which would end in my marrying Akam or another cousin of my family's choosing. Or be killed. A possible third option would be to report Dad's death threat to the police, but I was too scared to do this.

I have people on you, watching you. I have paid for them. They will bring you to me, alive or in a body bag. Dad and Ari had me followed. If they discovered I'd been to the police, they'd kill me. These men could kidnap and murder me as I walked to a police station. I remembered Ari's sickening words: 'Even the police are beneath me'.

I called Leyla, told her I had an upset stomach. 'I'm so sorry but I'll need to give today a miss,' I said. 'I feel awful.'

Leyla offered to come to the refuge instead. 'You can't be alone in that place if you're unwell. I'll come over and look after you, Becky.'

'No, no, thank you, but please, don't do that,' I said, my voice nasally from crying. I hated lying to my best friend. All I wanted to do was spend the day with Leyla, but no way could I risk dragging her into this patriarchal web of terror. That would put her life at risk too. 'I wouldn't want you to catch this bug, Leyla.'

'OK, Becky, but promise to call if you need anything.' I managed a croaky 'thanks' and hung up before I burst into tears again.

I had nobody to turn to. There were no staff members at the refuge at the weekends, and now that Chelsea had gone, I had no close friends there. Too afraid to go out, I spent the entire weekend in the refuge, smoking out of my bedroom window, hiding my face in a hoodie as I did so. Every time my phone rang or bleeped, my heart jumped into my mouth, but there were no more calls from the Evil Punisher – just Leyla, checking to see if I was OK. Dad's silence in itself enforced his death threat. He was expecting me to call him and say, 'I'm coming home, Baba.' *Don't make me ask again, Miss. They will bring you to me – even if it's only your head.* I was petrified. Did the people whom Dad claimed to have paid know where I was? Who were those men in the Volvo who drove past me near my school? I thought about our previous Hyde Park family picnics, when Ari had crowed about bringing more men from our family to the UK from Iraq. Now Ari's motive for doing this made sense. Most of these men were my cousins, from our Mirawaldy tribe. Ari had built a force of men – those he could marry us girls off to, and those who would kill us for dishonouring the Mahmod name.

On Monday morning, the first day of the October half-term school holiday, I approached Jill, a support worker at the refuge. I needed to confide in somebody – if only to confirm I hadn't imagined Dad's words. I went into Jill's office, and she listened to the voicemail. 'I'm sorry, Becky, I can hear "come home" mentioned but I don't understand the rest.' Jill was right. Those were the only two English words Dad spoke in his message: 'come' and 'home'. His actual death threat was in Kurdish, of course.

'But *I* understand what he's saying,' I said. 'You can hear him say "mirdû" – that means dead.'

Jill asked her colleague Theresa to listen to the message too. 'No, I don't understand the language,' she said afterwards.

'Yes, listen, Becky,' said Jill, 'you're in a safe place here. Why don't you change your number, destroy the SIM card and get a new one?'

I nodded, thinking, *if only things were that simple.* Then I went back to my room and packed my bag. I figured the best option for all concerned was for me to go home. Returning to 225 Morden Road was a risky move, and one I did not want to make. *What if they kill me as soon as I go in the front door?* But I suspected Dad now knew my whereabouts and I had to think about other people's safety too. What if Ari's Kurdish mob were to petrol-bomb the refuge? Or break in and murder every other girl before killing me. Seriously, I know this sounds overdramatic, but I would not have put any of these actions past Ari – or my father.

On my way out, I popped into Jill's office. 'I've decided to go home and try to sort things out with my parents,' I said.

'OK, but we're here if you need support, Becky. You can always come back if you need to. Stay safe.'

I walked outside, into the glorious golden light of autumn, head down, hoodie up. Every step I took felt like one step closer to my death.

Mum answered the front door and gasped. 'No, Allah, Bakha, my darling, my love.' She clapped her hands to her face, then reached for my hand, lifted it to her lips and kissed it. A warm wall of dolma-infused air hit me. 'Thank Allah you've come home. Mashallah.' Mum dropped to her knees and went to kiss my shoes. 'Bakha, my darling, my love.'

'Please, don't do that,' I said, stepping onto the plastic carpet protector in the hall. I took off my shoes, and when I looked up, Dad was there. Not taking his eyes off mine, he licked his lips, rubbed his moustache, then offered his hand for me to kiss. He greeted me in Arabic. 'Mashallah [Allah has willed], Subhan Allah (glory be to Allah) Mohammad Rasul Allah [the messenger, prophet of God].' Basically, Dad was saying, 'Allah has brought you home to me'. I swear to God, I would have eaten my vomit over kissing that bastard's hand.

A few minutes later, I was in Dad's bedroom, sitting on my shins by his feet, my bag containing my belongings on the floor to my left, and Mum kneeling to the right of me. Dad, strangely calm, did not mention his voicemail in which he'd blackmailed me with death to come home. 'So, where have you been?' he began.

'I went to a women's refuge,' I said. I was certain he knew this already, anyway.

'Who did you tell?'

'My friends. And my school knew.'

'Why did you run away?' *Really?*

'Because I was upset.' (I had to be careful what I said. I didn't want to highlight the Akam situation.) The questions went on, but still there was no mention of the voicemail.

'And why did you come home?'

'Because of the threatening voicemail you sent to me.' There, I'd said it.

Mum started laughing then. 'Oh, Bakha, what are you talking about. Your father wouldn't do such a thing.' I couldn't believe my ears. She had been there with Dad when he recorded that message, crying her eyes out as she begged me to come home. How could she be so delusional?

'Which voicemail?' said Dad, crossing his eyebrows. 'Show me your phone. I want to hear this voicemail.' I nodded, unzipped my bag, and fell into Dad's trap. I handed my phone to him and even told him my pin number to unlock the handset. Dad clamped my phone to his ear and replayed the message, narrowing his eyes as he listened, calm as you like. I could hear his voice on the recording, followed by Mum's harrowing pleas and sobs. When the voicemail ended, Dad deleted it. Then he handed the phone back to me. 'Now, behave yourself, Bekhal,' he said. He sounded just like Ari.

Mum smiled. 'Mashallah, Subhan Allah, Mohammad Rasul Allah. My darling, my love, Allah has brought you home.'

I silently berated myself for mentioning the voicemail.

Being back in the family home was strange. Everybody tiptoed on eggshells around me at first. If I went to do the dishes, for example, Kejal would stop me. 'No, no,' she'd say, her tone sarcastic. 'You sit down and rest. *I'll* do the dishes.' Mum cooked even more than usual, making pots and pots of my favourite dolma (with chunks of chicken breast and loads of pomegranate molasses and sumac). Dad's mood since I'd returned was smug. Our landline did not stop ringing – celebratory calls from relatives in the UK and Iraq, plus other members of the Kurdish community in London and beyond, applauding my return to the Mahmod household. 'Oh yes, Bekhal's back,' Dad would announce loudly. 'I brought her home. She's a good girl.' I'd watch him smile into the receiver, proud of his achievement, but questions a teenage girl should not need to ask fired in my mind. Did every one of those callers know of Dad's plot to have me killed? Would I be dead by now if I'd stayed at the women's refuge? Will Dad have me killed if I refuse to marry Akam? (If I did marry my cousin, I would also be forced to live with Akam and his parents in Iraq.) Will I ever escape this house alive and live the life of my choosing?

Kejal disbelieved Dad would have me killed. I'd sat on our bedroom floor, visibly shaking as I told her about his voicemail. 'I'm frightened. I'm really fucking frightened, Kejal. Kurdish men have been following me. I've seen them.'

My sister bit the corner of her bottom lip and slowly turned her head from side to side, looking at me like I was a delusional kid seeking attention. 'How could you say such a thing about Dad?' she said. 'Why would you make up evil lies about him? Do you not know how much stress you caused Mum and Dad? And now you've got everybody tiptoeing around you, making a fuss of you. It's not fair.'

'I swear to God, Kejal, Dad threatened to have me beheaded if I didn't come home. That's the only reason I came back. I'm frightened, Kejal, I'm…'

'Ha, if you believed in Allah, you would never have run away in the first place. Dad would never do such a thing.' Kejal got into bed and pulled a pillow over her head. I did not respond. There was no point. Kejal did not believe me. *If only I still had that voicemail as evidence.*

I did not tell my younger sisters about Dad's threat. How could I? It was the stuff of nightmares – and Ashti was only seven. But I did worry about Payzee and Banaz. Both girls did as they were told at home but, like me, I knew they dreamed of freer lives away from the locks and chains and misogyny of our culture. Banaz would be fourteen in less than two months and had resigned herself to the idea of an arranged marriage.

A few days after I returned home, while Kejal slaved in the kitchen as usual, Banaz and I got chatting in my room. It was so lovely to enjoy some alone time with her again, even though our conversation centred around marriage. We sat next to each other on the blood-red carpet, our backs against Kejal's bed. 'I wonder who I'll get as a husband?' said Banaz.

I picked at the carpet, frustration boiling in my chest. 'But if you could *choose* how to live your life, what would you do with your future? What do you want?'

Banaz rolled her head to face me, her chin dimpling as she smiled. Hope gleamed in her eyes. *Beautiful Nazca.* 'Xushawistyto [love and affection]. I want to marry a man whom I love – one who loves me back. Xushawistyto.' Banaz giggled and hugged her knees to her chest. 'Like, the kind of love that Ibrahim Tatlises sings about.' This made me giggle too. Ibrahim Tatlises is a Turkish actor and folk singer, of Kurdish descent, who's renowned for his heart-wrenching love songs. 'And I want to be a dayik [mum] and have lots of children. Oh, and I want to wear make-up all of the time.' I felt choked. Honestly, never in my life have I met anyone as kind and gentle and pure as Banaz. Not once did she mention money, a big house or a car. All Banaz wanted was to be loved, to give love, and bring new lives into this world.

'Oh, Nazca, you'll be a brilliant mum,' I said. While I hated living under the Evil Punisher's roof, I loved being close to my younger sisters again.

Around this time, I began to bond more with my brother. I admired Bahman and longed for the freedom he enjoyed. Sometimes, I wished I'd been born a boy – so I could make my own choices. I ran around after Bahman. I ironed his shirts, polished his shoes, and, in return, he would invite me into his bedroom for little chit-chats. Bahman's mysterious life fascinated me. He was always out and about, and his room reeked of JOOP aftershave. Now twenty, Bahman had grown a dark goatee beard, wore his hair in a fade cut, and was known to his friends as Tony Montana, after the Al Pacino character in the gangster film *Scarface*. Bahman, the only man I could trust in our house, would talk about his wild nights out in nightclubs and escapades with his friends. He gave me advice too. 'Keep your head down and try not to piss Dad off,' he said. 'And don't let him see you smoking. You need to watch your step, Bakha.'

Behind the closed door of Bahman's citrus-scented room, I confided in him about Dad's plan to marry me off and my reasons for running away. My brother already knew about the beatings Dad had given me over the years, but when I tried to tell Bahman about the death threat voicemail, he didn't believe me either. 'Come on, Bakha,' he said, passing me a fresh pile of shirts to iron. 'I know Dad's been an arsehole to you – and to me – but he wouldn't pay people to kill you. That's crazy, hardcore shit, man.'

'But this shit *does* go on in our culture, Bahman,' I said. 'I know what I heard – and Dad said he would have me killed for bringing shame on the family. I've been followed from school by Kurdish men.'

Bahman stroked his JOOP-soaked goatee. 'Stop fretting, Bakha, you're safe here.' Then he grabbed his jacket off the back of his swivel chair, thanked me for ironing his shirts, and headed to a better place in the outside world.

Why won't they believe me?

Within a few weeks, Mum and Dad were again talking about marrying me off to Akam. They tried to be covert about this, but I'd heard Mum on the phone to my aunty Sercan. 'Oh, Bekhal loves to clean. Nobody does the dishes like Bekhal does. She's very thorough.' Life at home returned to how it was before I ran away. Dad stalked me at work and school, trailing me in his red cavalier like a sleazy kerb-crawler. Once, he saw me walking with a male colleague, Simon, and almost ran the poor lad over as we crossed the street. I had bumped into Simon on my way to work on the road leading up to the supermarket, but Dad concluded my talking to this white English man meant I was romantically involved with him.

The beatings resumed, in the same style as before. Dad, smacking me around the head, pulling my hair, spitting in my face, pinching my legs. He used the same vile language: gahba, qehpik, accompanied by his favourite phrases: 'You look like you belong in a whorehouse,' and 'You look like you've just come out of your mother,' a nod towards my gelled, tonged hair. After the incident in the street with Simon, Dad interrogated me in his bedroom before battering and pinching me all over. However, most of the attacks followed conversations about arranged marriage. 'But I'm not ready to get married yet,' I argued.

Dad's death threat haunted and terrified me, but as the weeks went on, my defiant, rebellious streak returned, which counteracted my fear to a certain degree. I was sick of all this marriage talk. Plans to find a blood-relative husband for Kejal appeared to be on hold, yet my parents were determined to bundle me on the next flight to Iraq. Anything to get rid of the Troublemaker and earn those family 'honour' points.

No. Fucking. Way.

Convinced I was plotting to run away again, Dad started locking me in the house like a prisoner. I'd never known our family to have such a hectic social life. Dad took Mum and my siblings out at least four times a week – to the market, to Grandma Zareen's house, Kurdish community functions, and family get-togethers. Before they left, Dad would lock all the main windows – then lock the doors from the outside. Occasionally, he'd make Kejal stay in the house to watch me in case I tried to escape. I would climb onto the kitchen sink, then literally slither through the tiny top window that Dad had forgotten to lock. 'I'm telling Dad,' Kejal would yell, thumping the glass, while I leaned against the alley wall, laughing and smoking fags.

I hated my life, hated being a prisoner at home. Looking back, I was deeply depressed. As if I hadn't been harmed enough by my parents, I started cutting my legs with heavy-duty sewing needles. I would rip the sharp point along my thighs and shins, cutting deep enough to draw blood. It sounds crazy, but those red criss-cross scars filled me with a sense of achievement and control. Sometimes I'd draw bloody alphabet letters. This was my pain, inflicted by me, in private, on a part of my body that wasn't on show. My pain became my comfort and escapism from the emotional trauma that plagued my world.

One Saturday morning in early 2000, as the rest of my family were getting ready to go to the farmers' market, I came out of the toilet to find Dad waiting for me on the landing. 'Go into Bahman's room,' he said. 'I need to talk to you, Bekhal.' He gestured at Bahman's open door for me to go in first. Bahman was out as usual, so I wondered why Dad wanted this 'talk' in my brother's empty room. I walked towards the JOOP aroma regardless, hoping whatever Dad was about to say or do to me would be over quickly.

It was over in a flash.

As I stepped into Bahman's box room, the door slammed behind me. I wheeled round as the key rotated in the lock, *clunk-tickle-click.* Dad had locked me in the bedroom. I heard his stockinged feet thumping down the stairs. Dense, deliberate, measured steps. He closed the front door, but I did not hear the key turn in the lock. I stumbled to the window, sending Bahman's swivel chair in motion as I brushed past it, pulled back the net curtain, and watched my family – Mum, Dad, Kejal, Payzee and Ashti, as they piled into the red cavalier. Before getting into the car, Dad looked up at Bahman's window. I let go of the net veil before he could see my face, then I dropped to the floor and cried my heart out.

Time slipped by slowly and my tears subsided to fury. I pulled a pack of needles from my trousers pocket, lifted the fabric legs to my knees, and began drawing rapid lines on my shins. Blood dribbled wonkily over my skin until my shins resembled a Jackson Pollock painting. Miss Evans had showed us pictures of the American painter's splattered canvases in class last week. She said Pollock's work was termed 'abstract expressionism' and described him as a 'troubled man who struggled with inner demons'. I knew exactly how he felt.

As I scratched away, a thought interrupted me. *Dad left the key in Bahman's door. I can get out of here.* I shot to my feet, tore a sheet of paper from an A4 pad on Bahman's desk, and fed the sheet lengthways under the door beneath the lock, leaving an inch of the paper inside Bahman's room. Then, I gently poked the eye of my bloody needle in the lock and released the key. My heart ping-ponged in my ribcage as the key slapped the paper on the landing floor. In slow motion, I tugged the paper towards me. Fortunately, there was a small gap between the carpet and the bottom of the door – just enough space to accommodate the key. Oh my God, I lifted that piece of metal to my lips and kissed it. 'I'm out of here,' I shouted, and unlocked the door. I ran into my bedroom and packed my holdall. *I'm leaving for good this time*, I thought. Despite my previous fears about contacting the police, I found myself jabbing the nine button three times on my mobile. With a trembling voice, I poured my heart out to the female operator. The words jettisoned from my mouth. 'My Dad locked me in a bedroom. I need to get away from here. My Dad beats me. He calls me a bitch and a whore, and he pulls my hair. He's a strict Muslim, from Iraqi Kurdistan. I think my life is in danger. Please help me, please help me.'

I stood in Bahman's room, watching from the window. The police car arrived within ten minutes of my call. I nearly fell headfirst down the stairs in my rush to flee the house. Hoisting my holdall onto my shoulder, I opened the front door and bolted like a hare out of a trap to the yellow-and-blue car. At the same time, Dad pulled up in his red cavalier, brakes screeching as he stopped at an angle, obstructing the police car. I yanked the handle, opened the back door of the police car and tumbled into the back seat. 'Lock the doors, don't let him take me,' I cried, then, bang, bang, bang, Dad's fist on the driver's window. He was shouting but his words did not register through the glass. 'Please,' I said, 'put the music on. I don't want to hear him.' Dad was now trying to open the driver's door as I shrunk into the seat, pulled down my leather hood, and buried my face in my hands. 'Please, drive away, drive away.'

The driver floored the accelerator, hurling me backwards. Then he swerved around Dad's car and drove on, fast.

I kept my head down. When we arrived at Wimbledon Police Station, I was too scared to get out of the car.

Chapter Sixteen

LOOK AT US, BEAUTIFUL CHILDREN

Days later, I met the couple who would become my foster parents.

The smell of frying fish hit me as Valda and Peter, my assigned carers, welcomed me into their home, a four-bedroom house in a location that I shall not disclose for safety reasons. A social worker, Susan, accompanied me to Valda and Peter's, and stayed for a while to ensure I settled in OK.

A calm, homely atmosphere enveloped me as soon as I stepped into the house. Framed photographs vied for space on the walls, window ledges and all other available surfaces. The pictures looked to be family snaps. I recognised Valda and Peter in many, smiling and laughing as they posed with kids of varying ages. My parents had never displayed family pictures at home. They wouldn't even look at our annual class photos, let alone buy one. 'Why would I want a picture of whore children in this house?' Dad had snapped when I brought my Year Nine group shot home.

Valda and Peter, both in their early fifties, exuded warmth and kindness. Peter looked so chilled in his Pink Floyd sweatshirt and jeans, and when he smiled, you could literally hear his eyes go pop. I couldn't imagine Peter ever losing his temper.

Valda wore a gold crucifix necklace that she played with as she spoke. Her outfit comprised a thigh-length mauve jumper worn over black leggings, and a blue pair of Totes Toasties. 'Welcome to your new home, Becky,' she said in a voice as comforting as the spicy fish aroma. Her wooden bangles collided as she shook my hand. 'We hope you'll be very happy here.'

I felt chuffed that Valda used my Western nickname, and my eyes began to well at Valda's generosity. But I pulled myself together. I didn't want my new guardians thinking they'd taken on a crybaby. 'Thank you, I really appreciate this opportunity,' I said, and Valda smiled a motherly smile.

'I hope you like fried fish,' said Peter, extending his hand.

'Oh my God, I love fried fish.'

Peter's eyes widened again. 'Great, well, I'd best get back to the kitchen before I burn our dinner. Valda will show you around.'

I looked at Valda in confusion. 'Don't worry,' she said, 'Peter's a better cook than me. C'mon, I'll show you your bedroom.' I followed Valda up the peach carpeted stairs, still in shock. *A husband, doing the cooking? How wonderful is that?*

Was I really here, in this house, with these people who had effectively become my new parents? Less than a week had passed since I fled 225 Morden Road for the second time, but that ride in the police car felt like years ago. I panicked when we pulled up at Wimbledon Police Station. 'I can't get out, don't make me get out, they'll kill me,' I'd told the officers. Such was the extent of my terror. When I finally gathered the courage to get out of the car, I wore my coat like a blanket over my head. I looked more like a convict than a victim.

The officers took me to an interview room, but I initially couldn't speak for crying and shaking as I sat behind a table opposite a male officer and a WPC. Then I saw Dad through the brown glass window, shouting and trying to barge past two policemen blocking his path in the reception area. 'She's my child. Let my daughter go, now!' he hollered, interspersed with Kurdish spits of 'Mizir ker, mizir ker [fucking donkey].'

'Oh God, don't let him in, don't let him see me,' I said and doubled over in my seat, so my head was beneath the table.

'It's OK,' said the WPC, 'we can see out of the window, but your father can't see in. It's privacy glass.'

'But you don't know what he's like, what he's capable of.'

Silence. Slowly, I sat up. Dad was no longer in the window. 'Where is he, what is he doing?' I asked.

'The officers have taken your father into another room to speak with him. You're safe here, Becky. Now, are you up to giving a statement?'

I nodded. 'I think so.'

Through more tears, I told the officers about the abuse I'd suffered at home. I explained how my parents wanted to send me to Iraq to marry my first cousin, and outlined the repressive rules imposed on girls and women in my culture. I mentioned my FGM and the alleged 'honour' deaths of Jhara and Sahin in Iran. The only piece of information I withheld from the officers was Dad's threat to have me killed. Judging by the bewildered expressions on their faces when I described how Jhara was dropped into a barrel of tar 'for being naughty', I didn't think they'd believe my claim. *They'll think I'm a nutjob and send me away for wasting police time*, I thought.

To the officers' credit, they acted fast. I did not go back to Morden Road. Instead, I was placed in emergency care while the authorities obtained a care order and searched for suitable foster parents. And that's how I arrived here, in a new home with two big-hearted strangers who wanted to look after me.

My new bedroom was huge and beautifully decorated with rosebud print wallpaper and a fluffy green carpet. There was a white wood wardrobe and a shelf loaded with books – plus a hi-fi and a little television atop a chest of drawers. A massive window overlooked the back garden. I felt as though I'd stepped into a photo in *Ideal Home* magazine.

But I did not sleep well the first night. I could not stop thinking about my statement to the police and the impact my actions would have on Dad, Ari and the Kurdish community. Had I done the right thing? Would there now be a price on my head (again)?

Would I ever be safe, anywhere? I also felt overwhelmed by my new surroundings – this huge house, Peter and Valda, a television in my bedroom. *A television in my bedroom?*

The following morning, I broke down in front of Valda. We were sitting on the sofa in the lounge, discussing the new route I would be taking to school when I exploded into tears. (I had missed a few days of school due to my situation, but social services had liaised with my teachers.) I felt terrible for causing a scene. 'I'm so sorry,' I said, then Valda shuffled along the sofa and hugged me.

'Shh, don't apologise, it's OK to cry, you've been through a lot, Becky.' I melted into Valda's soft embrace. This was a whole new experience for me. My mum didn't cuddle me often. In fact, I couldn't remember the last time Mum hugged me, but I felt safe and loved in Valda's arms.

Adjusting to my new existence was both liberating and challenging. I loved that I could wear leggings at home without being battered and pinched. Watching television in my bedroom was also a luxury – even though I would jump and turn down the volume whenever I heard footsteps along the landing (old habits die hard). Valda said I could invite friends over, and I was allowed to socialise after school and at weekends, within reason. But despite my newfound freedom, I could not escape Dad or the hawk-eyed force of the Kurdish community. I remember attending a few meetings with social workers and my parents. Dad smiled and charmed and lied through his teeth in those meetings. 'Bekhal was happy at home,' he'd say. 'We never stopped her from doing things – she was free to come and go as she pleased – and will be free to do so once she returns.'

Sorry, but that's utter bullshit.

Then he'd pull a few old family pictures out of his pocket and slide them across the table to me. He'd show the social workers those photos too. Worryingly, one of the social workers, a Muslim woman called Tisha, appeared to be getting along too well with my parents. Tisha would see me once a week at my foster home, but she visited Mum and Dad too. I noted the little smiles Tisha gave Dad when he spoke. *I bet Mum feeds Tisha dolma when she visits.*

In May 2000, I went on study leave ahead of my GCSE exams, and while I loved living with my foster parents, I struggled with my schoolwork. Writing in English still felt foreign to me and there were so many words I did not yet understand. Art was the only subject I was good at, but I'd fallen behind with my coursework due to the upheaval and stress of leaving home. I missed Bahman and my sisters. For God's sake, I even missed Mum – and her amazing cooking. Although I had Valda, I daydreamed about sharing a loving relationship with my biological mum. Every daughter needs her mum, right?

I started calling home from phone boxes, choking on urine fumes as I connected to 225 Morden Road, remembering to punch 141 to withhold my number. Most times, Mum answered, but I never spoke. Crazy as this may sound, I just wanted to hear her voice. 'Bakha, is that you?' she'd say. 'Bakha, if that's you, please speak to me.' Then I'd hang up and run out of the phone box crying.

Once, Banaz answered the phone. 'Hello?' she said in her timid voice. 'Oh, Bakha, is that you?' It took all my strength not to reply as I was dying to speak to Banaz. She was the sibling I missed the most. 'Please, Bakha, if that's you, please speak to me. There's nobody near me – if you want to talk, now is a good time. I miss you so much. Please come home, Bakha.' Oh, I wanted to hug my Nazca, protect her, yet I could not be there to do either. I worried about the struggles she and Payzee might be going through at home now that I'd left. Every other day I'd call the house – then Dad must have got wise to my trick because, one day when I called, an automated message told me the landline no longer accepted calls from withheld numbers. Soon after, I received some moody calls on my mobile – also from withheld numbers.

My fear of being tracked down and followed by Kurds had never left me. While I remained in foster care, I was further discrediting the family's honour. Behind his smiles in those social services meetings, Dad would be scheming to get me home – or worse. Who knew how many family 'council of war' meetings had taken place, with Ari at the helm, planning my murder to the last detail.

This time the calls were from my cousins and other Kurds whose voices I didn't recognise. Dana's voice I knew as I'd seen him at a few family gatherings after Ari got him into the UK on a dodgy visa, or whatever. Dana hadn't changed much. He had merely grown into a bigger, slimier, red-faced monster than he had been as a kid. He called me a couple of times. 'Where are you? Are you happy with yourself? You're bringing shame upon this family, you whore.'

Eylo called too. 'Why are you bringing fucking shame on the fucking family?' I swear I felt his angry spit spurt through the phone. Some days, I'd receive several of these calls, then nothing for a week or so. Angrier rather than scared at this stage, I would hang up on the callers. I considered binning my SIM card but couldn't bring myself to do so. My sisters knew only my existing number – and I wanted them to be able to contact me. Also, our family friend, Amber, called me from time to time and no way did I want to lose touch with her. Amber was my go-to person for family affairs. If I wanted to get a message to my sisters, I would go through her. For this reason, I cannot identify Amber (not her real name) or reveal further details about her. I still fear for my life today, and if the Kurdish community discovered Amber leaked family information to me, her life would be in danger too.

I did not tell Valda and Peter about the phone calls as I did not want to scare them. But Valda was with me in the house one Friday afternoon when Tisha came round with a message from my parents.

Tisha breezed into the lounge, all smiles as she made small talk about the rainy weather. 'I can't believe this is May. I got absolutely drenched just walking to the car this morning,' she said. I sat on the sofa with Valda while Tish settled into the armchair opposite us. 'Anyway, Becky,' Tish went on, rifling in the shoulder bag by her feet. 'I've just come from your parents' house, and they asked me to give you this.' Tish produced from her bag a Jiffy bag, which she planted on the coffee table that separated us.

'What is it? Why would they send something to me? They're not even supposed to be in contact with me.' Curious all the same, I leaned forwards and picked up the envelope.

'It's just a couple of photographs and a cassette tape – they just wanted you to know how much they miss you, Becky.'

I shook the contents of the Jiffy bag into my lap. There were two family photos – one of me with my siblings in Iran, and a black-and-white shot of Mum and Dad looking all lovey-dovey in the mountains of Kurdistan. A blank TDK cassette tape also fell out of the bag.

Valda eyed the tape and shifted to the edge of the sofa. 'Excuse me one second, Tisha, but what is this? What's on this tape, what does it say?' I'd never seen my foster mum angry until now. Her already wild blonde-grey curls jumped in all directions from the bulldog clip that tried to tame them.

Tisha shrugged. 'I don't know what it says, but it's personal and private – from Becky's parents to her.'

'*Personal* and *private*? This is ridiculous. You've placed Bekhal in my care for a reason – because of her troubled home life. And now you want to give her this tape – and we don't even know what's on it? This is not allowed, Tisha.'

'Some things have to remain private, Valda. This is between Becky and her parents.'

I put the pictures and tape back in the Jiffy bag, which I then wedged between my outer thigh and the arm of the sofa. 'It's OK,' I said, 'I'll keep the tape for now, but I might not listen to it just yet.' That was a lie – how could I not listen to that tape? I wasn't expecting a recording of 'Take me Home, Country Roads' by John Denver. Far from it, but, after those dark calls from my cousins, I needed to know what was on this tape – if only to ensure Valda and Peter were not in danger.

The room darkened as a sudden storm hammered the house. Tisha looked up at the window, a misty grey rectangle, rattling with rain. 'Right, I'd better get going,' she said.

Valda advised me not to listen to the tape. 'It's your choice, Becky, but I don't think you should listen to it. You don't know what's on that tape. You've come so far – I'd hate for this to set you back.'

I pulled an apologetic face. 'I'll try not to listen to it.' Then I told Valda I had to study and went up to my bedroom. I flopped onto my bed and looked at the photograph of me with my siblings. In this one, taken before Ashti was born, Bahman is in the centre in his high-waisted jeans, a formal look on his face. I'm under Bahman's right arm as he wings his other over Kejal. Banaz is next to me, aged around four and sporting a funny Beatles-style haircut. She's in a pink jumper handed down from Kejal via me. Kejal is the only one of us girls in a hijab, while Payzee, with her short hair and quizzical expression, looks like a cute little pixie next to her eldest sister. Not one of us is smiling. A heavy, dragging sadness filled my chest and stomach. 'Look at us,' I whispered. 'Look at us, beautiful children. Who would want to hurt these innocent kids?' *What kind of parent would inflict pain on these little girls?* I put the picture back in the envelope, slipped the tape into the deck of the hi-fi, and pressed play.

I sat on the floor, close to the stereo, and dimmed the volume a little. Just like Dad's voicemail, this was another threatening recording, more sinister than his last. 'Bekhal, Miss, you're a whore. You've brought shame on this family,' Dad began, his voice slow and murderous. 'I've got people looking for you. And they will find you.'

He paused as Mum started wailing in the background again. 'Bakha, gyân [dear], please come home. Bakha, gyân, Bakha khoshawîst [beloved, dear love], Bakha gyân, don't do this to us, come home.'

Then Dad stepped in, louder this time: 'Bekhal, Miss. I will kill everyone in this house. I will kill all of your sisters, in order of age, from the youngest to the eldest. Then I will kill your brother, and your mother and, when they're all dead, I'll kill myself. And all of these deaths will be on *you*, Bekhal, Miss.' The recording ended. I pressed stop and curled into a ball on the floor, crying into my hands. *Who would want to hurt these innocent children?*

I cried all night and, the following morning, while my foster parents were out shopping, I called Kejal. 'Will you meet me?' I said, 'I'm coming home.' I did not doubt Dad's threat. Not for one second.

I left a note for Valda and Peter. 'I'm sorry,' I wrote, 'I've had to go home. Please don't worry. Love, Becky.'

When I arrived back at 225 Morden Road, Dad demanded I hand over the tape. Stupidly, I gave the cassette to him. That's the kind of power Dad had over me then. When I tried to tell my siblings about Dad's latest recording, they didn't believe me. I lasted two nights in that house – then I fled via my bedroom window again. *I will live the rest of my life in a permanent state of fear, anyway.*

I returned to Valda and Peter's. Valda went crazy when I told her about Dad's tape. 'How can a parent say such a thing?' she said. 'How could a parent possibly do that to their child? What kind of parents are they?' Valda paced around the breakfast bar, throwing her arms towards random objects as though they might answer her questions. The fridge, the kettle, the George Foreman Grill. Then she let out a deep sigh. 'You're safe here, Becky. Do not contact your parents. And do *not* answer if they call you.'

Once upon a time in Iran, I'd dreamed of becoming a police officer. *I'll release all the troubled girls like Avin from their horrible husbands and put an end to forced marriages for ever.* God, how I wished that dream had come true. I left Bishopsford High School with about four GCSEs. I remember being so stoned in my geography exam that I littered the paper in question marks, then walked out.

My life moved on, but I knew it would always be in danger. I spent the next year and a half living between my foster parents, Leyla's house and a hostel, before moving in with my then boyfriend, Ata, in 2002.

I met Ata when I lived at Valda and Peter's. I instantly warmed to him – he had a gentle, caring nature and his generosity knew no bounds. He was two years older than me and worked as a courier. Valda said I'd landed on my feet with Ata.

One Friday evening in March 2002, Bahman called me. This was not an unusual occurrence as we'd kept in touch since I'd last left home. But he called with good news. 'A cleaning job has come up and I could do with a hand. There could be a couple of grand in it for you. Fancy it?'

'Oh my God, I'd love that. Yes, definitely, I'm in,' I said, buzzing. Since leaving my supermarket job in 2000 (I left due to Dad stalking me), I had found it difficult to find work. I'd also dropped out of an art college course I'd started. Most jobs I applied for asked for a passport as proof of identification. My passport was at my parents' house and, despite going to their door with police backup on one occasion, they refused to hand over my document. Another time when I tried to retrieve my passport, Mum gave me the expired one on which Banaz and I had travelled to the UK. So, most of the jobs I went for tended to be cash-in-hand affairs. I had a part-time bar position and sometimes worked at Ata's sister Cheryl's hairdressers, but I struggled for money. Two grand would cover my rent for the next six months.

'Nice one,' said Bahman. 'It's tomorrow night though – is that OK?'

'Yeah, that's fine.'

Bahman told me to meet him in The Ravensbury pub car park on Croydon Road, near Mitcham, at 8 p.m. 'Oh, and do you have a suitcase?' he added. 'We'll need something to transport all the rubbish in afterwards.'

'Yeah, I've got one, I'll bring it,' I said.

'Cool, see you tomorrow, Bakha.'

I could not contain my excitement. Two grand – for a cleaning job? I love cleaning, too. I even vacuumed inside the suitcase and packed some cleaning products ahead of the job.

Ata drove me to the pub in his Ford Fiesta. Knowing about my culture and past, he was nervous about meeting Bahman. I went to hug Ata goodbye, but he recoiled. 'Are you stupid, Becky? Your brother will kill you. I should go before he arrives. Quick, get the suitcase from the boot and make sure your phone is charged.'

Just then, a man, head-to-toe in black, rocketed from the bushes next to the car and slammed his hand on the bonnet: Bahman's face gleamed beneath the car park lights. Ata's hand shot to his chest. 'Fuck, it's Tony Montana.'

I looked at Ata. 'You two know each other?'

This was weird. Ata and Bahman chatted outside the car for a bit while I stayed in the passenger seat. I thought Bahman would be furious at seeing me with a man, but he and Ata appeared to be getting along just fine. But what was with Bahman's outfit? He had on a black baseball cap, pulled low over his forehead, a black hoodie and jeans, and black leather biker gloves. He carried a bulging plastic Nike drawstring bag that weighed down his shoulder.

After ten minutes or so, Ata retrieved my suitcase from the boot and got back in the car. 'Call me if you need me,' he said.

I got out of the car and extended the handle of the wheely case. 'Which way are we going?' I asked Bahman.

My brother waited for Ata to drive away, then turned to me and said: 'Right, I need you to take the suitcase and walk in front of me, until we reach the house.' Bahman outlined the route, which would end at, 'A big cottage with black gates. Just walk and, under no circumstances must you look behind you – unless I tell you to.'

'Got you,' I said and started walking with my case.

When I reached the property, I called out to Bahman, 'Which way now?'

'Take the gravel path on the right.' Instinctively, I glanced over my shoulder.

'Don't look back. I fucking told you not to fucking look back,' yelled Bahman.

Oh my god, why is he being so aggressive? Why doesn't he want me to look back?

I continued, crunching along the dark path that ran alongside the cottage. I'd walked this path before – it gave way to a wooded area and the River Wandle. 'Where are we going? Why are we—'

Fast footsteps in the gravel sounded behind me.

Half laughing, thinking Bahman's playing a joke, I turn around. I see a streak of black, a raised arm, holding a dumbbell, and I shout, 'Bahman, no,' and the block heel on my right boot snaps when I try to run. My legs buckle as the weight crashes into the side of my head.

I fade into blackness, then, flash, I'm back and Bahman's on the ground with me, his arm clamped around my neck. My brother is trying to strangle me. *I can't breathe and my eyes burn and bulge with pressure. Somehow, I manage to move my chin and sink my teeth into the crook of Bahman's arm through the fabric of his hoodie. He yelps and releases his grip, but he's on me again, dragging me towards the woods by my feet. I kick my legs furiously. Blood streams into my right eye and a rush of air stings the gaping cut in my head. 'Bahman, stop,' I scream, 'you're going to kill me. How can you do this? I'm your sister, your flesh and blood.' Finally, one of my kicks connects with Bahman's knee and he drops my feet as he stumbles.*

I shuffle backwards on my bum and feet. The world sways above me in dull navy, grey and black. Skeletal trees spearing the clouds.

Everything is imperfect. Tarnished, dead.

I look at Bahman through blood and tears. He's crying too now. 'Don't you love me?' I ask.

Bahman sniffed and looked at the sky. 'I'm sorry,' he said. 'I have to do this. After Dad, I'm the man of the family, and I have to put an end to this shame.'

I began to hyperventilate. 'I'm your sister, I'm your sister.'

'I'm sorry. Let's sit over there and chat.' Bahman gestured at a bench a few metres from us, a brown smudge in the darkness. I tried to stand but my legs gave way. 'I'm not coming near you. You just tried to kill me.'

'I'm sorry, Bakha, I do love you – and I can't do what Dad asked me to do to you. I can't, but, please, let me talk to you. I promise I won't hurt you, Bakha.'

'Dad asked you to kill me?' I sounded shocked, even though I guessed Dad had ordered this hit. After all, he'd threatened to kill me before.

Bahman stood and took a few steps backwards. 'I'm so sorry. I won't do what Dad asked me to do. Please, Bakha, sit with me for a moment. Let's talk.'

I should have screamed for help – or grabbed my mobile, which was inside the suitcase with my bleach kitchen spray, and called Ata or the police. Instead, I crawled over the gravel to Bahman, who helped me onto the bench. He sat next to me, breathing hard, the Nike bag sandwiched between us. I opened the bag, felt inside it. 'For fuck's sake, Bahman, you brought a blanket,' I said as my fingers touched the woollen cloth. My head spun with pain and shock. 'If you'd hit me unconscious, you were literally going to strangle me to death, wrap me in this blanket and throw me in the river. How could you? How could you do that to your eighteen-year-old sister? How could you, how could you?' My voice dissolved into tears. I could not comprehend what was happening.

'I'm sorry, Bakha. Dad paid me two-and-a-half grand to "finish you off". Think about what you're doing to this family. You should come home.' With that bombshell, Bahman pulled something out of his pocket. Now I could see only blurred movements. This was how my cartoons looked whenever the signal fuzzed on the black-and-white telly in Iran. Beside me, paper slipped and shuffled. Bahman was counting money. I had no words. 'Here, take this,' said Bahman, handing me a slim wedge of notes. 'There's about 250 quid for you.'

I took the money and scrunched it in my trembling hand. 'Please,' I said, my face sticky with blood, 'can't you just tell Dad that you've killed me?'

'Trust me, Bakha, I would love to do that,' said Bahman through raw sobs. 'But I can't lie to Dad – he'll find out eventually.' He looked at me then, his tears glistening in the orange street light spearing the trees. 'Call a taxi and go straight home. Do not call your boyfriend, do not…'

'He's not my boyfriend,' I said quickly.

'I'm not stupid, Bakha, I know Ata's your boyfriend … do not call the police. Do not tell anybody about this. And do *not* go to hospital.'

I touched my head; it felt like a sponge. Blood poured from my wound.

'My head is open,' I said, 'but don't worry, I won't tell a soul. I'll go straight home, I promise.'

'Good. Let's go then.' Bahman got up, packed his dumbbell away, then we walked back the way we came. I could hardly see, yet I was still dragging that bastard suitcase. On Croydon Road, I stopped.

'I'm calling a taxi now, so you'd better go,' I told Bahman. 'My head is cracked. The driver will know you've attacked me if he sees you.'

'OK,' said Bahman, hoisting the bag containing his would-be murder weapon on his shoulder. 'But not a word, Bakha. Promise me?'

'Not a word, I promise.'

I watched my brother walk on ahead, until he disappeared into the night, then I called Ata.

'Fucking come and get me now,' I sobbed. 'My fucking brother just tried to kill me.'

Chapter Seventeen

WHAT CAN YOU DO FOR ME?

Ata's voice sounded like a furious tannoy announcement in my ear. 'I'll fucking kill him. I'm going after him. Tony fucking Montana, I'll smash *his* fucking head in.'

'No, please don't do that. He'll kill you – then he'll try to kill me again. Just pick me up and get me to hospital. I'm bleeding quite badly. I'm next to the pub. Please, Ata.' I leaned against a fence at the roadside near The Ravensbury, my stomach a whirlpool with nausea. Sharp pains speared my eyes and head, and my hair, drenched with blood, felt like wet seaweed clinging to my head. Dad had paid my brother to kill me, so Bahman claimed. Two-hundred-and-fifty pounds of that blood money was in my jeans pocket. I didn't know the weight of the dumbbell, but it had felt like a boulder crashing into my head. *How am I not dead now?*

'I'm on my way,' said Ata.

I cried when the nurse at the hospital shaved a section of my head around the wound, which needed thirteen stitches. 'So, you say you just fell in the street?' she said, pulling on her protective gloves.

'Will my hair grow back?' was my response through more tears. I cried and cried and cried, and would cry for days, weeks, months and years. God, I wanted to tell the truth, but I was petrified –

and psychologically damaged beyond belief. Would Bahman try to kill me again? My brother knew about my relationship with Ata, too; if Dad and Ari and other community leaders knew about this romance, they would be plotting to kill Ata and me as we speak. In their eyes, I was committing the most dishonourable, unforgivable act – by falling in love with a man whom they did not pick for me. A man who was not from the Mirawaldy tribe, too. It's an act that carries a death penalty in our community, for sure.

Picturing how Dad would react when Bahman told him he'd failed to kill me was too painful to contemplate. Or would Bahman lie and tell Dad that he'd wrapped me in the blanket and thrown my dead body into the river? A part of me wished that Bahman would lie – then at least I could live my life without the daily fear of being murdered.

'Yes, Bekhal, don't worry, it will grow back. Now, are you sure you don't want to report this to the police?'

I flinched as the razor scratched my scalp. 'No, it's OK.'

I looked like a criminal with my partially shaved head and rigid scar, but the emotional trauma of Bahman's attack affected me more than my physical injuries. Bahman plagued me with phone calls. Mostly, I ignored them, then, once, when I was at home with Ata, I answered Bahman's call. 'No, don't worry, I haven't told the police and I'm not going to. But if you ever come near me again, I will kill you.'

Ata then grabbed the phone out of my hand and let Bahman have it. 'Listen to me. You fucking come near her again and I'll fuck you up … Tony fucking Montana.' Ata gave a sarcastic laugh at Bahman's ridiculous nickname.

When I told Leyla about Bahman's attack and his claims that Dad paid him to kill me, she urged me to go to the police. 'What if he [Bahman] comes after you again?' she said, voicing my biggest fear. 'At least if the police know they can investigate. And it might scare your dad and brother off. The police are there to protect you, Becky.'

'But you don't know my family,' I said, crying again. 'They will kill me. Next time, they will kill me.' How could I go to the police? If I did report the attack and the case went to court, I would need to face my brother again. And who's to say I wouldn't be killed before then? However, a few months after the attack, I finally mustered the courage to walk into a police station and say, 'My dad paid my brother to kill me. My brother bludgeoned my head with a dumbbell. I think my life is in danger.'

Two policemen interviewed me but, to be honest, they did not seem interested in my account. I showed them my wound, which looked like a model railway track through prickly brown grass on my head. They did not ask to photograph this injury, and at the end of the meeting, the two officers basically told me that it was my word against Bahman's. 'If we're to pursue this matter, we'll need evidence. You should see if the area is covered by CCTV. If you find footage, by all means come back to us and we can look into it.'

I thought this was an odd thing to say. Was it not the police's job to investigate my report? Although, to be fair, I did not question their suggestion at the time. Like an idiot, I went to The Ravensbury and asked to see their CCTV footage from three months ago. 'Sorry, darling,' said the owner, 'we delete our tapes after one month. I can't help you, I'm afraid.'

I also asked at the adult learning centre, based in the cottage next to the path where Bahman attacked me. But the centre had no footage to offer either. I had no evidence. End of. Once again, the Evil Punisher had overpowered me.

My life was like a game of Russian Roulette. Seriously, most days, I'd ask myself, *Will today be the day they kill me?* I could not escape the evil clutches of the men in my family and community. Still, I'd receive threatening calls and voicemails. Sometimes, the caller did not speak at all. Once, my cousin Dana cornered me as I left the hairdressers in Mitcham. I lived nowhere near Mitcham then, but it was the only salon I could afford to go to. Dana was waiting for me outside the shop, a lanky streak in high-waisted trousers and a jacket whose arms were too short for him. He got right up in my face, walking backwards but in front of me. 'Where have you been? Your mum and dad have been looking for you. Go home and end this shame, now, qehpik.'

'My life is none of your business,' I shot back. 'You're not part of my family.' Then I pulled up my hoodie and ran. Dana: I hated the man-whore. And how did he know I would be at the hairdressers? I was being followed, of course.

More than three years after Bahman attacked me, I was still looking over my shoulder every time I left home. I had almost become acclimatised to living a nightmare.

Terrified though I was, I had to live my life, even though this meant estranging myself from my entire family, including my younger sisters, whom I loved so dearly. Not one day passed when I didn't think about my sisters. I prayed for them. 'Please, God, please don't let my sisters become victims of our brutal culture. Please keep them safe and well and let them lead happy lives,' I'd plead.

I escaped into daydreams of the past. I could be a baby again, eating Arabic sweets outside the university in Sulaymaniyah, as Mum and Dad, a big, fuzzy shape in the sun, chant, 'Bakha, Bakha, hello little one.' Other times I'd inhale the aroma of my clove-studded apple and imagine myself back in our mud house in Iraq, sitting on Dad's knee and playing with his moustache. Some nights, I'd giggle to myself in bed when a memory of Banaz and I making hand shadow puppets popped into my head. I pictured Banaz on the floor of my bedroom in Morden Road, her face aglow with hope as she spoke of her wish for xushawistyto (love and affection). *I want to marry a man whom I love – one who loves me back. Xushawistyto. Like, the kind of love that Ibrahim Tatlises sings about.* Her words had played in my mind before Amber called with news about Banaz and Payzee's arranged marriages in May 2005.

I'll admit, I snapped at my friend when she first told me about my sisters. I had tried calling Amber countless times over the last year or so, but she had not picked up or called back until now.

According to Amber, Banaz's wedding took place around March 2003 and Payzee married her husband, Tekan, six months later. 'Why the hell didn't you tell me this before, Amber?' I said. 'My little sisters were forced into child marriages – did you not think I would want to know about this?' I was raging. Of course, I had long hoped that Banaz or Payzee might call my mobile one day. Now I knew why they hadn't called – if their husbands found out they'd been in contact with me, Banaz and Payzee would be in serious trouble, I'm talking 'shameful, dishonourable' territory.

'I'm sorry, Becky,' Amber explained, 'but I didn't know about the marriages until a few days ago, when I saw Banaz. I don't want to say too much over the phone, but Banaz said her husband is abusive towards her. I'm worried about her, Becky. She wants to see you. I can arrange this if you like, but you must be careful.'

Tears streamed down my face. 'Oh my God, yes, please. I'm sorry. I must see her. I must see Nazca. This is all my fault, Amber.'

I went to Lewisham on that blazing May afternoon with one goal in mind: to leave with Banaz. And when Banaz told me in her own words how Binar beat her and treated her like 'his glove or his shoe … that he can wear whenever he chooses', I wanted more than anything in this world to get her away from that flat and her tragic life. Because nobody deserved xushawistyto more than our delicate, caring, soft-spoken Nazca did.

During my conversation with Banaz in her bathroom, she told me that Kejal too was in an arranged marriage, and lived in Sheffield with her husband's family, as is often customary in our culture. 'Kejal seems happy with her arrangement,' said Banaz.

'And what about Payzee's husband, what is he like?' How could I even be asking this question? Payzee had just turned thirteen when I last saw her. She was not even eighteen yet.

'He's not so bad. Like, he's completely different to my husband. Payzee's husband doesn't hit her. But there's nothing I can do about Binar. If I fight him, he beats me. Or he calls Dad and tells him I'm being disrespectful – that I'm not fulfilling the duties of a wife. Then Dad says I need to try harder and be a better wife.'

Before Banaz and I left for the shop, she gave me her mobile number. 'If I don't answer it's because Binar's around. He doesn't let me speak to friends on the phone, and I can only see my friends when he's away or at work. Like, a few times, Binar smashed my phone – because he thought I'd been speaking to friends.'

I entered Banaz's number into my phone under 'Nazca', but I was still secretly hoping I could persuade her to leave her husband. Sadly, I was unsuccessful, and watching Banaz run back to that flat and the barbaric life she'd described to me tore me apart, literally. Banaz would need to reach the flat before her husband arrived home – otherwise, he would beat her, she'd said. Believe me, I did not want to leave Banaz that day. Stepping onto the bus I felt as though I'd betrayed her. I sat on the top deck, hood covering my weeping eyes, thinking, *I should have done more. I* could *have done more to help Banaz. Why didn't I drag her onto this bus with me?* I went over and over my last conversation with Banaz at the bus shelter, remembering how her long eyelashes had glistened with tears in the sunlight.

Can I see you again, Bakha?

I hope so, let's try.

I love you, Bakha. Goodbye, my love.

My circumstances had changed over the last couple of years. Ata and I split up in 2003 but we remained friends and I continued to work occasional shifts at his sister's hairdressing salon. I had a new partner now, whom I'll name Imran, a Moroccan, and lived in a B&B at a location in South London. The council placed me in this temporary accommodation until they found me a proper home, which was proving to be a long, frustrating process.

I went to the housing department every day, desperate for a move to a flat elsewhere. You see, I did not feel safe at the B&B, where I'd seen Kurdish men loitering outside, watching me. As I said, I spent every waking hour of my life looking over my shoulder.

I could not stop thinking about Banaz – and Payzee – and how Dad had forced them to marry those men, whom I believe are second cousins to us girls. Both husbands were several years older than my sisters, but age is not an issue for men where arranged nuptials are concerned. Honestly, a father will give his daughter to a man who's about to take his last breath if she isn't married by the age of twenty. I've seen this happen.

The ceremonial bullshit associated with arranged marriages in my culture is debasing towards women. For example, on her wedding night, the bride must prove she's a virgin to her husband and in-laws. The bride and groom will have sex on a clean, white sheet while the husband's mother and father wait for the result in the next room. And God forbid if there's no blood on that sheet afterwards. It's sickening.

Over the summer, I continuously tried to contact Banaz, but her mobile was often switched off or would ring out. Her answerphone message featured the same crying baby ringtone that had sounded when Banaz's husband had called. Dear Banaz, she couldn't wait to become a mother. Then, in October, I discovered that I was pregnant with Imran's child. I was thrilled with this news; like Banaz, I longed to have many kids too. But I would need to be extra vigilant from now on. Should news of my relationship and pregnancy reach Dad, he would have me and my unborn child killed without hesitation or remorse.

Unbeknownst to me, while I was comprehending my baby news, Banaz had bravely walked into a police station and made rape and abuse claims against her now ex-husband. Apparently – and again, I would not discover this until months later – Banaz had finally divorced Binar and moved back into 225 Morden Road.

I later watched a recording of Banaz's police interview, which took place on October 5, 2005, at 2.15 p.m. In the footage, Banaz, visibly petrified, also tells how Kurdish men had been following her. 'Still now, they follow me, people from my dad's side of the family. That's why I came to the police. In the future, if anything happens to me, it's them.'

Towards the end of the interview, the female officer asks Banaz, 'Is there anything you'd like to ask me?'

And my darling sister, clutching her notebook of evidence – her diary in which she'd documented every allegation of abuse, car registration numbers, addresses and phone numbers that could assist the police – looks at the officer with her big, scared eyes, and says: 'Now that I'm giving this statement, what can you do for me?'

This would not be the only time Banaz reported her fears to the police.

So, I now knew that Banaz and I were simultaneously followed by male members of our family. If only I'd known this at the time. October slipped into November, then December, and I continued to call Banaz's phone, each time hearing the haunting cries of a non-existent baby. Amber did not return my calls either. I hoped this silence meant that Banaz was OK as I was sure that Amber would have contacted me if, heaven forbid, anything untoward had happened to my sister.

One early evening, days before Christmas, I found myself in the diner opposite the housing department, sobbing into a bowl of salad. Once again, I had sat from 8.30 a.m. until 5 p.m., in the council offices, with my deli-style ticket, suitcase and blanket, waiting to speak to an official about my housing situation. Alas, I waited and waited, but the office closed before my number came up. 'We'll be closed for the festive period, so I suggest you come back in the New Year,' a female staff member had informed me.

The Pogues' 'Fairytale of New York' gargled through the speaker on the wall above me as I hunched over my food, shielding my forehead with my hands. My tears puddled on the Formica table and plopped into the bowl, diluting the mountain of coleslaw I'd craved all day. Now, loaded with pregnancy hormones and despair, I felt too sick to eat. A radio DJ spoke over the closing bars of The Pogues' song, his voice full of festive cheer. I kneaded my eyes with the heels of my hands. *Get a grip, Becky.* Then another voice spoke over the DJ.

'Hey, Bekhal khan [Bekhal, madam], are you OK?' My heart thrashed at an alarming pace. When I looked up, I came eye to eye with a Kurdish man I'd seen before. He had a skinny, oily face, topped with a plasticky quiff. 'Hey, Bekhal khan, don't cry, don't be sad.' He sat down opposite me and leaned across the table.

I pushed back in my chair. 'Who are you?'

'I'm Elend,' he said. 'And you're Bekhal, Payzee's sister.'

'No, that's not my name. I don't know what you're talking about – I have to go,' I said, and as I turned in my chair to get my suitcase, another man walked towards the table and sat next to Elend.

'Hello, Bekhal khan,' said the second man, 'I'm Tekan, your sister Payzee's husband.' Warm saliva filled my mouth as I assimilated the two Kurds. I recognised Elend; he was one of the men I'd seen loitering outside my B&B. Tekan smiled. He looked old enough to be Payzee's dad with his Friar Tuck bald head. 'Elend is my nephew,' he went on. 'Payzee has told us all about your problems and we want to help you. Why don't you come to our flat and we can talk? We're your family too – and Payzee would love to see you. Wouldn't you love to see your sister?' God, Tekan's voice, low and gluey, creeped the shit out of me. I knew full well this was a trap. No way had Payzee sent her husband to rescue me.

'Don't cry, Bekhal khan,' repeated Elend, 'We're only trying to…'

'Bekhal is not my name.' I put on my best South London accent and tried to look calm as I stood up, grabbed my case, and made for the door. Once outside, I slid and tripped over icy pavements with my suitcase until I reached the nearby town centre, where I caught a cab to a friend's flat outside the area. I could not risk going back to the B&B tonight.

In the New Year, the council finally offered me a home in another part of London. I moved into the sixth-floor, one-bedroom flat on January 24, 2006, unaware of the heartrending significance that date would forever hold. While delighted about my new home, something didn't feel quite right about the place initially. I couldn't quite put my finger on it. Maybe it was my paranoia taking over or pregnancy symptoms at force, but every so often, the flat would turn bitterly cold, and I'd shiver all over for a few seconds. It felt kind of ghostly in there.

Three days later, around 8 a.m., a loud knock on the door woke me and my new boyfriend, Marcus. (Imran walked out on me soon after we discovered I was pregnant.) I threw on my dressing gown to the sound of more insistent thumps. I called from the hallway, 'Who is it?'

'It's the police,' came a man's voice. 'Please open the door.' A quick look through the spyhole revealed a man in a suit and two women. I released the chain lock, opened the door, and the trio strode into my flat, flashing their identification badges.

'I'm DS Andy Craig,' said the man. 'Are you Bekhal Mahmod?'

'Yes, why? What's going on, why are you here?' I said, folding my arms over my small baby bump.

One of the women, who introduced herself as 'Sarah Raymond, family liaison officer', shared concerned looks with her colleagues. 'Your sister, Banaz Mahmod has been reported missing. I'm sorry, but we'll need to search your property.'

'Missing?' Pins and needles prickled my face. I couldn't think what to say next.

'Becky, what the fuck's going on?' that was Marcus.

'Who's in there?' said Andy, nodding towards the bedroom. 'Are there any weapons in the flat? Is Banaz hiding here?'

'My boyfriend's sleeping in there,' I said. 'Why would I have weapons? Where has Banaz gone? Who reported her missing?' More questions blurted from my mouth as the officers flew around my tiny home, rifling in cupboards and drawers. They looked under my bed, searched the bathroom and even checked the small balcony off the lounge. Then, satisfied Banaz was not hiding in my flat, Andy, Sarah and the second woman, Keilly Jones, filled me in on some of the information they'd gathered regarding Banaz's disappearance.

To be fair, after all the commotion, the three officers could not have been any nicer. Sarah, in particular, had a motherly way about her that instantly put me at ease. She said nobody had seen or heard from Banaz since January 23. Banaz did not take a change of clothing or passport with her and had not withdrawn a penny from her bank account since she vanished, Sarah explained.

When I asked whether my parents had reported Banaz missing, Sarah shook her head.

'Then who did report this? Her husband? My sisters?'

'We can't go into too many details just now,' Andy interjected. 'Our investigation is still in its early stages, but we will update you on developments as they arise. Now, when was the last time you saw or spoke to Banaz, Bekhal?'

I looked at the ceiling, crying again. 'I last saw her in May, at her flat. She was washing her husband's clothes in the bath,' I began. Marcus came in and out of the room a few times, giving me looks as though to say, 'What's with all this drama?' I told the officers about the Kurdish culture, explained how I'd left home to escape horrific beatings from my father and an arranged marriage to my cousin. 'My dad would beat me and call me a whore for wearing leggings or tweezing my eyebrows.' Keilly and Sarah looked up from their notebooks in disbelief. 'The men can do whatever they like in our culture, but the moment a woman so much as voices an opinion, or "dishonours" the family name, she's punished for it.' Again, I asked questions: 'Has anybody been arrested?' 'Have you spoken to my parents or siblings?' 'Have you spoken to Banaz's husband?'

'As I said, we're making several inquiries, but I assure you, Bekhal, we will leave no stone unturned,' said Andy. I nodded into my lap, thinking, *they're keeping something from me.*

'I don't get it,' I added. 'Banaz isn't like me. I'm known as the troublemaker in our family, but Banaz is the most gentle, kindest person I know. We call her Nazca, which means delicate and beautiful in Kurdish. She would not run away. She just wouldn't. Banaz would not want people to worry. She's not that kind of person. Oh God, where is she?' I wiped my eyes with the sleeve of my dressing gown. 'Please find my sister, please find her,' I cried.

Sarah placed a hand on my shoulder. 'I promise we'll find Banaz.'

When the officers left, I checked my mobile phone and noticed three missed calls from Amber. I called her back and she picked up this time. 'What's going on, Amber? I've been trying to call you for months and you didn't return my calls. The police have been here – they say Banaz has gone missing. What do you know? Tell me what you know.' By now I had visions of Banaz lying in a ditch or by a roadside somewhere. *Maybe she's been hit by a lorry and has broken her neck or back – but if so, she'll be OK. Anything so long as she's not dead.*

Amber cried down the phone. 'I'm sorry, Bekhal, I was too scared to call … there's been so much horrible stuff going on … with Banaz…'

'Just tell me what's going on, please, Amber. Is it her husband? Has he hurt her?'

'OK, but don't tell anyone I told you. Please, Bekhal, this can't have come from me.'

The fear in Amber's voice was palpable. 'I promise,' I said, then rocked back and forth, phone in one hand, my other on my pregnant belly, as a tsunami of dread washed over me.

'Banaz divorced her husband, Bekhal. She moved back to your parents. Then she fell in love with another man, from a different tribe. A sweet Iranian man called Rahmat Suleimani. Oh my God, Banaz and Rahmat are so in love, Bekhal, but your parents are against their relationship. That's all I know, I swear. And now Banaz is missing.'

I couldn't speak.

'I'm sorry, Bekhal, if I hear anything, I'll call you.'

'Please do,' I said, and hung up.

That night I called Banaz's phone at least thirty times. It went straight to the crying baby answerphone. I left a message, 'Please, Nazca, please pick up. Please let me know that your safe. I love you, Nazca.'

Chapter Eighteen

HOW COULD THEY DO THIS TO YOU, NAZCA?

While the police continued to treat Banaz's disappearance as a missing person inquiry, I believed my sister to be alive. I concocted all kinds of scenarios in my head. *Maybe she just needed a break? She's in the Lake District and has fallen while walking in a remote location? Maybe she's broken a leg – or both legs? Her phone has died too. Perhaps she's fled the country with Rahmat Suleimani? Banaz has found xushawistyto and will live happily ever after in a secret location, away from the Kurdish community?*

Hope is a powerful emotion, isn't it? Looking back, I knew in my heart that I was clutching at straws with my hypotheses. Banaz would not dare to run away to the Lake District, especially while living under the Evil Punisher's roof. She had just returned to the family home after leaving her husband. I could not bring myself to imagine how Dad and Ari and Banaz's ex-husband had reacted to her leaving her arranged marriage – and then falling in love with an Iranian man. Who was this Rahmat Suleimani?

I did not sleep all night after the police told me about Banaz's disappearance. I sat in the kitchen, dialling Banaz's phone while the sky outside went from black to blue to sugar-almond pink, then I called Amber again.

Understandably, Amber was reluctant to speak, but managed to provide a few more details about Rahmat. 'I'm pretty sure Banaz met him at a family function,' she said. 'But I do know that they've been trying to keep their relationship a secret – because your dad disapproves of Rahmat. And now … oh, I don't know whether or not I should say this.'

'Go on, please,' I urged.

'Well, I don't know whether this is true, but I heard that somebody from the community followed Banaz and Rahmat – and photographed them kissing outside Morden Tube station.'

Oh, Nazca, what have they done to you? I immediately shook that thought from my head. At the same time, a sudden wave of morning sickness overwhelmed me. 'I have to go,' I stuttered. I made it to the bathroom, then vomited, violently.

Later that day, the police were at my door again. This time, Sarah and Andy – or Craigy as he was known to his colleagues – were joined by DCI Caroline Goode, who was leading the investigation on behalf of the Metropolitan Police Homicide and Serious Crime Command. Caroline's dedication to her job shone through as she assured me her team would do everything in their power to find Banaz. 'We *will* find Banaz,' she said several times, reiterating Sarah's promise the previous day. She said officers had already searched several addresses in London, Birmingham, and Sheffield, where Banaz's ex-husband Binar now lived. Several men had been arrested, she explained, but did not elaborate.

'Have you arrested my dad or my uncle Ari?' I asked.

'At the moment, we can't say who's been arrested, but we are questioning family members.' This confirmed to me that, yes, the police had arrested Dad and Ari.

Sarah sat beside me on my IKEA sofa while Caroline and Craigy fired questions about Banaz and my family from their hard kitchen chairs (there was only enough space for one comfy seat in the small lounge).

'I love my sister,' I said, 'but I can't even see Banaz because I could put her in danger. We took a huge risk when we met in May. Banaz was terrified her husband would catch us together. I begged

Banaz to come with me, to leave her husband, but she was too frightened to do so.'

Caroline did confirm the romance between Banaz and Rahmat Suleimani – and also mentioned the photograph of them kissing. Apparently, Rahmat had reported my sister missing to police on the morning of January 24 when she failed to send him a 'loving text as usual'. On that day, Banaz had been due to attend an appointment at Wimbledon Police Station regarding an earlier 'complaint' she'd made. However, Banaz did not go to the police station. My parents, when questioned, told police that Banaz was not at home on the morning of January 24, I later learned. 'Banaz often disappears,' Dad would tell detectives. 'She's free to come and go as she pleases.'

Tears dropped from my chin. What was the complaint Banaz made to the police? God, I felt so helpless. Sarah, bless her, passed me a tissue. 'Just take your time, Bekhal. We know how difficult this must be – but we're here for you.'

'I'm not in touch with my family. But that's not by choice. I *want* to see my sisters. Have you not seen my name on your files? I was taken away from the family home in a police car – then put into foster care. This was because my dad beat me and threatened to send me to Iraq to marry my cousin – when I was *fifteen*. In 2002, I went to the police again when my brother smashed me over the head with a dumbbell. He said my dad had paid him to kill me.' Once I started talking, I couldn't stop. I told Caroline about the Kurdish men who followed me and the death threat voicemail and tape from Dad. 'I live in fear, every day,' I said, 'but I will do anything to help you find Banaz.'

'We will find Banaz,' Caroline said again.

Days passed, but still no sign of Banaz. Sarah visited or called me every day. She was a huge comfort, listening with sympathy when I described the excruciating details of my FGM in Iran and the torturous punishments I'd endured for challenging the restraints of my culture. Each time I spoke to Sarah, I'd remember another incident – another moody phone call, Tekan and Elend confronting me in the diner, and Ari's threat to turn me to ashes. Although I did not want to believe it at the time, I suspected Ari and Dad had played a major part in Banaz's disappearance.

I called Banaz's number day and night, crying into the phone. 'Banaz, if you're out there and you're scared, just call me. Just let me know you're OK.' She never replied, and as time went by, my theories about Banaz breaking her legs or neck or jetting off to a secret location seemed less and less likely. I wondered what my mum had said to the police. And Kejal too. (My elder sister was then staying at 225 Morden Road and was in the house on the morning of Banaz's disappearance.) What would Grandma Zareen make of Banaz's disappearance? Could it be that Banaz was alive and had been held against her will somewhere? Caroline said the team had been working on this assumption, which would then explain why Banaz had not replied to calls and text messages. At this stage, I clung to every glimmer of hope that Banaz was alive, however grim the circumstances.

But February brought more distressing news when a 29-year-old Kurdish man, Mohammad Marid Hama, was charged with Banaz's murder. Press reports said police were treating my sister's death as a 'possible honour killing'. Police had arrested eight other men, but Dad and Ari were out on bail. But while Banaz's body had not been found, I refused to believe she was dead.

Looking back on the weeks that followed, I don't know how I coped. More threatening phone calls flooded my personal mobile. Kurdish men: voices I recognised from previous intimidating calls. Once, I heard Ari's voice, 'Bakha, how are you, my dear?' he said with a snigger, trying to intimidate me. Some callers would breathe heavily down the phone but say nothing. The most terrifying call came late one night in March when I was alone in the flat. 'Bekhal, you are being followed. You are the next girl to be killed. You will get the same as Banaz.' My whole body convulsed. I tried to hang up, but my hands were trembling so much I stabbed every button on the handset apart from the end call one. His voice crackled through the mic, 'You're next, Bekhal.' Three beeps sounded. He was gone. I cradled my bump, crying in that way where it sounds like you're laughing. Each jagged breath saturated with grief and shock and immeasurable fear. *What have they done to you, Nazca?*

My days were upside down, back to front, yet all the same. Those men had my phone number. Did they also know my address? If so, they could break in at night and murder me in my sleep. Too scared to sleep at night, I slept only in the daytime, and those were brief one or two-hour naps fractured by nightmares. More death threats followed. The calls, as usual, were mostly from withheld numbers, but occasionally I'd get some from Manchester or Birmingham codes. When I told Sarah about the calls, the investigation team installed a CCTV system and panic alarms in my flat and gave me a new mobile phone to call them on. But despite the new security measures and police presence, I still didn't feel safe.

Soon after I received the 'you're next' threat, Tekan, Payzee's then husband, called me. 'Bekhal khan,' he said, 'this is Tekan, your brother-in-law. I really think we should meet for a chat. Payzee wants to see you too. Why don't you come to the flat?'

I told him, 'No, leave me alone.' But I worried that Payzee – and Ashti – might also be in danger. I would subsequently learn that Ashti, then thirteen, was being followed by Kurdish men as she walked to and from school.

Towards the end of April, my bump was huge. Whenever I left the flat, I would conceal my pregnancy under an extra-large man's coat, but this became trickier as my stomach blew up even more. One morning, I received another call, from a woman this time. I could tell she was trying to hide her Kurdish accent. 'Hi, Bekhal, have you had your baby yet? I just wanted to...' I cut her off. For fuck's sake, even my unborn baby was being watched by these bastards. By now, I should have been hanging the bunting, shopping for baby clothes, and looking forward to becoming a mum. Instead, I thought, *Someone could kill me before I get to bring this new life into the world.* Meanwhile, Caroline and her team continued to search properties up and down the country for Banaz. Then, on Sunday afternoon, April 30, I received the call I hoped I would never receive, bringing a message that would emotionally kill me more than those death threats ever could. The call was from Sarah.

I was on the private balcony, sending another text message to Banaz, when Sarah's name and number flashed on the screen. I quickly hit the accept call button. 'Sarah, what is it? Any news?' A few seconds' silence followed. 'Sarah, what is it?' Agitation rose inside me, my body a composition of springs, needles and piano strings.

'I need to see you, Bekhal.' Sarah's voice was even softer than usual. I'd heard this tone used by hospital doctors in television dramas, in scenes when they confront the victim's family and say, 'I'm sorry, we did everything we could, but…'

'You've found Banaz, haven't you? You've found Nazca.'

'I'm coming to see you, Bekhal. Are you at home? Do you have a friend you can call? I think it might help if a friend is with you.'

'Yes, please hurry. Can't you give me an idea? Is Banaz alive?'

'Bekhal, just let me come to you. I'm five minutes away.'

I called Savanna, who lived on the same estate. I'd only known Savanna since January, but we'd become close friends. 'Please can you come over?' I sobbed. 'I think they've found my sister.'

'I'll be right there.' I dropped my phone, pushed my fingers through the hexagonal holes in the chicken wire fence above the balcony wall, then wailed all over London, 'No, no, no, no.' I shook the fence as hard as I could, trying to detach it from the wall. 'Let me go, let me jump, I want to die,' I yelled. 'Let me go, take me away.'

In those few seconds, I wanted to jump. I was ready to die. Thankfully, my baby saved me. Instinctively, I let go of the fence, felt my bump and suddenly realised, *no way can I kill my child.* I stepped away from the wall and went into the lounge, hands clamped to my belly, breathing hard. I jumped when the intercom buzzed.

Sarah did not need to utter a word. Her watery eyes and tilted head said it all. I fell into her open arms and sobbed and sobbed into her shoulder. I think Keilly, plus a male detective, came to my flat with Sarah that day, but I can't say for certain. But I do remember sitting on the black-and-white polka dot IKEA sofa, hugging a purple space hopper (Savanna's son had left it at mine a while back), my stomach hardening as Braxton Hicks contractions wrenched my womb. Sarah and Savanna sat either side of me. 'I'm so sorry, Bekhal,' said Sarah, 'but we have found Banaz's body.'

Even though I expected to hear that sentence, I was not prepared. I let out a noise somewhere between a scream and a growl. My throat tightened and swelled, like I had a whole apple stuck in my windpipe. Squeezing the space hoppers' horns with all my strength, I pushed my face hard into the inflated ball. I wanted to empty all my hurt and anger and loss into that bouncy toy. I cried into the space hopper for a good minute or so, its rubbery scent strong in my pregnant nose, then I turned to Sarah. 'What did those animals do to Nazca?' I asked.

Sarah couldn't say how Banaz died, but she told me where they found my darling sister, who they identified through dental records only. Bile burned my throat as I heard how the kindest, most delicate human being I'd ever known, was discovered foetal in a suitcase buried six feet down in the back garden of a house in Birmingham. A discarded fridge freezer covered the crude grave behind 86 Alexandra Road, Handsworth.

'Let me see her?' I asked. 'I need to see this for myself.'

'We do have some photographs, but you don't have to look at them. It's entirely up to you,' Sarah explained, 'but I will warn you, they're graphic and upsetting.'

'I want to see them,' I said. 'If you don't tell and show me everything, how am I supposed to grieve?'

I know it sounds grim, but I had to see for myself that this tragedy had happened. I needed to know, if only to get it into my head: *She ain't gonna come back any time soon.* I thought the pictures might help me deal with the reality of the situation. But they did not make me feel better. Ringing sounded in my ears, like a horror-film soundtrack, as I turned the pages of the A4 book of colour photographs. The police estimated Banaz had lain in the ground for three months. 'Are you sure you want to see the next picture?' Sarah asked at every page.

'Yes, you're the police, but I'm the sister. I'm the one hoping that she's still alive or will be found with a broken leg or back but … not … this … not … *that.*' I gestured at the suitcase picture in my lap and broke down. 'Let me see Nazca,' I said. 'Let me see her one last time.'

Savanna, Sarah and Keilly came with me to Birmingham. Even when we arrived at the mortuary in the police car, they were trying to talk me out of seeing Banaz's body. 'Are you sure you want to do this?' asked Sarah.

'Remember you're pregnant, Bekhal. This will put a lot of stress on you and the baby,' added Savanna.

'Please,' I said, 'let me say goodbye to my sister.'

After a three-hour wait, in which police, solicitors and mortuary staff further tried to dissuade me, I went to see Banaz.

Savanna held my arm as we walked into the cold room. I remember holding my belly and hearing somebody say, 'She's just over there.' And as I turned and saw Banaz on the table, I stopped breathing for a few seconds. Just seeing her, the body God gave her, destroyed. *They've ruined her body, ruined what she looks like*, I thought. But I could still see Nazca. I saw her high cheekbones, the dimple in her chin, her hair. I took a step closer, but my legs gave way. Savanna managed to steady me, then hugged my shoulders as I cried. 'Nazca, my baby, my gorgeous baby sister. How could they have done this to you, Nazca?'

I closed my eyes and pictured Nazca's face as I had known it. I remembered our sneaky make-up sessions at home and heard her voice in my head. 'Can you do contouring? And I want, like, the big red lips. Oh, jwana, jwana.'

I opened my eyes. 'Goodbye, Nazca. Goodbye, my love.'

As I left the room, I felt my baby kick for the first time.

Three days after Banaz's body was found, Ari Mahmod was charged with her murder. Dad was arrested on the same day. 'Your father is in custody at Lewisham Police Station,' Sarah said, again handing me a tissue as we sat on my IKEA sofa. I felt sick to my stomach. I knew all along that Dad and Ari were involved. My beautiful sister, murdered for falling in love, would never have the family she so wished for. Those whore-pig men – including our father (yet to be charged at this stage) – had snuffed out Banaz's life and labelled their heinous crime 'honour'. How the fuck could they contemplate such an evil act?

I looked at Sarah. 'You know, Ari, my dad, all those men in the community will be celebrating Banaz's murder. They'll be celebrating on the streets of Iraq right now, slapping each other on the back. I'm not kidding. That's how sick and fucked-up this culture is.'

'I'm so sorry, Bekhal. I can't bring Banaz back, but we will continue to fight, and we *will* find justice for your sister.'

'I know,' I said, blowing my nose again. A sudden coldness in the room, the same icy sensation I'd felt when I first moved into the flat, caused me to shiver. 'I want to be a mum and have lots of children. Oh, and I want to wear make-up all of the time,' I said out loud in Kurdish. I hadn't spoken my language in years.

Sarah looked taken aback at my sudden outburst. 'What does that mean?'

'Oh nothing,' I said. 'I was just thinking about Nazca. She would have made a brilliant mum, you know.'

Dad was released on bail – and subsequently arranged Banaz's funeral, which I could not go to even. That callous bastard told police that Banaz would be laid to rest at London Central Mosque, so Caroline and Sarah headed to the Regent's Park venue. En route, the undertaker called them to say the funeral would now be held at Tooting Mosque. But listen to this: the Evil Punisher had made no prior arrangements with the Tooting venue, which did not receive bodies. So, Mahmod left his murdered daughter's hearse parked in a side street while he and the family went into the mosque to say prayers. This did not surprise me, but it shattered my heart, nonetheless. Eventually, Banaz was buried in the Muslim quarter at Morden cemetery, in a grave marked only with a plot number. *How could they do this to you, Nazca?*

Although I spoke to the investigation team most days, they couldn't tell me specific information about their inquiries. They would not reveal what other members of my family had said in interviews. I asked, 'How did she end up in Birmingham?' But again, they could not tell me. All I knew about the case so far was that Banaz had left her husband, who she claimed (to me) raped and beat her, and had fallen in love with Rahmat Suleimani, an Iranian Kurd. I also knew she had been due to go to the police station regarding an earlier complaint she'd lodged. At this point, I did not know the nature of this complaint. My father disapproved of Banaz and Rahmat's relationship – and Banaz was now dead. My sister's killers left her to rot in a suitcase which they then buried in the garden of an abandoned house. Banaz had just turned twenty. She had her whole life ahead of her. I wanted justice, of course I did – and I would join that fight to the bitter end, but no amount of justice would ever bring Nazca back.

Detectives battled to find answers in the tight-knit, secretive Kurdish community. Women, too petrified to speak out, would say they'd never heard of Banaz. Men lied and threw obstacles in the way of the investigation. They gave false alibis, pledging allegiance to the suspects and the sickening 'honour' Banaz's death symbolised in the community. Caroline Goode identified fifty men linked to my sister's murder.

Throughout the investigation, Caroline, Craigy and DS Stuart Reeves would run suspects' names by me. Did I know Mohammed Saleh Ali? 'I don't recognise the name,' I said, 'but I might recognise his face.' (Turns out Mohammed Saleh Ali is my cousin.) Omar Hussain? Yes, I'd heard this name mentioned in the past but, again, I could not put the name to a face. But when asked, 'Does the name Dana Amin mean anything to you?' my blood turned to lava. 'Oh yes. Dana's my cousin, unfortunately. He watched, laughing and jeering as I almost drowned in a river in Iraq when I was six. He refused to help me. Dana is one of the Kurds who's been following me and making threatening calls.' It would later transpire that Dana helped in the disposal of Banaz's body. Mohammed Saleh Ali and Omar Hussain had conveniently fled to Iraq.

Behind the scenes, Ari's minions were plotting to kill me. I received more calls, some silent, others again warning, 'You're next.' I was petrified – and I now had two lives to protect. As my due date approached, I suffered panic attack after panic attack, convinced one – or more – of those callers would murder me before I made it to the hospital. Then, two weeks before I went into labour, a fairy godmother came into my life. Literally.

Dr Hannana Siddiqui, a long-standing member of the Southall Black Sisters (SBS), had been drafted in by the Metropolitan Police to support me. Hannana came to my flat one morning with Sarah and, oh my God, I clicked with her from the get-go. Petite and motherly, with a calming voice, Hannana was – and still is – highly regarded for her campaigns around honour-based violence. You know when a person appears in your life at just the right time? That was Hannana. And I know this sounds childish, but I swear I saw a golden halo crowning her soft black hair.

As we sat down, I remembered how I'd initially approached SBS the first time I fled 225 Morden Road, so that felt like a fitting place to start the conversation. 'When I was fifteen, I ran away from home because my dad beat me and tried to force me into an arranged marriage,' I began. I talked and cried a lot, but Hannana, like Sarah, came prepared with packets of tissues (bless those two – they always had the tissues at the ready for me). Hannana had a knack for assuaging my fears with her calm and collected manner. She reminded me of a kind aunty whom I'd known all my life. I wanted to ask Hannana if I could live with her, but I knew that wouldn't be allowed.

I remember Hannana called to congratulate me just days after I gave birth to my baby daughter. 'What wonderful news, you must be so proud,' she said, and that meant the world to me.

Unfortunately, I can't say much about my daughter, other than she was born amid high security. I went into hospital under a new name and gave birth in a private room guarded by police officers. Sarah arrived at the hospital when I reached the final throes of pushing. 'I heard you screaming when I was in the lift,' she said.

When my daughter was minutes old, I whispered in her little ear, 'I love you with all my heart and I want you to be happy, no matter what. I want you to make your own choices in life, travel the world and be with whomever makes you happy. Enjoy your freedom.' Then I kissed my baby's head and said a silent prayer for her aunty Banaz.

My emotions whirled as I embraced my creation and grieved Banaz. Still, I could not believe or accept what had happened to my sister. I kept expecting Banaz to walk through the door, smiling her pretty smile. Reality kicked in when, in August 2006, our dad, the Evil Punisher was charged with Banaz's murder. Caroline asked whether I'd be prepared to give evidence for the prosecution, which would mean testifying against my family and the Kurdish community. The risks involved were insurmountable. By now, the police had moved me and my daughter to another secret location amid further death threats. The thought of facing Dad and Ari in court terrified me to the core but securing justice for Banaz outweighed all the risks.

'Yes, I'll do it for Banaz,' I told Caroline. 'But they cannot see my face in court.'

Chapter Nineteen

NOTHING BUT THE TRUTH

St George's Hospital, Tooting, London, New Year's Eve, 2005.

Lying on a hospital trolley, Banaz rolls her head from side to side, licking her dehydrated lips as she relives the moment the Evil Punisher attempted to kill her in Grandma Zareen's house – while forcing her to drink brandy and watch the *101 Dalmatians* film.

Banaz lifts a bloodied arm to her brow. Her beautiful hair is all dishevelled and her eyes, rimmed black with smudged make-up, move drowsily, floating into her forehead at times. 'I was so scared,' she says.

My sister, who does not drink alcohol, is intoxicated, but sheer terror trembles in her little slurred voice. She looks up at her boyfriend, Rahmat Suleimani, who's filming this unthinkable conversation on his mobile phone. Banaz is speaking in Kurdish interspersed with a few English words. 'Baba took me to grandmother's house. He took everything away from me. He asked for my phone, everything I had on me, then gave me a suitcase and told me to carry it "with your right hand" from the car to the house. He [Dad] told me to go into the lounge. I held it [the case] in my right hand and went into the room. Baba talked more than usual, but I didn't talk much. He said, "Uncle Ari is coming." The curtains were shut, and it was dark, and Baba said, "Sit and turn your back to me," but I turned around every now and then because I didn't trust him. Baba left the room, then came back. He was wearing Reebok trainers and rubber gloves. The gloves were different colours, one yellow, the other blue, and he had a black bag with a Kurdish flag on it. He asked, "have you drunk alcohol before?", and I said, "No, I don't drink alcohol, because of my beliefs." He put the *101 Dalmatians* on the TV and told me to sit on the floor with him, made hafhafa, hafhafa [rustle, rustle], noises with the bag. He gave me the bottle. "Don't get up," he said, "drink it, drink it, slowly, slowly".'

Rahmat then asks Banaz, 'How can your dad make you drink? Does he not love you? Does he not take care of you? He's a religious man, he prays.'

Banaz's head lolls to her left. 'I don't know – you're asking me, my love? I told Baba, "I've not had alcohol before" and he said, "Don't lie to me. Don't be a donkey." I heard hafhafa, hafhafa, the bag, then he made me drink. Brandy, eight units. He said, between 3.30 p.m. and 4 p.m. you must drink half the bottle. He asked, "Are you hot?" I said, "Yes, I want water." The room started to turn. He said, "Do you want to sleep now?" Then he went out, he left the key in the back door.'

Rahmat says, 'Where was your dad?'

'In the next room. I got up and opened the garden door and ran outside. I made a run at the wire fence, went over it, and fell to the ground in the neighbour's garden. I was dizzy, the alcohol made me stumble. I put my hands through the neighbour's window and shouted for help. Nobody answered. I ran to the neighbour's gate at the side entrance, opened it and ran into the street. There were cars coming left and right.'

Rahmat then asks, 'Why would your dad do this to you? What is his reason?'

Again, you see the cuts on Banaz's arm as she runs her hand through her hair, exhausted, petrified. 'Because I didn't listen to him,' she replies.

Watching this harrowing footage today, I want to reach through the screen and scoop Banaz in my arms. If only I could. I wish I could kiss Nazca's face and touch her hair and inhale her floral Kenzo perfume. Pausing the video, I cry as I instead kiss my fingertips and touch Banaz's lips on the screen. This is the nearest I come to being with my sister again. I trace the contours of her face and sob, 'I'm so sorry, Nazca. I should have done more. I should have rescued you.'

The dialogue above is my translation of the terrifying account Banaz told from St George's Hospital on New Year's Eve, 2005. In the clip, she recounts the sickening scene which happened earlier that day at 11 Dorset Road, Wimbledon, in Grandpa Babakir's former lounge. So, the Evil Punisher was going to kill his daughter in his parent's house, in the very room where his father spent his dying days. Did Grandma Zareen know about this? Was she at home when it happened? I don't know the answers to those questions, and Zareen died a few years ago, but instinct tells me she knew of the plot to kill Banaz.

I remember when Bahman showed us around 11 Dorset Road on the day we arrived there, fresh off the plane from Iran. I'd noted the lack of exits from the house and thought, *it would be difficult to escape from here if I were trapped.* Little did I know Banaz would find herself in this situation almost eight years later. Dad lured Banaz to 11 Dorset Road on the pretence of a meeting with her estranged husband to discuss a divorce. At the beginning of the hospital footage, Banaz tells Rahmat how Dad earlier hurried her away from 225 Morden Road. 'He [Dad] told me to go and "get dressed appropriately" – because "we're going to meet Binar and your uncle to discuss your talaq [Islamic divorce]".' Just as I had fallen for Bahman's false affection on the night he attacked me, Banaz was also tricked into Dad's murderous trap. His plan, I believe, was to strangle her to death with his rubber-gloved hands – possibly with Ari's help when he arrived at the house. The only saving grace on this occasion, was the door leading to the garden. Banaz managed to escape. She vaulted the garden fence, then smashed a neighbour's window with her bare hands, slicing open both arms on the jagged glass as she did so. When nobody answered, poor Nazca ran, barefoot and bleeding, along the street, screaming for help, and eventually collapsed outside a café, where staff called for an ambulance.

Like I was too scared to get out of the police car when I fled Morden Road, Banaz was so frightened she told the ambulance crew, 'Please don't let me out. My dad and uncle are trying to kill me.' Banaz would not leave the ambulance until a security guard assisted. But what sickens me, is how the police reacted to Banaz's claims on New Year's Eve, 2005.

A female police officer arrived at the hospital to interview Banaz. That woman dismissed Banaz's claims and accused my sister of being 'manipulative and melodramatic'. She then wanted to charge Banaz with criminal damage for breaking the neighbour's window. Don't even get me started on this. How I wish the police had checked their systems and made the connection between Banaz Mahmod, Bekhal Mahmod and 225 Morden Road. The family background was there for them in black and white: Bekhal Mahmod, aged fifteen, ran away from home to escape her controlling father who locked her in rooms, beat her and called her a whore. Bekhal Mahmod was subsequently placed into emergency foster care owing to the violence she suffered at the family home – 225 Morden Road, the same address where Banaz lived in December 2005. Then, Bekhal Mahmod, aged eighteen, reported to police how her brother tried to kill her – at her father's behest. The writing was on the wall, for God's sake. If the police had shown me that video of Banaz at the time, I would have told them: 'You need to act now – otherwise, my sister will be dead within weeks. My dad and uncle will make sure of this.'

I believe Banaz would still be alive today if the police had listened to her claims from the outset. But no. The authorities failed my sister. The police did *not* listen to Banaz in the final months of her short life. And I will never forgive those officers for this.

The distressing hospital footage was played to the jury in the early stages of Banaz's murder trial, which began at the Old Bailey on March 5, 2007. Being a witness for the prosecution, I would not be allowed to watch the trial until I'd given evidence.

As my family liaison officer, Sarah would support me throughout the trial but could not reveal any details about the police investigation or Banaz's murder. 'We can't be seen to be influencing you in any way,' she explained. 'There will be reports in the press, once the trial begins, but please do not read them.'

'No, I don't want to,' I said. 'There's no way I want to fuck this up.'

Although I was not allowed in the court at the beginning of the trial, I can now, based on my knowledge of the case and court reports, tell you what the jury heard in my absence in courtroom ten of the Old Bailey.

Sitting in the dock, sneering, was Mahmod Babakir Mahmod, the Evil Punisher, and my man-whore uncle, smug Ari Mahmod. Both had pleaded not guilty to killing Banaz. Ari also denied conspiring with others to pervert the course of justice. A third man, Darbaz Rasul, joined Dad and Ari in the dock. He too pleaded not guilty to conspiring to pervert the course of justice.

Mohamed Hama had pleaded guilty to Banaz's murder and conspiring to pervert the course of justice. The two other suspects, my cousins Mohammed Saleh Ali and Omar Hussain, were still at large in Iraq.

The court heard that my beautiful sister Banaz was strangled in a so-called honour killing in the lounge of 225 Morden Road on January 24, 2006. The killing itself was carried out by Mohamed Hama, who was described as 'close family friend'. Banaz's body was then stuffed in a suitcase and buried in the garden of 86 Alexandra Road, Birmingham.

Victor Temple QC, prosecuting, described Banaz's murder as a 'cold-blooded and callous execution' arranged by Dad and Ari. Mum and Dad left the family home so the killers could commit the crime, the QC suggested. When police found Banaz, a bootlace ligature was still around her neck, the jury heard.

Victor Temple QC explained the tight-knit dynamics of the Kurdish community in South London, where, if a family name is shamed, 'Retribution often merciless must follow, especially if the family member is a woman.' He said: 'Women are not treated as equals. Banaz was killed for no other reason than she chose, after an unhappy marriage, to associate and fall in love with another. Her father was indifferent to his daughter's fate and showed no remorse from first to last, perceiving the loss of reputation was more important than his daughter's life.'

Next, the jury watched the footage recorded by Rahmat at St George's Hospital. Banaz's account 'Had all the hallmarks of an early attempt to kill her,' Victor Temple said. I'm told that Dad and Ari sniggered throughout that tragic six-minute clip. Evil, fucking bastards. I'm glad I wasn't in the courtroom to witness that despicable show.

Rahmat broke down in the witness box when he watched the chilling New Year's Eve video. Describing his love for my sister, he told the jury, 'I don't think I have ever loved anyone as much as I loved Banaz. She was my first love. She meant the world to me.'

Banaz was clearly madly in love with Rahmat too. In text messages she'd called him 'My prince, my shining one.' The court heard how Banaz had finally found the courage to walk out on the husband she claimed beat and raped her. In Rahmat, however, she had found a kind, loving and 'open-minded' partner whom she'd hoped to marry.

It broke my heart when I heard how Banaz and Rahmat were forced to keep their relationship a secret – all because Rahmat was not an Iraqi-Kurd or a strict Muslim from the precious 'Mirawaldy tribe'. The hypocrisy of this never fails to astound me. Grandma Zareen was more Iranian than Iraqi, for heaven's sake.

But early in December 2005, Banaz and Rahmat were spotted together by a car full of Kurdish men – Ari's minions – who followed the couple to Morden Tube station. One of those Kurds whipped out his mobile phone and snapped Banaz and Rahmat kissing. When Ari found out about the picture, he decided Banaz should pay for her 'shameful' freedom with her life.

I had already brought shame on the Mahmod name by refusing to conform to the family's fucked-up regime. Now, Banaz had further discredited the tribe by daring to fall in love with an 'unsuitable' man. On December 2, Ari called a family meeting. The conclusion following that 'council of war' gathering was to kill Banaz and Rahmat.

The court heard how Ari then called my mum and told her how he and other family members planned to kill her daughter and Rahmat. To Mum's credit, she warned Banaz and Rahmat about Ari's double murder plot, and, two days later, Banaz walked into Mitcham Police Station and reported Ari's threat.

Banaz went to the police four times in the seven weeks leading up to her death. But the jury did not hear about the letter Banaz handed to officers, naming the people she feared would kill her, including Hama, Mohammed Saleh Ali and Omar Hussain.

Giving evidence, Rahmat also explained how on January 22, 2006, just two days before Banaz was killed, a group of Kurdish men tried to abduct him from a street in Hounslow. One of the men told Rahmat: 'We are going to kill you and Banaz because we're Muslim and Kurdish. We're not like the English where you can be boyfriend and girlfriend. We're going to leave but we'll be back.'

Now I know the nature of Banaz's 'complaint' on January 23. While Rahmat reported the attempted abduction at Kennington Police Station, Banaz returned to Mitcham Police Station to report further threats to their lives.

Admittedly, when police offered to house Banaz in a women's refuge, she refused this option, saying she felt 'safer at home'. The defence later had a field day with that remark, but I knew what Banaz had inferred by it. As Banaz told one of the nurses when she discharged herself from St George's Hospital the following day: 'If I run away, I'm dead; if I go home, I'm dead.' Also, she stressed to police that she was only going home because 'my Mum is there'. In my opinion, the police should have placed Banaz (and Rahmat) in a safe house there and then. Banaz's appearance at the police station on January 23 was the last time she was seen alive.

Phone evidence showed Dad spoke to Ari after leaving the home with Mum and my sister Ashti on the morning of January 24. Further calls – analysed by Keilly – showed Ari and Dad informing Hama, Mohammed Saleh Ali and Omar Hussain when it was safe to go into 225 Morden Road. Kejal was at home and upstairs at the time, the court heard.

Mum and Dad showed no interest when police informed them of Banaz's disappearance. Again, Dad would smirk and tell his standard lie: 'She's free to come and go as she pleases.'

Even once the trial started, I was still receiving silent phone calls, so, again, the police moved me to another part of London and increased security measures. Meanwhile, as my moment in the witness box loomed, Sarah assured me that every precaution was in place to protect me at court. I would be travelling to and from the Old Bailey in a police car with Sarah and other team members. 'You will enter the court via a separate entrance, away from the public,' she said, 'and security has been stepped up inside and outside the court. Your safety is our priority, Bekhal.' Sarah had also arranged for me to visit the court beforehand. A screen would be erected around the witness box to shield me from the public gallery and dock, she said, but I would still need to walk into the courtroom to get to that box. There was no way I could let Dad or Ari or any other Kurdish man in that court see my face.

'I have no choice,' I told Sarah. 'I'll need to wear all the traditional gear – hijab, niqab and abaya.' A niqab is the traditional Muslim face veil, while the abaya is a square of fabric that drapes from your shoulders to your feet.

Sarah agreed. 'Whatever makes you feel most comfortable, Bekhal. I'll sort this for you.'

Oh my God, Sarah, bless her, went to Green Street in East London and bought me a black face veil, hijab, and abaya. I remember Hannana came to my flat with Sarah when I tried the gear on. Hannana looked both horrified and amused. There I was, cloaked head to toe in black cloth, the only part of me visible being my eyes through the rectangle hole in the face veil. I stood in the lounge, sweating in the thing, glancing from Hannana to Sarah, to Hannana again through my spy box. Then they both burst out laughing. 'What?' I said, spreading my arms in the shapeless fabric. Seriously, ten of me would have fitted inside that tent.

'Oh, Bekhal, it's fine. I think you look fine. And it will serve its purpose on the day,' said Hannana. 'It's just a *little* bit ironic though as the hijab and veil, all that stuff, goes against what we're campaigning for – women's freedom.'

I laughed too then as Hannana's observation sunk in. 'Oh don't, stop it, Hannana.' I think it did us all good to laugh for a minute or two.

On March 29, in a private witness room at the Old Bailey, I worked myself up into the worst panic ever as I prepared to testify against the Evil Punisher and Ari. I swear I wore out the hard blue carpet in that room, pacing nervous circles around Sarah in my abaya and headgear, chanting, 'Oh my God, they're gonna kill me, they're gonna kill me, they're gonna kill me. They *will* kill me.' My head was a tumble dryer, churning thoughts as black as my hijab, niqab and abaya. *What if Dad and Ari get off? What if one of them leaps from the dock while I'm giving my evidence? What if there's a Kurdish man in the public gallery, armed with a knife, ready to storm the witness stand and slit my throat? Will the jury believe me?*

'It's OK, Bekhal,' said Sarah, 'we won't let anybody harm you.' I stopped pacing and looked at Sarah, sucking the material of the niqab as I breathed. I was literally suffocating in that thing. 'You will be fine, Bekhal. Just remember, you're doing this for Banaz. You're a brave woman – you can do this.'

I nodded, yes, tears soaking my veil, and fell into Sarah's open arms. 'I'm doing this for my sister,' I said. 'I think I'm ready now.'

Sarah walked with me and the security guards through the corridors of the Old Bailey to the court. I hugged Sarah one last time, then, with legs as hollow as empty tin cans, advanced with two security guards into courtroom ten.

The first people I noticed were Dad and Ari, both in grey suits, watching my every step, as always. Ari gave me one of his smug smiles, tilting his head to reveal his disgusting hairy nostrils. I'll never forget that look. It said: 'I'm going to win this case – then kill you, Bekhal khan.' The Evil Punisher crossed his brows, his hatred for me palpable in his menacing stare. I quickly averted my gaze to the blue screen around the witness stand ahead, aware that every pair of eyes in that packed courtroom were on me. *Breathe, Becky, breathe. Do this for Banaz.* Sounds echoed in the room: papers shuffling, muffled coughs, my feet climbing the steps to the witness stand. I felt as though I was the one on trial. *They're gonna kill me, they're gonna kill me, they're gonna kill me.* As I stood behind the screen in the witness box, a voice, from somewhere, said: 'Bekhal Mahmod, would you mind removing your veil so the jury can see your face?'

Hands trembling, I lifted my niqab, and the clerk handed me a book. For the life of me, I cannot remember whether it was the Holy Bible or the Quran, but whichever that title, I meant every word that issued from my mouth. I swallowed hard, looked at the jury, and said, 'I promise to tell the truth, the whole truth, and nothing but the truth.'

Chapter Twenty

SLEEP TIGHT, MY DARLING NAZCA

My heart died. I heard my voice, but I couldn't feel my lips moving. I was supposed to be addressing the jury, yet I kept looking at the judge, Brian Barker, the common sergeant of London. 'My father used to beat me. He would beat me regularly, with his hands, shoes, a belt or a stick. He punched me, kicked and pinched me,' I said after Victor Temple asked me what Mahmod Mahmod was like as a father. 'He pulled my hair, spat in my face and called me a whore and a bitch – just because I wanted to wear Western clothes. My father would beat me for not wearing a hijab. I did not want boyfriends or to do anything wrong that would upset my parents. I just wanted to live my life – to have friends and give my opinion – very small things British girls take for granted.'

During fraught pauses between Victor Temple's questions, I imagined Dad and Ari on the other side of the screen. The mantra repeated in my head: *They're gonna kill me, they're gonna kill me, they will kill me.* Honestly, with every slow second that passed, I expected Dad or Ari to jump over the dock, rip down the screen and strangle me. *Were they in handcuffs? I have no idea.* Inside my head, those two had power. I'd seen their power when I walked into this courtroom. Ari's arrogant posture, one arm slung leisurely over the back of the bench, just how he used to sit on his show-off-y buttoned leather sofa in his house. *If I had my way, you'd be turning to ashes by now.* And the Evil Punisher's crossed brows that tortured me for years. *Gahba, qehpik, they will bring you to me. Even if it's only your head.* There was no doubt in my mind: had I not escaped and estranged myself from this family, I would be dead by now. Dad and Ari still wanted to kill me. There would be several other Kurdish men in this room willing to do the job, too. *I'm going against them all. I'm giving damning evidence about the people who want to kill me.* Those thoughts crowded my mind as I tried to focus on Victor Temple's next question, about the time Bahman smashed me over the head with a dumbbell.

My voice wobbled and cracked but I kept going, telling myself, *I've lived with this fear all my life, anyway. Do this for Banaz.* This time, I looked directly at the jury and told them how Bahman had lured me with his cleaning job lie. 'He [Bahman] told me to bring an empty suitcase,' I said. 'He made me drag the suitcase while he walked behind me. Bahman told me "Just walk and, under no circumstances must you look behind you – unless I tell you to".' I then relayed how I'd momentarily blacked out after Bahman bludgeoned me with the training weight. 'He [Bahman] dragged me along the path by my feet. I kicked my legs and eventually he broke down. He cried like a baby – then told me: "Dad asked me to do this. He paid me to do this to you".' I told the court that Dad had paid my brother to 'finish me off'.

Victor asked me about Ari next, so, in accordance with my statement, I recalled the meeting in my bedroom at 225 Morden Road, when Ari had threatened to turn me to ashes. 'He [Ari] said, "If I was your father, you would have been turned to ashes by now. He [my father] is scared but I am not. Ask the police. Even the police are beneath me. Your father's your father. I would have done it by now. I would have killed you by now, got rid of you".'

Another pause, then Victor asked me, 'Did you believe what was being said?'

'Yes,' I replied. At this point, I did not know about Ari's threats to Banaz and Rahmat or Dad's attempt to kill Banaz on New Year's Eve 2005.

Next, the QC questioned whether I'd received any other threats from my family. My eyes watered as I spoke of the terrifying voicemails Dad recorded on my phone after I left home, and how he'd threatened to have me beheaded. 'When I was in foster care, my father sent me a tape recording,' I added. 'He gave the cassette to my social worker. She brought it to me when she visited my foster home. In the recording, Dad said, "I will kill everyone in this house. I will kill all of your sisters, in order of age, from the youngest to the oldest. Then I will kill your brother, and your mother and, when they're all dead, I'll kill myself. And all of these deaths will be on *you*, Bekhal".' I looked at the judge again, but he was busy writing notes. *What was he writing? Did he believe me? Did the jury believe me?*

Victor gave me a polite nod. 'Thank you, Miss Mahmod,' he said, then turned to the judge. 'I have no further questions, your honour.'

Next came the part I'd been dreading most – my cross-examination by Dad and Ari's defence team. And just as I'd gained a little courage in the witness box, I soon fell apart. Ari's lawyer, David Lederman broke me with his opening question: 'Isn't it true that you have a baby?' My knees gave way. I literally collapsed in the witness box. My gasps and sobs echoed in the courtroom, that fucking abaya a lead cloak, cementing me to the floor in a cruel reminder of the restraints I'd battled my entire life in this warped culture. How could he have mentioned my daughter? *How could he?*

Two security guards helped me out of the witness box and escorted me out of the courtroom. I kept my veiled head down until I reached the witness room, where I fell onto the sofa, shaking and crying uncontrollably as Sarah tried to calm me. 'I've fucked it up. I'm so sorry, I've fucked it up,' I said between sobs. 'How do they know about my daughter? Don't let them hurt my daughter. They can't hurt my daughter.' Police had arranged childcare for my baby throughout the trial, but now I feared for her safety.

'Your daughter is safe, Bekhal. We're here to protect you both. And you haven't fucked anything up.' Sarah sat beside me, rubbing my back and passing me tissues as I told her about David Lederman's question. 'Your reaction was completely understandable, Bekhal. You've done nothing wrong.'

Eventually, after hearing that the judge had now banned the defence lawyers from asking further questions about my personal life, I returned to the witness stand. *I'm doing this for Banaz*, I reminded myself.

I managed to keep it together as, again, the defence tried their best to discredit my evidence and reputation. Lederman and Dad's lawyer, Henry Grunwald, QC, clutched at straws, suggesting I was a liar, thief and a drug addict. They even implied Sarah had bribed me with 'mobile phones and housing' to testify against my family. Their theories were ridiculous, lame attempts by the Evil Punisher and Ari to intimidate me via their lawyers. And in a way, their accusations helped me. My feisty teenage defiance returned. 'When the police first came to me, I was frightened to speak for putting Banaz in danger,' I said. 'I wanted my sister to come home. I believed her to be alive then.' The lawyers pressed on, trying to persuade me to agree that Dad had been nothing but a 'loyal, loving father'. *Really?* I wanted to ask, 'Would you say beating your daughter, sitting on her face until she can't breathe, pulling her hair, calling her a whore, and threatening to kill her is "loving father" behaviour?' Instead, I told the defence about the time a police officer had accompanied me to my parents' house – just so I could ask them for my passport. 'I was petrified of my father,' I said. 'Women in the Kurdish community are not allowed to do anything. They're ruled by men – and the men can do whatever they want.'

The defence team finally ran out of questions. Brian Barker QC thanked me and said my evidence was now over. But I felt as though I hadn't done or said enough, so I asked the judge: 'Please, Your Honour, can I just say something to the jury before I leave?' To my surprise, the judge said yes. I faced the twelve people who would decide Dad and Ari's fate. 'You're probably wondering why I'm wearing this,' I said, pointing at my hijab. 'I don't normally dress like this, but I am going to be looking over my shoulder for the rest of my life.'

Walking back to the witness room with Sarah and the security guards, I still didn't think I'd done enough to win justice for Banaz. 'I should have said more,' I told Sarah. 'What if the jury thinks I'm a lunatic?' Again, Sarah, ever supportive, reassured me. Just before we reached the witness room, she took me to one side.

'What you did took real guts, Bekhal. I'm so proud of you.' Oh my God, I started crying in my veil again. *Would I ever stop crying?*

I pulled the niqab over my head. 'What happens now?'

'Well, it's your decision,' Sarah said softly. 'You can watch the remainder of the trial via CCTV link, on the television in the witness room, or, if you feel that will be too difficult, you don't need to attend court from now on.'

'No, no, I *want* to watch it. I *have* to watch it.'

'That's absolutely fine,' said Sarah, then, taking my hand in hers, added, 'There's somebody waiting for you in there.' She tilted her head towards the door to the witness room. 'Would you like to meet Rahmat?'

I squeezed Sarah's hand. 'Yes, I want to meet him.'

Rahmat rose from the sofa when I walked into the witness room. Instantly I could see how he and Banaz were a perfect match. Gentle in his posture and expression, he needed no words to prove his love and heartache for my little sister. Oh, his face said it all. His dark eyes, bloodshot and swimming with tears and pain and loss. The way he held himself as he came towards me, like he was walking away, injured and confused, from the wreckage of a bad accident. His arms fluttered in his navy jacket as he extended them. He did not look me up and down how other men from my culture would do but looked directly into my eyes. 'I've been longing to meet you, Bekhal,' he said, and, for a moment, I felt as though Banaz was there in the room, saying, *Look after my prince, Bakha, tell Rahmat that I love him.* I stepped into Rahmat's embrace, both of us crying.

'I know how much you and Banaz loved one another,' I choked.

Until now, I had been unable to share my grief for Banaz with anyone who knew her. I did not speak to my family, and I had not spoken with Amber since she told me about Banaz and Rahmat's romance (it would be too dangerous for Amber and me to contact one another now; in any case, soon after, Amber lost touch with me and the family after marrying outside of the community and moving away). Meeting Rahmat was upsetting and comforting at once. He looked truly broken; I felt so sorry for Rahmat, but the connection we shared, Banaz, brought a little piece of her back to me somehow.

After Banaz's murder, Rahmat was given a new identity under the witness protection programme. Even Rahmat's parents, who lived in Iran, had received death threats. 'Banaz and I fell in love. We didn't commit a crime. How could they do this to her?' he asked as we sat chatting in the witness room that day.

Rahmat spoke of his and Banaz's wish to marry and have children. They had even picked baby names together. 'Banaz really wanted a daughter,' said Rahmat through a tearful smile, 'so we agreed on Rose for a little girl.' Oh God, I could not speak. I replied with more tears, remembering how Banaz loved her flowers. I loved Banaz with all my heart. I should have done more to protect her.

I looked at Rahmat. 'It's not your fault. You made Banaz happy. She would hate for you to feel guilty. You did not kill Banaz.'

Rahmat leaned forwards, covering his face with his hands. 'My life means nothing without Banaz.'

The witness room at the Old Bailey became my second home for the next three months. Every morning, I'd run out of my flat in my abaya, hijab and niqab and jump into the awaiting unmarked police car, exhausted but jittering with nerves. Some days, I'd get into that car having had no sleep. When I did sleep a reoccurring nightmare would wake me. In this dream, lions would chase me around the corridors of the Old Bailey and into courtroom ten, where Dad and Ari would appear, smirking and rubbing their hands together. This nightmare still haunts me today.

I missed Hannana. We were not allowed to contact one another during the trial for security reasons. But I knew she was there, observing from somewhere in the public gallery while I watched the proceedings on the CCTV link with Rahmat.

While I'll never forgive the initial police failures, I must also praise the detective work of those officers who worked tirelessly to find Banaz. Via the CCTV link, I watched as Keilly McIntyre produced evidence of all the telephone calls she'd meticulously analysed. Banaz's killer transported her body in a hire car, unaware that it had a satellite tracking device. Keilly had studied the data from this device, which proved the car had been to 225 Morden Road on the day Banaz disappeared and later to 86 Alexandra Road in Birmingham, where her body was found.

Various police officers gave evidence, telling how Dad gave varying accounts about the last time he'd seen Banaz. Dad told one officer he'd seen Banaz in 'a T-shirt and jeans' on the morning of January 24. I shouted, 'You fucking liar' at the screen when I heard this. Since when did the Evil Punisher allow his daughters to wear T-shirts? Dad told another officer, 'I didn't see her [Banaz] that morning.'

My father told another pack of lies when his turn came to testify – via an interpreter. Seriously, like he needed a translator. Dad, for all his 'only Kurdish must be spoken in this house' crap, spoke better English than any one of us Mahmods put together. I sat on the edge of the sofa, my eyes almost touching the screen, watching that vile thing spout untruth after untruth after untruth. 'I'm like a friend to my daughters. I would never harm my children,' he said, all grey moustache-y smiles and chuckles. I wanted to tear my hair out at that remark. It got worse, in a desperate attempt to woo the jury, Dad produced photographs of me, taken years ago in the family home. In those pictures, he pointed out, 'Bekhal is not wearing a hijab.' There were no men in those pictures. And besides, we were allowed to remove our hijabs indoors in front of immediate family. Dad would beat me for not wearing my headscarf outside the house. And so, the lies continued:

'I was happy about Banaz marrying Rahmat.'

'Banaz would often spend the night with Rahmat.'

'My children are free to come and go as they pleased.'

But when Victor Temple challenged Dad, the jury witnessed a glimpse of his temper. 'Your questions are ridiculous,' he shouted in Kurdish. 'You don't have any evidence – they're blaming me because they can't catch who did it.'

My innards weaved into plaits as Kejal gave her evidence for the defence, painting Dad as the perfect, 'loving' father. She told the court that she had been at home on the morning of January 24. 'I was upstairs, feeding my baby and having a bath,' she said. Phone records showed multiple calls from Mum and Dad (on their respective mobiles) to Kejal's number that morning. However, not one of them had tried to call Banaz.

My uncle, of course, tried to turn the court case into the fucking Ari show. Also speaking via an interpreter, Ari, smug as ever, shrugged and half-laughed and gave it 'I can't be arsed with this shit' expressions when probed by Victor. I gestured at Ari, a tiny, insignificant person on the screen, and said to Rahmat, 'Look at that murderous, disgusting parasite. How fucking dare he. Evil, lying, manipulative, heartless son of a bitch.'

Ari denied every allegation put to him by the prosecution and, like Dad, made himself out to be a perfect, liberal father. When asked about the meeting when he threatened to turn me to ashes, he shot back, 'Did she [me] record it?' He then denied his call to Mum, in which he warned that Banaz and Rahmat would be killed. 'Banaz did not make any allegations against me,' said Ari. Can you believe it? He wasn't so smug when the jury heard the statement Banaz gave to police on January 23, which included details of Ari's death threats and the events of New Year's Eve 2005. In her statement, Banaz said how Ari had 'brainwashed my family'. 'He [Ari] seems to be in control of every decision my father makes,' she had told police.

I think I expected the trial to go on forever, and a part of me didn't want it to end. In my mind, going to court every day and seeing Rahmat kept Banaz's name alive. I'd heard about the campaigners outside the front of the court, waving their banners and chanting, 'Justice for Banaz', which proved how much Banaz's tragic story had touched people's hearts. But, on Friday, June 8, 2007, the judge sent the jury to another private room in the courthouse to consider its verdict.

Oh my God, I was a wreck, sweating, shivering, crying, and in and out of the loo every few minutes. 'What if they get off?' I kept asking Sarah. 'I've gone against my family. If they get off, they're gonna kill me. They *will* kill me.' The jury did not reach a decision that day. A long, agonising weekend followed. Then, on the afternoon of Monday, June 11, the twelve people who had sat in a private room, discussing almost four months' evidence, finally delivered their verdict.

Rahmat and I were allowed in the courtroom to hear the jury's decision. We sat beneath the balcony of the public gallery with Sarah, shielded by security guards. Through the rectangle of my veil, I stared at Dad and Ari, who both eyeballed me back. Ari's expression, as always, was one of pure arrogance. I wanted to run to that dock, thump my hand down his throat and rip out his heart.

When the jury filed into the room, a rush of heat shot from my heart to my scalp. I felt faint, like I was about to pass out, and my hands, coated with sweat, slithered and trembled in my lap. I heard the judge speak. 'Would the defendants please rise.' And the Evil Punisher and Ari showed no emotion as they stood. They looked like two bored men waiting at a bus stop. Next, the spokesperson for the jury rose and my heart thrummed in my ears as the judge spoke again. 'On the charge of murder, do you find the defendant Mahmod Babakir Mahmod guilty or not guilty?' I squeezed my eyes shut. *Oh God, please don't let them walk free.* Silence, filled with whisperings from the gallery above...

'Guilty.'

'Yes!' I shouted through my niqab. I grabbed Sarah's hand as Rahmat punched the air.

'On the charge of murder,' continued Brian Barker QC. 'Do you find the defendant Ari Mahmod guilty or not guilty?'

'Guilty.'

I burst into tears as the jury further found Ari guilty of conspiring to pervert the course of justice. *We've done it,* I thought, *but what happens now?* Gasps and protests in Kurdish jumbled above me. I pictured Mum, covering her eyes with her hijab as she cried. She was in the courtroom, but I was glad I couldn't see her. The judge slammed his hammer. 'Take them down.'

A mixture of emotions hit me. First came relief, quickly overshadowed by fear and pain. I thought, *Fuck, we've done this, but we're the ones who're going to get it now. They're gonna kill me, they're gonna kill me, they* will *kill me.* Then came a deep, gut-wrenching sadness as the Evil Punisher cast me one final look of contempt. I looked away. I could not begin to conceive the reality of what he'd done to Banaz. How could he watch his daughter, whom he brought into this world, grow into a beautiful young woman – then deny her of any happiness before ending her life? All the justice in the world could not bring Nazca back.

Over a month later, I sat in that same courtroom with Rahmat after learning how my darling Nazca was tortured and raped in the final two-and-a-half hours of her precious life. This time, another man stood in the dock alongside Dad and Ari: Mohamad Hama, who had previously pleaded guilty to murdering Banaz. All three killers would be sentenced on that Friday, July 20, 2007.

At a pre-sentencing hearing the previous day, Hama's acts of unspeakable depravity were revealed. On the blood-red carpet of 225 Morden Road, the home in which my sister should have felt secure and loved by her family, Hama kicked and stamped on Banaz's neck before raping her and strangling her to death to 'get her soul out'. Hama, then 31, was recorded in telephone calls from prison, boasting and laughing to a friend. Referring to the bootlace he strangled Banaz with, he said: 'The wire was thick, and the soul would not just leave like that. We could not remove it. All in all, it took five minutes to strangle her. I was kicking and stamping on her neck to get the soul out.' I do not wish to waste any more words on that callous bastard's horrific crime.

Before Judge Barker sentenced the murderers, I read from my victim impact statement. In my hijab, niqab and abaya, I stood behind a screen, trembling as I told the court of the last time I saw Nazca in 2005:

I find it really hard to say how much Banaz's death has affected me. Words just do not say enough … I left home when I was fifteen, but I stayed in touch with [my sister] Banaz. I knew what was happening to her, and how unhappy she was in her marriage. The last time I saw Banaz alive was in 2005. She did look rundown … I have nothing of Banaz except two pictures, and I find it very hard to grieve for her. As I am separated from my family, I have no one to share my memories or share my grief with.

I wish with all my heart I had taken her with me in 2005 because she would then still be alive. Banaz was a smart, fun and attractive lady. She had a very caring personality and got on with everyone. Above all she wanted to be happy and have a loving husband and children. Since her disappearance I can honestly say there's not been one night without having nightmares about what has happened to her. Banaz herself does not come into my dreams or nightmares, and that upsets me; I would like to see her again. Because of the circumstances of Banaz's death, I know I shall never be safe again, and constantly have to look over my shoulder.

I cry and become very upset when I think what's happened to her. My life will never be the same again. If there's one thing I could wish for, it would be to have Banaz back. I miss her and love her. Banaz was very dear to me and a special sister and friend. The world was not good enough for Banaz; at least now she can rest like an angel.

After reading my statement, two security guards escorted me back to my seat in the courtroom. I remember shouting, 'No' when the judge sentenced the Evil Punisher to life, with a minimum tariff of twenty years in prison. Ari, who ordered and planned Banaz's 'honour killing', was sentenced to a minimum of twenty-three years, while the heinous pig who raped and strangled my baby sister was handed a pathetic seventeen years. I didn't understand. I thought a life sentence meant just that: life in prison – you die behind bars. Again, Dad and Ari showed no emotion in the dock as Judge Brian Barker told them: 'You are both hard and unswerving men for whom apparent honour in the community is more important than the happiness of your flesh and blood and for whom killing in the name of honour is to be put above tolerance and understanding.'

'Rot in hell, you bastard pigs,' I said under my breath as the Evil Punisher and Ari were led away to begin their life sentences. *I hope you both get the crap beaten out of you in jail.*

A few weeks after the sentencing, Rahmat and I visited Nazca's grave for the first time. Police drove us to Morden Cemetery in separate unmarked cars. They even locked the gates, while several plain clothes officers guarded the graveyard.

I met Rahmat and we walked together to Banaz's grave. My arms were full of flowers – two bunches of lilies (Banaz's favourite), one yellow, the other pink, and a bouquet of orange roses. The mouth of a green vase poked out the top of my shoulder bag, which Rahmat offered to carry. As we walked, with officers trailing our steps, Rahmat again spoke of his grief for Banaz. We stopped for a moment in the spitting rain, a few feet shy of the mound of earth that marked Nazca's resting place, and I glanced up at Rahmat. God, he looked as though he hadn't slept for weeks. His eyes, circled with purply shadows, were swollen from crying. 'Oh, Rahmat, I know how much you miss Banaz,' I said. 'I miss her too, and I know I can't magic her back, but I am here for you, if ever you need to talk.'

Tears tumbled down Rahmat's cheeks. 'Bekhal, can I ask you something?'

'Of course.'

'Would you live with me? I don't mean like boyfriend and girlfriend – just as friends. We can help one another and keep Banaz close to our hearts.'

Oh, what could I say? I felt so helpless. Much as I wanted to help Rahmat, I could not live with him. My eyes filled up as I searched my mind for the right words. 'I'm so sorry,' I said finally. 'That's such a lovely offer but I can't. I have a daughter now and I have to consider her safety. But I am still here for you.'

Rahmat nodded. 'I understand,' he said, then, proffering my shoulder bag, added, 'Please, you should spend some time with your sister. I'll leave you in peace to say goodbye.'

I thanked Rahmat, thinking, *How typical of Banaz to choose such a polite, caring man.* I stepped forwards, then knelt in the soggy grass. There was no headstone, only a small plaque emblazoned with a plot number, so I placed my vase where the headstone should be and began to arrange Nazca's flowers. As I did this, I remembered Banaz admiring the daffodils outside our house in Morden Road. 'I love flowers, Bakha. Yellow and orange are my favourite colours. Jwana, jwana.' And I sobbed as I thought of her delicate fingers touching those petals. I filled the vase with the yellow lilies and orange roses, then sat back on my heels and whispered my final farewell.

'Oh, Nazca, if you were here, the whole world would be orange and yellow. I love you, my darling sister. Sleep tight, my angel.'

EPILOGUE

Years ago, when we lived in Iran, Banaz climbed a twenty-foot ladder while sleepwalking. I spotted her from our bedroom window, a swaying figure in her Aladdin trousers, clinging to the top part of the ladder that led to the roof of our house.

I ran into Mum and Dad's room, panicking. 'Quick, help, Banaz is stuck. She's on the ladder.' I was petrified Banaz would fall and smash her head on the concrete below. Banaz was about eight at the time, and this was not her first sleepwalking episode. Dad flew out of bed and ran outside. I followed and watched through my fingers as he then climbed the ladder and rescued my little sister. Banaz was still asleep, but Dad managed to talk her down, step by step, all the while standing behind her.

The point I'm making is this: Banaz could have died that night, but Dad saved her. What happened to that man? How could he go from protecting Banaz to orchestrating her murder twelve years later? I ask myself this question every day.

Sadly, Dad's conviction and jail sentence does not end the trauma he and Ari inflicted upon Banaz and me – and my younger sisters Payzee and Ashti. Not one day passes when I don't think about Banaz. On every anniversary – that of her birthday, the day she disappeared and the day she was found,

I light a candle and cry for the future she never had with her 'prince', Rahmat.

In 2012, I gave an interview for a documentary about Banaz's so-called 'honour killing'. *Banaz: A Love Story*, produced and directed by Deeyah Khan, which included footage from the five visits Banaz made to police to ask for help. These videos were not shown at Banaz's trial and viewing them for the first time broke my heart. One of the clips shows Banaz reporting allegations of rape and abuse against her ex-husband. 'When he raped me, it was like I was his shoe that he could wear whenever he wanted to,' she explained. 'I didn't know if this was normal in my culture, or here. I was just seventeen then.' This is Banaz, speaking beyond the grave. When Banaz told me about her husband in 2005, she had used almost identical language to describe his alleged attacks: 'It's like I'm his glove or his shoe ... that he can wear whenever he chooses.' Why weren't Banaz's allegations taken seriously by police? I can't watch these videos without crying or screaming at the screen or thinking, *What if?*

In 2008, the former Independent Police Complaints Commission found serious failings in the handling of Banaz's case. The IPCC was particularly critical of two Metropolitan Police officers who attended Banaz on New Year's Eve 2005. However, the female police officer and her superior, an Inspector, were only issued with 'words of advice' by the police disciplinary body. This outraged me beyond belief. Banaz is dead. She died twenty-four days after confiding in officers that Dad tried to kill her – but the staff who dismissed Banaz's claims as 'melodramatic' get to walk away with just a slap on the wrists? Adding to this injustice, the female officer was then promoted to sergeant. I mean, really?

Following the IPCC's ruling, Dr Hannana Siddiqui, and solicitors, helped me launch a civil action against the Metropolitan Police regarding the force's failures. I can't reveal specific details of this action, but I can confirm the Met made an out-of-court settlement.

I must stress, however, that my criticisms do not extend to the Metropolitan Police Homicide and Serious Crime Command, who went above and beyond to find Banaz and bring her killers to justice. Indeed, DCI Caroline Goode made legal history when she secured the extradition of my cousins, Mohammed Saleh Ali and Omar Hussain, from Iraq Kurdistan. At a second trial in November 2010, they were both found guilty of murder and sentenced to at least twenty-one years. Ali was easier to find because, get this: he'd been arrested in Iraq after killing a sixteen-year-old boy in a hit-and-run motorbike accident.

My other cousin, Dana Amin – the one who followed me, sent me threats and laughed when I nearly drowned as a child – helped to dispose of Banaz's body. He was jailed for eight years in 2013 and has since been released.

As I said in my witness impact statement in court, I will never feel safe. I'll always be looking over my shoulder. Days after the trial ended, I got a call from Cheryl – the hairdresser sister of my ex-boyfriend, Ata. She had read about the case in the press and recognised Ari's face. In December 2005, that man-whore had walked into her salon, where I used to work, had his horrible moustache trimmed, got a haircut, and asked questions. 'I recognise your uncle, Ari Mahmod. He came into the salon – just before Christmas in 2005,' said Cheryl. 'He kept asking about the women who worked here – he asked for names, which I thought was odd. He was really creepy. It was definitely the same man.' Oh yes, that was Ari, for sure. So, he was looking for me at around the same time he was planning Banaz's murder. But this doesn't surprise me – I've always been on Ari's hitlist.

Towards the end of 2007, I entered the witness protection programme. I did not want to do this, but, if I refused, there was a good chance my daughter would be taken into care for her safety. My life is difficult. It's a lonely life. I never wanted to cut ties with my family, but circumstances meant I had to. God, what I wouldn't give to see my younger sisters. Nowadays, I suffer panic attacks and nightmares and, to be honest, I will never be fully happy again.

In May 2016 I heard the shocking news that Rahmat had committed suicide. According to press reports, he had tried to take his life twice before. Poor Rahmat, I truly believe that he could not live without Banaz.

I have no love for my father, the Evil Punisher, but I live in fear of the day when he and Ari are released from jail. But I hope they never get out. I want the Evil Punisher to suffer a slow, painful death in jail. As Judge Brian Barker said when he sentenced Dad and Ari, where is the honour in a father putting his status in the community before the life of his own flesh and blood? Today, with my dear friend Hannana, I continue to campaign for awareness around honour-based violence. We are fighting for a Banaz's law, which will recognise 'honour' as an aggravating, not a mitigating factor in cultural crimes.

Banaz was a beautiful young woman, who had her whole life ahead of her, yet her hopes were quashed and buried by the people who were supposed to love her. My sister committed no crime. As I've mentioned several times in the pages of this book, Banaz was the softest, kindest person you could hope to meet. She would have made a wonderful mum and if my father, uncle and male cousins had let her have a life, Banaz would have lived it to the full in the most honest way.

Every night before I go to sleep, I kiss one of my existing photographs of Banaz, which is taped to the inside door of my wardrobe. On birthdays and anniversaries, I read a poem to Banaz, which sums up my emotions for my sister. A poem by Roisin Loughran, called *Don't Cry for Me*. These last two verses always make me cry:

So please don't cry for me,
I can see all that you do,
Although you thought I was gone,
I was always with you.

I can't wait for the day
For your eyes to see,
The person who wiped your tears away,
Has always been me.

POSTSCRIPT

Bekhal was known as the 'troublemaker' from childhood, her defiant spirit constantly getting her into hot water, earning her not only verbal chastisement but also cruel beatings when her family was living in Iraq and Iran. In the UK, as a teenager, while her father continued to be violent, her uncle Ari added to the controlling and threatening behaviour. He threatened to turn her into 'ashes' and her brother, emotionally blackmailed and financially bribed by the father to be the 'man of the family', attempted to kill her.

Shockingly, Bekhal's sexuality came under security and control from the age of six, when she was first beaten for innocently touching an adult male cousin's odd-looking fingernails. At the time, she was confused as to why this was 'wrong' or why her loving parents at times became unfamiliar monsters; no explanations were given, which made it difficult to predict how to avoid a beating. This forced Bekhal to live with fear and uncertainty, while she tested the waters when she could. But even she did not expect that herself and her female siblings and cousins would suddenly suffer the amateur surgery of female genital mutilation. It was this experience, when Bekhal nearly died after her half-blind hostile grandmother cut a nerve, that made Bekhal realise that in order to survive, she had to fight for her rights as a woman. This became the turning point, when she decided the traditional life was not for her. Later in England, she found 'girl power' and avenues to escaping abuse, such as contacting women's organisations. She even once called Southall Black Sisters. Although the advice is normally to move to a new location, changing school or employers, this is not always wanted by or possible for victims. Bekhal was referred to a local Council run service and placed in a refuge, as she did not want to leave the area.

Banaz, on the other hand, remained truly innocent and 'delicate', as her name implies, and consequently became a victim of an honour killing. However, like most people, it would have been hard for her to imagine that those who you trust, would kill you. Banaz returned home after leaving her husband. Initially she was told she was not a 'good wife' to the 'David Beckham of husbands' even though, according to Banaz in a video of the police interview she gave in 2005, he treated her as his 'shoe'. She also alleged that he told her family that he only raped her when she said no. Divorce, however, would be shameful as Banaz herself said in the interview that 'all the blame goes to the female'. In any case, leaving a cousin or a betrothed marriage is almost impossible. So, she went back to her husband. Banaz later hoped that her parents would support her and returned home; subsequently developing a relationship with Rahmat. Her husband pronounced an Islamic *talaq* (divorce), accusing her of adultery. Banaz wanted to re-marry to Rahmat, but the couple were forced to pretend that their relationship was over when he was deemed 'unsuitable'. The extended family and community, however, remained suspicious, following and controlling her. Her fate was sealed when the couple were photographed kissing outside a Tube station. This was following a night that Banaz had not returned home. The day before had been Banaz's birthday and so, for the first time, the couple had spent a night together. Her Uncle Ari made threats to kill her, and there was a family 'council of war' meeting to conspire and consolidate a plot to kill.

Banaz, despite her innocence, did fight back when faced with extreme danger. She had clung on to life as long as she could, as the killers describe in secret recordings in prison how her soul would not 'discharge'. Prior to her death, Banaz knew that she was not safe at home or outside of it, but nevertheless bravely sought help from the police – *five times*. She even wrote the names of five suspects who did indeed later murder her. Earlier, 'If anything happens to me, it's them' is what Banaz predicted in the police video, clutching her notes.

Banaz returned home after her own father attempted to kill her on New Year's Eve in 2005. Despite Rahmat's mobile phone footage where, in fear and distress, Banaz describes the details of the murder attempt, disbelief from the police would have shattered her confidence in the authorities. Dismissed as being 'manipulative and melodramatic', Banaz faced charges for criminal damage instead. In the earlier 2005 police video, Banaz also speaks to us, but even in silence when left alone for a while, she looks terrified, but hopeful of help. It reminded me of the time later on when Banaz was left alone in a dangerous situation at home while the police investigated further threats to kill her after the murder attempt. She would have hoped for protection then too. She died on the day she was due to make another statement. This was a failure in basic policing, which became colossal in effect.

Banaz was betrayed by some members of her family and community. But the lack of protection by the police meant Banaz was failed twice over, this time by the state. The police, who may have ignored her pleas in order to be culturally or religiously sensitive, were ironically, racist in the process. Indeed, I would argue that the case shows institutional racism in the police force as great as that shown after the racist murder of Stephen Lawrence in 1993. In Stephen's case, the police failed to conduct a proper investigation, initially resulting in all suspects escaping justice. There was a public Inquiry as well as a public apology by the Metropolitan Police Commissioner. In Banaz's case, racial discrimination intersected with sexism, creating multiple forms of discrimination, something that is commonly experienced by black and ethnic minority women. Although Bekhal has received a private apology by a lower ranking officer following a successful civil action, I would also argue that a public apology from the Police Commissioner is long overdue, as is a wider Inquiry on violence against women and girls in black and ethnic minority communities.

It is ironic that Bekhal had once wanted to be a police officer so that she could stop violence against women and girls. I also could not help but notice the irony in my recommendation that victims should continue to call the police on the ITV Chat Show *This Morning.* Afterwards, Yvonne Rhoden asked me why I had advised that given Banaz's experiences. I had said, 'Where else do victims go for protection, particularly in an emergency?' Despite her anger with the police, Bekhal also feels that the police need to improve their response. As a result, just after the trial, we both used to train the police on honour violence. Even though we provided this training free of charge, the police later took training in-house and forgot about the survivors and experts. Inevitably, many other police failures followed. And they are not alone in these failings. Bekhal was pressured by social services by being told to 'listen to her parents'. The social worker mediated with her parents and even gave her a cassette tape from her father, a recording of him threatening to kill the whole family if she did not return home.

The killers were hailed as 'heroes' by many in their community in the UK and Iraq for raping and killing Banaz and restoring their honour. Their boasting, however, was their downfall – it helped to provide the smoking gun of admission of guilt while these claims were being secretly recorded in prison. But, regardless of the legal outcome, the killers felt no remorse. Instead, they joked and felt justified in showing Banaz 'disrespect' by torturing her for over two hours; raping her and stamping and kicking her neck when her soul refused to leave the body. They strangled her with a shoelace, stuffed her in a suitcase and buried her in an abandoned house, under a discarded fridge. Ari, a powerful community leader, said: 'I am not in here for anything I am ashamed of. I have done justice.' The horror of what they had done to Banaz seemed to have passed them by.

In many Middle Eastern and Asian countries, this cold-hearted attitude is the same. Brutal murders in the name of honour are state sanctioned and killers have immunity. Even where these actions have been declared illegal, the criminal justice system turns a blind eye to the problem. That is why two of the suspects in Banaz's case fled to Iraq. This is also precisely why some honour killings have a transnational element where the victim is killed overseas, or the perpetrators leave the UK in order to evade justice. While we obtained convictions in the case of Banaz, this is not true in all honour killings. Although there are an estimated twelve honour killings per year, we do not know how many women resident in this country have been killed whilst overseas. Even in the UK, some escape justice where killings are disguised as suicides or accidents.

The issues of honour killings and forced marriage were not debated in the mainstream British media or on the government's radar until the death of Rukshana Naz in 1998 and Heshu Yonis in 2002. Rukshana's case mainly highlighted the scandal of forced marriage after she was strangled at the age of nineteen by her brother, while her mother held down her feet. Like Banaz, she had refused to stay in a forced marriage to a cousin. Instead, she became pregnant to her lover and resisted a late abortion. Heshu's case, however, was the first to be widely called an 'honour killing' by the press, the police and the courts. Like Banaz, Heshu was another Iraqi Kurd, who was stabbed to death by her father at the tender age of sixteen for having an 'unsuitable' boyfriend. Like Bekhal, she had refused to marry her cousin and her father had also subjected her to a history of restrictions and domestic abuse. As reported by *BBC News*, in a letter to him before her death when she was planning to leave home, Heshu wrote: '*Bye Dad, sorry I was so much trouble. Me and you will probably never understand each other, but I'm sorry I wasn't what you wanted, but there's some things you can't change... Hey, for an older man you have a good strong punch and kick. I hope you enjoyed testing your strength on me, it was fun being on the receiving end. Well done.'*

In another case, Surjit Kaur Athwal was killed in 1998 when she was aged twenty-seven after being lured to India in an honour killing organised by her husband and mother-in-law. This case first highlighted transnational murder. Surjit had wanted a divorce due to domestic abuse from her husband. This, and the possibility that she was having an affair, was seen as too shameful and like Banaz, her death was arranged after a 'council of war' meeting. Surjit's brother, Jagdeesh Singh, campaigned for justice for over a decade with the support of Southall Black Sisters. The culprits were not convicted until 2007 (a case I juggled to support at the same time as Banaz's trial) when Sarbjit Kaur Athwal, a woman married to the husband's brother, bravely came forward with new evidence. This was supported by the good police work by the dogged determination of a 'cold case' officer, DCI Clive Driscoll, who, in 2012, also successfully uncovered evidence to prosecute two of the suspects in the Stephen Lawrence case. Surjit's body was never found, and those responsible in India have yet to be prosecuted. Jagdeesh continues to campaign for justice and calls for a public inquiry into 'outsourced' transnational honour killings.

These cases show the continuum of violence women from minority communities experience from a young age from their own families and then in marriage from their husband and in-laws. In honour killings, there is often a conspiracy to kill, or to cover up afterwards, as was the case in Banaz's murder. Honour killings and other abusive acts like rape and violence, aim to preserve or restore honour, but they also act as warnings to other women and girls who may step out of line. Samaira Nazir's blood was splattered onto her two young nieces as her brother and young male cousin stabbed her to death at home in Southall in 2005. There was a plan to kill Bekhal so that her sisters could be controlled, but when this was not possible, Banaz and Payzee were married off as child brides to counter the dishonour.

Although men have, as Bekhal says, 'limitless freedom', they can also sometimes become victims of honour killings if they are regarded to have 'corrupted' a woman. Rahmat was fortunate to escape a kidnapping and murder. On the whole, men are the perpetrators, but some may be reluctantly involved. Underaged men in particular are encouraged or forced to do the killing, since they are likely to receive a lighter prison sentence. Bekhal's younger brother may have been used to attempt her murder in an effort to use his youth in such a plea of mitigation. His reluctance, however, was clear as he wept and aborted the attempt when Bekhal struggled. He was also the only man to have cried at Banaz's funeral.

Although women can be involved, the reasons may be mixed. Surjit's mother-in-law was portrayed as the matriarch behind her killing, but this ignored the fact that codes of honour are defined and maintained by male power. The husband, who had greater power, would have been able to stop the murder if he had so desired. Women too can have strong instilled conservative value systems, like Rukshana's mother who believed that her daughter's death was in her 'kismet' (fate); that women cannot escape suppression or abuse. Although Banaz's mother warned Banaz and Rahmat, her motives are suspect because she supported the father after the murder. Some women, however, may be victims themselves and unable to protect their children. Only one mother, Hanim Goren, bravely and unusually gave evidence in an honour killing against her own husband, which led to his conviction for the murder of their fifteen-year-old daughter, Tulay, in 2009. Only two daughters have given prosecution evidence – against their parent or parents, one being Alesha, the sister of Shafilea Ahmed who was killed in 2003 but her case did not come to trial until 2012, and the other was Bekhal. So, the evidence that Bekhal gave was rare indeed, and her actions extremely courageous.

The problem of honour killings and other gender-based violence has never been addressed by self-styled community and religious elders or leaders, who tend to be male and conservative.

POSTSCRIPT

On the contrary, such abuse has been encouraged so that they can maintain their power base through the subjugation of women. They often mediate and reconcile women back into abusive situations, rather than encourage separation or divorce or trying to obtain state protection for victims and sanctions for perpetrators. Indeed, as leaders, they act as the 'gatekeepers' between the community and wider society, and argue, under multicultural policies, for non-interference from the government or statutory agencies like the police and social services. The community, they argue, is 'self-policing' and 'self-governing'. To interfere would be intolerant, even racist, they say. In turn, the state agencies have historically colluded and refused to intervene to protect women in order to be culturally sensitive for the sake of good community or race relations. Indeed, Shafilea Ahmed's parents evaded justice for nearly a decade, in part by describing the police investigation as 'racist'. The failure of the British police to investigate when Surjit Kaur Athwal's case was first reported and regardless of our meetings with officials and the Foreign Secretary, the Foreign Office did not robustly demand action from the Indian government. These were the result of 'cultural sensitivity', trying to avoid allegations of imperialism and inviting bad international relations, or just plain racism. These failures are less common in cases of white nationals being murdered or in trouble abroad. Indeed, they delayed and almost denied justice of any kind in Surjit's case.

Although we do need to avoid racial and religious stereotypes, and encourage anti-racism, this version of multiculturalism nevertheless needs to acknowledge gender inequality and power differentials within communities. Bekhal has some very strong criticisms of her 'fucked up' culture and religion, but these have to be understood in the context of her life and experience – she suffered the more conservative end of these value systems and traditional practices, interpreted and imposed by men and elders within a male dominated community.

Bekhal enjoys many other parts of her culture such as food, music and some traditional dress. She also believes in God. She is not without religious or cultural sensibilities, but she rightly questions and challenges the way her culture and religion has been used to degrade and discriminate against her and other women in her family and community. At great personal cost, she had upheld basic humanity and respect for women's rights, which is a litmus test that many fail. To her, and to many others in her position, this is true honour.

Multiculturalism was briefly re-envisioned in 1998 as 'mature multiculturalism' by a Home Office Minister, Mike O'Brien. Memorably, he said: 'Multicultural sensitivity is not an excuse for moral blindness.' O'Brien had been influenced by Southall Black Sisters in this new vision. I had called for a public inquiry and was invited to be a member of the first Home Office Working Group on Forced Marriage established by O'Brien in the wake of Rukshana Naz's death. The Working Group reported in 2000 and for the first time in British history, forced marriage was recognised as an abuse of human rights. However, although most of my recommendations in the Working Group were incorporated in the report, I nevertheless resigned just before publication as the Co-Chairs supported mediation and reconciliation as a legitimate option when handling forced marriage. I objected because the practice placed pressure on victims to return to abusive situations at home. I was later able to influence forced marriage and honour violence guidance for professionals, which opposed mediation and reconciliation, and helped to introduce the Forced Marriage (Civil Protection) Act 2007. Despite these reforms, however, honour violence as a wider problem has not been well addressed. In spite of years of training and guidance on this issue, the HMIC Inspectorate reported in 2015 that the police response to the problem was still poor and inconsistent, with only three out of forty-three police forces being fully prepared.

It seems that agencies are now also hesitant to intervene if an abusive act is justified in the name of faith for fear of being religiously insensitive or Islamophobic. Within a context of growing religious fundamentalism (in all religions), failings in state response and cuts in services and legal aid, the male leadership and clergy are increasing their stranglehold on communities, especially on young women, who they fear they will lose through 'westernisation' and the growth of black feminism. They are now controlling women through the use of 'bounty hunters' and networks of men, shopkeepers and taxi drivers to find wayward women. Alternatively, women are being diverted away from the criminal and civil justice system into community-based resolution, through religious arbitration tribunals or Sharia Courts. So even where a woman complains of forced marriage and domestic abuse, or just wants an Islamic divorce, these bodies tell them to go back and try harder to please their parents or husbands. Once again, mediation and reconciliation are attempted but the abuse is unchallenged and lives are put at risk. These dangerous practices can be reinforced by agencies who may also become involved in, or turn a blind eye to the dangers, as happened in Bekhal's case with social services. Astonishingly, in 1991, Vendana Patel was stabbed to death by her husband during a mediation meeting organised by the police. These practices and the discriminatory effects of religious law on women are now being ignored or endorsed by the state in their multi-faith policies, which respect religious difference at the expense of women's rights.

So while the leaders within communities gain power without responsibility or accountability to women, the state too has abrogated its responsibility and accountability to women in minority communities. As a result, these women, particularly young women/girls and migrant women who have an insecure immigration status or no access to public funds, are being failed twice over. Their double jeopardy situation is also compounded by intersecting discrimination on multiple fronts because of race and gender inequality, and often also poverty. It is therefore not surprising that Asian women are three times more likely to commit suicide and have higher rates of self-harm than women generally. Minority and migrant women also have a disproportionately higher rate of domestic homicide. This is because they face greater barriers to escaping abuse and can be trapped for longer than women generally. One thing we always tell professionals in training is about the 'one chance' rule – that they may have only one chance to spot and help a victim, and so they must take every opportunity they have to support them. So why did Banaz get turned away five times by the police? Bekhal was also let down by social services, who as Payzee says, also failed to protect the siblings. Their intervention could have prevented her and Banaz's 'child marriages', when their father exploited a loophole in the law which allows parents to 'consent' to marriage for those aged sixteen to eighteen.

How is it possible when the government says it wants to protect women from honour violence that we have fewer resources and inadequate responses from agencies? This is particularly so with the Covid-19 pandemic-induced recession after ten years of austerity. Specialist frontline organisations like Southall Black Sisters in minority communities, historically under-funded, have been the hardest hit. They have been forced to close or reduce their services. How do we prevent the very preventable deaths we witness in honour killings? How do we fulfil our promise to protect and respect women's human rights, as outlined in human rights conventions to which Britain is a signatory, and effectively respond to what Banaz hauntingly asks in the police video: 'What can you do for me?'

More education is needed to inform victims of their rights and to change attitudes. Good practice guidance and the law should also be enforced through improved inspection and disciplinary action for systemic and individual accountability – so that you do not have officers only receiving 'words of advice' for serious failings, as they did in Banaz's case. Services no doubt need better funding and improvements in housing, benefits, legal aid, and health (including mental health) and social care are all required, especially for young and migrant women. Specialist provision by secular human rights-based minority women's rights organisations in particular need wholehearted financial and political support from the state. At the moment, despite some support, there is a hostility or lip service from the community and government for these groups; and a lack of will to make promises good.

In 2021, in memory of Banaz, Bekhal and I proposed a 'Banaz's Law' which prevents the use of misogynous cultural defences in the murder of women or femicide. Bekhal's father received a minimum sentence of twenty years, and her uncle, the instigator of the murder, received twenty-three years. Normally, these sentences would be considered lengthy for murder, but Bekhal does not think they are long enough. In addition, although they were convicted and imprisoned, they were nevertheless treated as 'heroes' who had 'done justice'. They explicitly justified the killing in the community and implicitly in the British legal system. In some cases, cultural justifications have been explicitly, even successfully, used as mitigation in honour killings to reduce murder to the lesser offence of manslaughter, or to lower sentencing. For example, in Rukshana Naz's case, the brother felt confident about pleading provocation to reduce the murder charge to manslaughter, and although he was unsuccessful, this defence was accepted in 1998 by the Crown Prosecution Service in the case of Tasleem Begum, killed by her male cousin in 1995. As stated in the *Bradford Telegraph and Argus,* in the latter case, passing a lenient sentence of six and half years, the judge said, 'It is clear she was having an illicit relationship with Mr X and that would be deeply offensive to someone with your background and religious beliefs.' In 2003, the judge in Heshu Yonis's case took account of 'cultural differences' in mitigation when setting her killer's minimum tariff of fourteen years.

Banaz's law will turn mitigation into an aggravating factor, attracting longer sentencing, and will not only cover homicide. It should also be used in all forms of gender-based violence, including suicide and self-harm driven by abuse, which should be treated as criminal offences. Both Bekhal and Banaz had contemplated or attempted suicide, and both also self-harmed. Even in Rahmat's suicide, Banaz's killers were complicit. Banaz's Law will also extend to family law and influence best practice, as cultural or religious sensitivity could not be used to avoid providing protection to victims. In family courts, violent fathers have argued for their right for child residence so that they can arrange 'traditional marriages' of their daughters because it protects their family honour. The police and social services also play into the hands of perpetrators who impose excessive restrictions on the lifestyle choices of women and girls, or inflict obvious abuse, in order to respect minority cultural and religious rights.

Payzee, who is now boldly campaigning against child marriage, talks about how all agencies involved in her wedding did not even question why a sixteen-year-old was marrying a man twice her age. The signs of abuse were missed and the 'one chance' rule ignored as it is assumed that marriage for a woman at such a young age is culturally acceptable. As a result of the campaign, however, the government is now introducing legal reform by raising the age of consent to marriage to eighteen and removing the current provision which allows parents to give permission for those over sixteen. Although 'forced marriage' is already illegal, the burden to prove coercion is on the victim, and so the new law would remove pressure on young victims, who are still children for safeguarding purposes, to convince the court that they were forced into marriage. This reform will also help to change attitudes within minority communities on forced marriage and child abuse.

Banaz's law will also send the right message to the community, promoting human rights values and the empowerment of women. It can also benefit those from other communities as it challenges all forms of cultural defences based on hating women, such as treating them as men's 'property'. Indeed, it should be incorporated in a new law treating misogyny as a hate crime, so that it is regarded as an aggravating factor in the same way as it is currently possible to argue race hate to increase sentencing powers. Together the two hate crime offences would fill a gap for minority women who experience intersectional discrimination based on their race *and* gender. The law, however, must be supported by resources and enforcement mechanisms to make it effective.

Like the murder of Sarah Everard in 2021, which was a turning point on violence against women and girls more generally, the early cases, including that of Banaz, were turning points for honour killings in minority communities. For the first time, they created a national debate on the use and abuse of honour, and the failure of both community and the state to protect minority women. That debate continues with recent cases of honour killings, like those of Samia Shahid, Seeta Kaur and Mayra Zulfiqar. For me, mature multiculturalism needs to be revived and extended to 'mature multi-faithism' to fight intersecting race, religious and gender discrimination. This would uphold the human rights of black and minority women.

Bekhal's greatest regret is not taking Banaz home with her when she last saw her in 2005; and her greatest guilt? That her sisters, Banaz and Payzee, were forced into child marriages to save the 'honour' of the family after she had been accused of having 'shamed' them. But I would say to Bekhal, you have nothing to regret or feel guilty about – you were more failed than failing. Like your sisters, Banaz and Payzee, and other victim-survivors, you are the real heroes of our times in the fight against *dis*honour crimes.

Dr Hannana Siddiqui
14 July 2021

Acknowledgements

Bekhal Mahmod:
Writing this book has been a highly emotional and heartbreaking experience for me, but also an extended form of therapy. Being in witness protection means I'm unable to talk to many people about my childhood or family or the acts of evil committed by my father, uncle and male cousins. I can't tell new friends about my beautiful, caring little sister. Nor can I cry to them on Banaz's birthday or the anniversary of her death. Therefore, I'm hugely grateful for the opportunity to share this deeply painful – yet important – story. A story that would not be possible without the help of many dear people.

Massive thanks to Dr Hannana Siddiqui, my 'adopted' aunty and angel who has supported me from the very beginning. Hannana, I don't think I would have coped had we not met. I will be forever thankful and appreciative for your comfort and continual, indefatigable support, throughout the trial and beyond. Please know, I will always remember everything that you've done, and continue to do, for me. Honestly, I cannot thank you enough.

Likewise, a huge thank-you to everyone at Southhall Black Sisters. Your kindness and dedication to Banaz's case means the world to me.

Thanks also to Sarah Raymond. Sarah, you will always be in my heart for your outstanding support and work during and after the trial. Banaz's case affected you deeply and I know how much you cared about winning justice for my sister. I would have asked you to adopt me were it not for your professional job.

To Nicola Stow for bringing my story to life. Nicola, this was meant to be. This book couldn't have happened without you. The experience of working on my story with you is a memorable one. The blood, sweat and tears that has gone in to putting this book together by you is amazing. You captured everything exactly as I told it to you, and more. Thank you.

Special thanks to Amber for her support and encouragement. You risked your safety when you arranged for me to meet Banaz in 2005. Without your help, I would never have got to tell my darling sister that I loved her one last time. Amber, I'll be forever in your debt.

Also to Ata – you were my guardian angel by taking me to the hospital after I was attacked by my brother. I will always remember you.

I could not write these acknowledgements without thanking my foster mum, Valda. Thank you for taking me in and treating me with so much love and kindness – and for always putting my safety first. God bless you for the love you have given to all the kids you have cared for over the years. You're one of the most independent and inspiring women I have ever known.

To Leyla, for being a true friend and making my teenage years fun, despite my troubles at home. Thank you for treating me like a sister, even sharing your bedroom with me when you and your family took me in years ago.

And to Neats, for supporting me through those dark times and sleepless nights. For always being there emotionally and listening to me during long, late-night phone calls during those challenging times. Friends are the family you choose.

Thanks also to Nehir for your friendship and support in ending the bullying at school, and to Chelsea for making my fearful days at the women's refuge feel a bit safer and for letting me tag along with you. It made me more independent.

Also, thanks to my old friends Shell, Shan, Jo, Raa, Em, Son, Kel, Chelles and Max. You were all a tower of strength during my darkest days, helping me through numerous breakdowns.

The friends I have not mentioned by name, you all know who you are. I will never forget your generous love and support throughout those hard times. Tremendous love to you all.

A special thank-you to the Metropolitan Police murder investigation team. What an outstanding job. Every single person in this team was wholly devoted to achieving justice for Banaz. Thank you from the bottom of my heart.

Thank you to all the women's aid groups for all your hard work on helping women and men in need. Without your work, the lives of many more beautiful people would be lost.

Many heartfelt thanks to the talented team at Ad Lib Publishers. Thank you, John Blake, for your endless enthusiasm and sensitive approach throughout this book project. Big thanks also to Jon Rippon, Duncan Proudfoot, Rob Nichols, Martin Palmer, Kaz

Harrison and Mel Sambells. Without your passion and vision for my story, this book would not exist.

To Raju Bhatt and Carolynn Gallwey from Bhatt Murphy Solicitors. Thank you for your hard work and commitment throughout my civil case.

Huge thanks to my therapist for the dedication in supporting me over a decade, always there when I needed you. I appreciate everything you have done for me.

And last, but by no means least, thank you to my angel, Banaz. Losing you has been the hardest thing I have had to endure in life. No pain compares to the empty space left in my heart without you. No day goes by that I don't miss or think of you. You should be right here with me, but the devil had other plans. Although I live on, I look forward to the day I will see your beautiful face, hear your soft voice again and get a long-overdue hug. Until then, thank you for the time I had with you, for your kindness that knew no bounds and for all that you taught me. I will always love you, my darling Nazca.

Dr Hannana Siddiqui:
Writing this book with Bekhal has been a huge privilege for me. For years, Bekhal and I dreamed about penning her incredible story – and there are many people I must thank for finally making *No Safe Place* a reality.

Firstly, to Bekhal, I would like to express deep gratitude for your unfailing love and friendship. It was a true honour to share this book telling your painful and inspiring life story. I am sure that that it will play a vital part in helping countless others to escape abuse, and in bringing closure and justice for victim-survivors and those bereaved by the loss of their loved ones in honour killings and other forms of gender-based violence.

To the wonderfully talented Nicola Stow, thank you for your friendship and endless hours of writing support – and for telling Bekhal's story with outrage and heart. Thanks also for your valuable editorial support in my sections.

Thank you to the determined Metropolitan Police team who investigated the murder and went to the ends of the earth to achieve justice for Banaz. In particular, many thanks to the Family Liaison Officer, Sarah Raymond – your constant gentle support made it possible for Bekhal to give evidence in court. Your aftercare was also above and beyond.

I thank Southall Black Sisters and my work colleagues, especially Meena Patel, for enabling me to provide support to Bekhal to give evidence in court to achieve justice for Banaz and in the subsequent civil action and complaints against the police and social services, who had failed Banaz and Bekhal. Support from Southall Black Sisters has also helped in campaigning for Banaz and for legal and social reform.

Many thanks to Raju Bhatt and Carolynn Gallwey from Bhatt Murphy Solicitors for your commitment, sensitivity and excellent work in assisting Bekhal to make complaints against the police and social services, and on other legal matters; and for winning the civil case against the police and holding those who failed Banaz to account.

Thanks also to all at Ad Lib Publishers for publishing and publicising this book. Without John Blake approaching me, this book would not have been possible. Additionally, I would like to thank the many journalists and media who have covered the story of Bekhal, Banaz and Payzee over the years, creating national awareness of and pressure to end honour violence.

Finally, to partners, family, friends, survivors, bereaved and supporting families and friends of victims, women's groups, professionals, allies and activists who have all kindly supported us on the long journey to achieve justice, to produce *No Safe Place,* and in the on-going campaign for Banaz's Law and for wider change so that *all* women and girls can find a safe place to escape gender-based violence.

Southall Black Sisters

Southall Black Sisters is a black and minority women's organisation, founded in 1979, to combat violence against women and girls in black and minority communities. It provides direct services to survivors and also campaigns and conducts developmental and policy work to create wider change. The resource centre can be contacted for assistance – details and other information is on the website: www.southallblacksisters.org.uk. Donations are welcomed.